# Introduction
# To
# Manuscriptology

# Introduction To Manuscriptology

R.S. SHIVAGANESHA MURTHY

SHARADA

SHARADA PUBLISHING HOUSE

DELHI

*First Published 1996*



ISBN. : 81-85616-26-4



*Published by :*
B.L. Bansal
SHARADA PUBLISHING HOUSE
(Publishers on India's Past and Present)
40, Anand Nagar, Inderlok,
DELHI-110035
Phones : 5117390, 5116763

*Laser Typesetting by :*
Compu-Media The D.T.P. People,
43, Banglow Road, Delhi-110007
Phone : 2911869

*Printed at :*
Santosh Offset, Delhi-110035

# CONTENTS

*Acknowledgement* ix
*Introduction* xi
*List of Illustration* xv

*CHAPTER I*

**WRITING IN ANCIENT INDIA** 1
Antiquity of Writing in India 2
Theories about the origin of Brāhmī 3
Literary Evidence :
Indian Sources 6
Foreign Sources 10
Other Evidences 11
Brāhmī-invented in 3rd cent. B.C. ? 12
Scripts in the Manuscripts available now 13
Peculiarities 16

*CHAPTER - II*

**WRITING MATERIALS** 24
(i) Materials 24
(A) Material for Writing Books 25
(1) Palm Leaf (Tālapatra) 27
Preparation of Palm Leaf 27
Antiquity of use of Palm Leaf 29
Some Early Specimens 30
Peculiar Manuscripts 31
(2) Birch Bark (Bhūrja Patra) 31
Preparation 31
Antiquity 32
Some Specimens 33
(3) Sāñcīpāṭ or Samucīaṭ 33
Tūlīpāṭ 34
(4) Paper 34
Antiquity of Paper Manuscripts 35

(B) Other Materials 36
(1) Metals 37
(2) Non-Metals 42
(ii) Writing Instruments 49
(iii) Other Instruments and Materials 50
(iv) Ink 52

*CHAPTER - III*

**COLLECTION OF MANUSCRIPTS** 67
Discoveries of Manuscripts in Central Asia 70
Major Manuscripts Libraries : India 71
Abroad 72

*CHAPTER IV*

**PRESERVATION AND CATALOGUING** 77
I. Preservation 77
A. The Need 77
B. Causes of Destruction of Manuscripts 78
Climatic Conditions 78
Environment 79
C. Remedies 82
Fumigation 84
D. Repair of Manuscripts 86
Lamination 87
E. Mechanical Reproduction 90
II Cataloguing 92
Card Catalogue 93
Book-Form 94
Sheaf-Form 94
Form of a Manuscript Catalogue 97
Descriptive Catalogue 98
Catalogus Catalogorum (CC) 99
New Catalogus Catalogorum (NCC) 100

*CHAPTER V*

**WRITING IN MANUSCRIPTS** 103
A Manuscripts : Their Form and Size 103
B. Technique 104
Pagination 106

Punctuation 106
Abbreviations 107
Colophon 107
Illustrations 107
Decoration 108
Corrections 109
C. Scribe 110
D. Kinds of Texts 112
Recension 116

CHAPTER VI

VARIOUS READINGS 121
Their Causes and Types 121
Types of Errors 125
a. Deletion or Omission 125
(i) Simple Omission 125
(ii) Omission of Serifs 126
(iii) Haplography 126
b. Addition 127
c. Substitution 129
d. Orthographic Confusion 131
e. Transposition (Anagramatism) 131

CHAPTER VII

CRITICAL RECENSION 134
Method 135
A. Lower Criticism 136
(i) Heuristics 136
Siglum 137
Collation 138
Secondary Sources of Evidence 140
(a) Commentary 141
(b) Translations 141
(c) Anthologies (Florilegia) 142
(d) Quotations 144
(e) Obvious imitations 144
(f) Epitomies and adaptations 144
(g) Parallel Versions 145

(ii) Recensio 145
(iii) Emendation 146
B. High Criticism 146

*CHAPTER VIII*

**PROCESS OF CRITICAL EDITING** 149
1. Genealogy of Manuscripts 149
2. Emendation 155
3. Canons of Critical editing 158
4. Problem of Prakrit Texts 161
5. Other Editorial Tasks 163
Manuscript and related material 163
The constituted Text 164
Critical Apparatus 165
Editorial Signs 166
Higher Criticism 167
Indexes 168

**Notes On Some Manuscripts Collections** 170
Central Asian

**Appendix-I** 177
List of Manuscripts Libraries
Indian 177
Outside India 187

**Appendix-II** 190
*Glossary* 190
Some Technical Terms
(i) English 190
(ii) Sanskrit 196

*Bibliography* 208

*Index* 231

*Scripts* (Alphabets and numerals)

*Illustrations*

# ACKNOWLEDGEMENT

A number of institutions and individuals have provided various pictures, drawings and photographs to Dr. R.S. Shivaganesha Murthy for inclusion in this book, for which Dr. Murthy had requested. Some of them have been printed in this book. It is not specifically known from which sources these materials were procured, owing to Dr. Murthy's sudden demise even before the book was printed. Hence specific acknowledgements could not be made in respective places of the book. However thanks are due to all those who obliged Dr. Murthy with the required materials used in this book.

The suggestion and co-operation of many friends and colleagues of Prof. Murthy are hereby gratefully acknowledged. Thanks are due to Prof. Satkari Mukhopadhyaya, New Delhi, Vidvan H.S. Phatak of the ORI, Mysore, Prof. K.V. Sarma, Madras, Vidvan Heramba Bhat, Mysore, S. Rangachar, Mysore, Dr. H.L.N. Bharati, Mysore and many others who have co-operated in many ways in writing this book and later during its printing.

Sincere thanks are also due to Messrs, Sharada Publishing House, Delhi who readily agreed to publish this book and to Messrs Santosh Offset .Delhi. for the neat get up of the book.

# INTRODUCTION

The study of ancient writing system technically called palaeography, leads to the origin and history of the alphabets. Clear evidence for the writing system in ancient India is available as may be seen from numerous manuscripts written on palm-leaf and other writing materials. The available manuscripts are generally not older than 600 years (only in a few cases, it may be 1000 years or more) because of the fragile nature of the material used for writing. Numerous epigraphs and inscriptions also reflect the history of writing system. There are also literary evidences that lead to the knowledge of the existence of writing from a hoary past.

The ancient manuscripts have a link between the past and the present. Sanskrit was for a long time the medium of instruction, particularly higher education. Hence Sanskrit works are a repository of the multifarious facets of knowledge. These ancient works are still available to us in manuscript form. It is therefore necessary to preserve them.

Any intellectual evolution could get explicit expression for the advancement of knowledge and induce intellectual thought among the people. After the advent of writing system, such a knowledge was transformed into written records to serve as a permanent guide to the orally transmitted knowledge. It become a speciality to create a record of important subject information on a writing material. Such matters of intellect amounted to be a enormous, requiring classification into specific subjects. That way, hundreds of manuscripts were available to the younger generations as written documents. Such ancient writings required to be studied extensively for a reconstruction of Indian literary tradition. In this direction, ancient manuscripts, inscriptions, coins, etc., were unearthed, collected and preserved by various agencies set up for a historical study.

The ancient documents have revealed striking informations in all the intellectual areas reflecting the scientific knowledge of the older generations in modern contexts. Such documents required, at the outset, a systematic classification and arrangement to tackle with, for an exhaustive study in order to draw significant conclusions. This systematic and scientific approach towards research in the area came to be known as "textual criticism."

Critical editing of ancient manuscripts is a process of selecting the most acceptable reading of a work, which its author might have written. This is done on the basis of various readings available in the copies of the manuscript of a work collected from different sources. In the presence of copies of a manuscript, it is worthwhile to examine them from various aspects of the subject and language to avoid possible corruptions in the text. Therefore, each copy of the manuscript of the text is to be studied thoroughly from the point of view of orthographic peculiarities and scribal stylistics, in determining the trustworthiness of the codices. Almost all texts in Sanskrit have commentaries written on them. Many commentaries are earlier than the available codices and they provide clear evidence of the readings accepted during their times. Though these commentaries also have come down to us in a line of transmission, chances of corrupt readings are very rare. The commentators often discuss the variant readings and add to the editor's knowledge of the situation. Secondly, the translation of a Sanskrit work into any target language, anthologies, quotations, obvious imitations, epitomes, adaptations, parallel versions, etc., should be consulted as important documents.

Critical editing of texts in India is lagging behind for several reasons. Most of the editors have neither proper training nor guidance to qualify them for this type of work. Many of the texts published in India show very little acquaintance with modern scientisfic methods of editing. The editor's application of the techniques of editing in bringing out a final credible text of a manuscript must be endorsed by his scholarship, critical acumen, decision-making and confidence in what he concludes as final. Textual criticism is an essential part of Manuscriptology. The other aspects, right from collection of manuscripts to cataloguing them, also form an important as well as an essential part of this area of study. With the decline in interest and capability to study ancient manuscripts, manuscriptology has taken a back seat.

The aim of this monograph is to show with reference to Indian conditions the principle feature of the science of manuscriptology to enable the future editors to master the modern methods of critical editing of manuscripts. The academic needs of professionals as well as beginners in the field have been kept in view by Dr. Murthy, while preparing this monograph. Almost all aspects of manuscriptology have been covered in this book to cater to such needs.

Dr. R.S. Shivaganesha Murthy, Professor and Head, Dept. of Studies in Sanskrit and Director, Oriental Research Institute, University of Mysore, Mysore, has to be congratulated, posthumously, for this valuable contribution to the field of manuscriptology. Unfortunately, he did not live to see his book in print. If the book fulfils the needs of scholars and students even to a little extent, then the efforts of Prof. Murthy will be amply rewarded.

Dr. H.L.N. BHARATI
Editor (retd.)
Central Institute of Indian Languages
Mysore - 570 006

## List of Illustrations


Pl. 1. Nāgarī Script, Bīlhaṇacaritam (Courtesy ORI, Mysore)

Pl. 2. Nāgarī Script, Bīlhaṇacaritaṃ (Courtesy ORI, Mysore)

Pl. 3. Nāgarī Script, Bālakavacam (Paper Mss.) (Courtesy ORI, Mysore)

Pl. 4. Nāgarī Script (Courtesy ORI, Mysore)

Pl. 5. Nandi-Nāgarī Script, Vālmīki Rāmāyaṇa, 31st Canto in Sundara Kāṇḍa

Pl. 6. Nāgari Script, Sīddhānta Kaumudi (Courtesy ORI, Mysore)

Pl. 7. Nāgari Script

Pl. 8. Nāgarī Script

Pl. 9. Grantha Script, Sīddhānta Kaumudi (Courtesy ORI, Mysore)

Pl. 10. Kannada Script, Sankhya Ratnakośa

Pl. 11. Kannada Script, Gīta Govinda

Pl. 12. Copper Plate with dotted lines

Pl. 13. Copper Plate with dotted lines

Pl. 14. Sohgaura Copper Plate, 4th cent. B.C.

Pl. 15. Tulu Script, Devīmāhātyam (Courtesy ORI, Mysore)

Pl. 16. Malayalam Script, (Courtesy ORI, Mysore)

Pl. 17. Kannada Script, Deśavarṇanam

Pl. 18. Drawings in Palmleaf Manuscripts (Courtesy B.M.S.M. Foundation, Bangalore)

Pl. 19. Drawings in Palmleaf Manuscripts (Courtesy B.M.S.M. Foundation, Bangalore)

Pl. 20. Drawings in Palmleaf Manuscripts (Courtesy B.M.S.M. Foundation, Bangalore)

Pl. 21. Geometrical Patterns in writing

Pl. 22. Patterns in writing

Pl. 23. Oriya manuscript containing Viṣṇusahasranamastotra, etc.

Pl. 24. Jaina Prakrit manuscript, Mahavira Preaching

Pl. 25. Jaina Prakrit manuscript, King Sanjaya stoots the deer

Pl. 26. A sage reading a palm-leaf manuscript

Pl. 27. Muttara [Image in stone of Piṅgala, attendant of Sūrya, holding pen in his right hand and an inkpot in left (Gupta Period)]

Pl. 28. Gautama at school, Ajanta Painting, Cave No.XVI, c. 6th cent. A.D.

Pl. 29. Sculpture showing Vaiṣṇava Guru and his royal disciple holding in his right hand a manuscript with his attending guards shown below.

Pl. 30. Scroll (Courtesy Dr. Veerendra Heggade Dharmasthala)

Pl. 31. Knife with ivory handle (Courtesy Dr. Veerendra Heggade Dharmasthala)

Pl. 32. Stylus used in writing on palmleaf and a stylus case

Pl. 33. Stylus (Courtesy Dr. Veerendra Heggade Dharmasthala)

Pl. 34. Stylus (Courtesy Dr. Veerendra Heggade Dharmasthala)

Pl. 35. Stylus (Courtesy Dr. Veerendra Heggade Dharmasthala)

Pl. 36. Inkpot Top view (Courtesy Dr. Veerendra Heggade Dharmasthala)

Pl. 37. Inkpot Front view (Courtesy Dr. Veerendra Heggade Dharmasthala)

Pl. 38. Inkpot, (Courtesy Dr. Veerendra Heggade Dharmasthala)

Pl. 39. Headless Saraswati

Pl. 40. Khajuraho - Woman writing letter on palmleaf

Pl. 41. Lady writing inscription, Śiva Temple, Bidar Dist.

Pl. 42. Pandit holding a palmleaf in the left hand explaining to a citizen, 16th cent.

Pl. 43. A saint holding a manuscript, decorated manuscript box is also seen

Pl. 44. A Jaina saint holding a palmleaf in left hand is seen with a disciple

Pl. 45. Jaina saint holding palmleaf under his left arm

## CHAPTER I

# WRITING IN ANCIENT INDIA

As we deal with manuscripts, the question rises naturally as to when the first manuscript could have been written. This leads to the problem of antiquity and origin of writing in India. The study of writing is itself a very vast field. Writing in various styles or decorative lettering comes to be called 'calligraphy' and the study of writing of ancient times is 'palaeography'. Thus the history of the alphabet is strictly the field of palaeography. For manuscriptology, neither the origin of scripts nor its development through the ages is required in detail but a general outline of history is essential because the manuscripts are also written documents in historical succession. And it is this that differentiates epigraphy and manuscriptology. While decipherment and editing of a text is common to both, the stress on decipherment is more marked in epigraphy which is very close to palaeography. Most of the manuscripts date from about 13th century. Thus, the question of antiquity of writing is dealt with here as a prelude to the study of manuscripts. The various evidences, literary and otherwise found in India, bearing on the topic as well as the views of modern scholars on the origin of Indian writing are set forth in brief.

Though the clear evidence for writing in ancient India is available as early as 5th century B.C., the manuscripts now available are not generally older than about 600 years (only in a few cases, it may be 1000 years or more) because of the fragile nature of the material used for writing. Though many manuscripts of the earlier period are not to be had, the history of writing can easily be traced, thanks to the numerous inscriptions and epigraphs. While almost all of them are dated, they are also available in large numbers almost continuously throughout the period from 3rd century

B.C. to date in various parts of the land from Kashmir to Kanyakumari. Indian palaeography has been well developed by a number of devout scholars.[1]

## Antiquity of Writing in India

The earliest positive evidence available for a full-fledged script are the inscriptions of Aśoka (3rd century B.C.) found all over the country.[2] The inscriptions are found to be written in two scripts in the main : Brāhmī and Kharoṣṭhī. While those in Brāhmī are distributed all over the country, those in Kharoṣṭhī are restricted to North-Western parts. The Brāhmī, the wide-spread script, shows variations in the formation of letters. In other words, there are local variations (for example : 'a' is said to have ten forms).[3] The language of the edicts is the same but with regional differences. These writings were meant to be read and understood by the masses. That is why they were written on stone slabs and rocks found in open places. This establishes two points : (1) the script, Brāhmī, was in vogue in all parts of the country and (2) that all people could read and understand a written document.

Earlier to Aśokan edicts, we come across some evidence extending for about two centuries. It is in the form of coin legends, casket inscriptions, etc.:

(a) There are two coins with legends : The Eran coin, so called because it was found in Eran, Jabalpur district, is of the period earlier than 4th century B.C. to which period the other, Taxila coin, also belongs.

(b) The date of Piprahwa Vase Inscription discovered in Basti district (U.P) is 5th century B.C. (487 or 483 B.C.) The Bhattiprolu relic Casket Inscription (A.P) belongs to 4th century B.C.[4]

(c) A stone plaque Inscription discovered in Bogra district (now Bangladesh) called 'Mahasthana Stone Plaque Inscription' is pre-Aśokan (320 B.C.)[5] and an inscription called 'Badli Inscription' found in Ajmer district, is assigned to 483 B.C.

(d) The pre-Aśokan (2nd half of 4th century B.C.)

copper plate called 'Sohgaura Copper Plate' was discovered in Gorakhpur district (U.P.).[6]

Immediately earlier to these stray instances, we have no material evidence extant but have to go back by about 3000 years for any. There are the Harappan seals discovered in plenty. These contain symbols which have been deciphered as alphabets. They date from about 3000 B.C. The lack of any concrete evidence in a vast gap of time makes it difficult to relate these with the Brāhmī. Recently, however, excavations in Dwaraka have brought out brown earthenware pottery of the post-Harappan period on which there are some 'letters' which resemble Aśokan scripts. It may now be possible for linking Indian script with Brāhmī.[7]

Going further back, we have the markings which are taken as alphabetic signs, found on pre-historic pottery dug out in Hyderabad and other places. However, the link between these and Brāhmī cannot be traced and established on concrete grounds.[8]

There are, indeed, literary evidences, Indian and foreign, that point to the existence of writing activity from a hoary past. But, in the early stages of Sanskrit studies undertaken by European scholars, these evidences were not forthcoming and hence the scholars were led to believe that writing was not indigenously developed but was borrowed from abroad.[9] No less a scholar like Max Muller wrote in clear terms that Pāṇini, the great grammarian who lived not later than the 4th century B.C., did not know of even a single word that might indicate the existence of writing. This opinion coming from an authority, though baseless, held the ground for a long time. Thus, we find many scholars subscribing to the foreign origin of Indian alphabet. But they are divided in their opinion as to which that source was.

### *Theories about the origin of Brāhmī*

Before going through the evidence in Pāṇini and other works, we may consider very briefly the theories regarding the origin of Indian alphabet as held by some modern scholars.

Joseph Prinsep, who succeeded first in deciphering the early Brāhmī in the 1830s felt that Brāhmī was derived from Greek. Though there are a few close similarities between the two and some scholars supported Prinsep, the theory is beset with chronological and other problems. It was given up long ago, as being not sound.

Rhys Davids writes[10] :

> Writing was unknown in the age of the Buddha and probably for long after his time. In all probabilities, just as the Indians learnt from the Greeks, not the art of coinage, but the custom of issuing a legally authorised coinage, so it was from the Greeks that they acquired, if not their earliest alphabet, at least the knowledge of the utility of writing.

Lassen viewed that Indian alphabet was indigenous. This was supported by Edward Thomas (1866) who felt that it must have been the invention of Dravidians of South India. Alexander Cunningham tried to show properly that it evolved from a picto-graph of ancient India. Following them, Dowson further tried to establish Cunningham's conclusions.

By about 1806 (Jones) it was put forward that the Indian alphabet had a Semitic source. Kopt (1821) spoke of the Semitic source. He was followed by Lepsices (1834) and Weber (1856). Benfey, Max Muller and Whitney felt this theory to be probable. There were also scholars like Westergaard who were hesitant. Weber, Buhler and others held that the Indian alphabet was the direct descendant of North Semitic script. This is the ancient Phoenecian and is known from the Singarli Stone Inscription, the long document of Mesa, the King of Moab. The Inscription is believed to be of about 850 B.C. This theory is wide-spread. It was Weber who suggested first that Indian script originated from the Phoenician. Buhler argued establishing this on firm foundation and incidentally contributed a lot to Indian Palaeography.

Cunningham pointed out that the Brāhmī which was written from left to right could not have originated from the

Phoenician which was written from right to left. Buhler brought the Eran coin discovered by Cunningham, to the attention of scholars. The legend on it consists of letters written in the reverse fashion and therefore to be read from right to left. Even in the edicts of Aśoka, certain letters are sometimes written reverse which is clearly a reminiscent of writing from right to left, says Buhler.[11] The form of conjunct consonants too supports this view. However, it is not yet established beyond doubt how there was contact between the ancient India and Phonecia.

The discovery of Yazdani has turned the tables.[12] He came across about 131 different markings on the pre-historic pottery dug out in Nalgonda District and on those collected from the southern states and exhibited in Calcutta and Madras Museums respectively. It has been shown that these are alphabetical signs and not mere markings. A few of them-about five - are identical with Brāhmī. There are two neolithic finds deposited in Indian Museum, Calcutta. The one, Green stone chisel, found in Assam, has four letters marked on it in a line. Another is a palm-shaped himatite stone discovered near Ranchi. The three letters written on this have very close similarities with Brāhmī but are reversed. Thus, it is possible to trace the development of Indian alphabet indigenously and a foreign source need not be posited. This can be conclusively proved by further pre-historic archaeological studies.

David Diringer in his comprehensive book, *The Alphabet*, writes[13] that "the early Aramaic alphabet" 'is the prototype of Brahmi'. Further on, he writes :

> We need not assume that the Brahmi is a simple derivative of the Aramaic alphabet. It was probably mainly the idea of alphabetic writing which was accepted...It is generally admitted that the earliest known form of the Brahmi is a script framed by Brahmins for writing Sanskrit, and it may be assumed that they were the inventors of this essentially national alphabet, regardless of the problem concerning the original source of the idea.

S.R. Rao has tried to show that the Indus script was the fore-runner of Brāhmī.[14] The new discovery of post-Harappan scripts at Dwaraka has strengthened his proposition. It has narrowed the gap between the Indus script and the Brāhmī.

We may now proceed to examine what the traditions in India and elsewhere have to say about Indian writing adding the evidence in literature to establish the existence of writing as a well-grounded art.

**Literary Evidence : *Indian Sources***

The Smṛtis (about 5th century A.D.) attach high antiquity to the script. It was created by Brahmā, so that thoughts could be recorded, as otherwise, they would be forgotten in course of time. *Nārada-Smṛti* (4.70) says : "Had not Brahmā created writing, the best vision, then this prosperous trend of the world would not have been there." Bṛhaspati: "In six months' time, one will have confusion regarding one's earlier commitments and therefore, the writing on leaves was created by Brahmā." Śukra too says similarly. The Yājñavalkya-Śikṣā decries a person who reads a written text as such, *yathālikhita-pāṭhaka.*[15]

Kālidāsa considers the alphabet as the pathway leading to the ocean of learning. He also refers to writing on *'bhūrja-patra'* and royal seal and maintaining files.[16]

Bhāsa in his *Avimāraka* makes the Vidūṣaka hide his inability to read the writing on the ring by saying that it was not in his book. Yaugandharāyaṇa intends sending a written message to Udayana in *Pratijñā-Yaugandharāyaṇa.*[17]

In his *Arthaśāstra,* Kauṭilya (4th century B.C.) gives evidence to confirm that writing was a well-established factor in human life during his time. Learning of alphabet and numerals (saṅkhyāna) began at the age of four (1.5.2). A time was set apart in the daily routine of a king for attending to correspondence (*patrasampreṣaṇa*) (1.19.6) It was mandatory to maintain varieties of records. There were professional scribes whose qualifications were set forth. In the Royal courts, they were employed to write the Royal edicts and charters. Their services were also utilised in the law courts in writing down the plaint etc. (2.9.28; 2.10.4-9). It is ordained that a well-partitioned 'Record room', *Nibandha-pustaka-sthāna*, shall be built wherein records of information - assets, earnings etc. - of all the officials including the prince and the queen, and other government records were to be maintained. Secret codes (*saṁjñā-lipi*) were developed for the use of the intelligence department (1.12.8). *Akṣara-kalā* (calligraphy), *Pāṭhyakalā* (art of recitation) were among the arts to be learnt by *gaṇikas*, their maid servants and stage-actors (2.27).[18]

*Nātyaśāstra* suggests that the heads of drama troupes should seek the aid of a *'lekhaka'* and *'gaṇaka'* to record the points of success of a stage performance.[19] *Kāmasūtra* includes *akṣarakalā* (calligraphy) as one of the 64 arts.[20]

Existence of books at the time of Pāṇini is indisputable. He makes use of the terms *lipi* and *lipikāra*. The word *'grantha'*, a book, occurs not less than four times. The term *'likha'* is an instance for the analysis in 3.1.135. The scholars are of the opinion that the *Mahabhārata* was also known to Paṇini as a *'grantha'* (6.2.38). Similarly, the Vedic literature, it is shown, was also available to him in manuscripts.[21] The sūtra *'adarśanam lopaḥ'* (1.1.60) defines *lopa*, elision, as disappearance and this very clearly points to written symbols.

The *Rāmāyaṇa* and the *Mahābhārata* make use of the terms *likha, lekha, lekhana* and *lekhaka*. An instance from the *Rāmāyaṇa* which refers to a written name may be quoted here : Hanūmān shows the ring to Sītā asking her to see the name of Rāma engraved on it.[22]

The *Vāsiṣṭha-Dharmasūtra* and the *Viṣṇu-Dharmasūtra* speak of *likhita* (written document) as an evidence. *Gautama-Dharmasūtra* (13.4) refers to the signature of the witness on a document.[23]

The Āraṇyakas and the Upaniṣads speak of grammatical terminologies : *varṇa, mātrā, bala, sandhi, saṁhitā, svara, ūṣma, sparśa, antastha, vyañjanā, ghoṣa, mūrdhanya, dantya,* etc. They refer to *akṣara*, the written symbol, so named because, a mark made on wood, stone or any such material was indelible. The morpheme *'kāra'* (e.g. *hiṁkāra*) is employed to denote a speech sound.[24]

The Saṁhitas have words like *paṅkti, dvipadī, tripadā,* etc., in connection with the metres. The terms suggest that the written text was before them. The hymns are spoken of as being fashioned as one would fashion a chariot.[25]

While the script, symbol for speech-sound, is one aspect of writing, another aspect is counting symbols for numbers. Conception of very high numbers on the one hand and of fractions on the other, point to the fact that the symbols were being used. We find the numbers counted in geometrical progression in terms of tens, the highest figure reached being 100,000,00,00,000 (13 places) called *'parārdha'*. The lesser figures are also given names; thus we have *daśa, śata, sahasra, ayuta, niyuta, prayuta, arbuda, nyarbuda, samudra, madhya, anta* - each being ten times greater than its previous one. In another context, we have multiples of twelve. Conversely, we have the terms like *ardha* (1/2), *pāda* (1/4), *śapha* (1/8) and *kalā* (1/16). In SB (12.3.2.1) a day is divided into 15 *muhūrtas* : then follow the divisions : *kṣipra, etarhi, idānīm,* and *prāṇa* each of which is 1/15 of its preceding one. These intricacies could not have been arrived at without having some corresponding written symbols.[26]

*Bījākṣaras* and *yantras,* mystic syllables and symbols are the basic elements of Tantra thought. These are written or inscribed on various recommended materials. Thus, they also offer evidence for writing. The *Vārāhi-tantra,* for example, speaks of five types of *lipi,* writing' -- pen-script, chisel-script, that written on sand, flour and so on.[27]

The Buddhist literature too provides very interesting information regarding writing in ancient India. We understand that literacy was widespread. *Lekhana* is spoken of as an honourable profession. Among the activities in which Bhikkus are not to indulge, *Sutta-piṭaka* includes *akkharikā,* probably, a game played by children. It consisted of recognising letters written with fingers on one's back or in the air *(Suttanta,* 1.1; *Brahmajāla-Sutta* 14;

*Sāmaṇṇaphala-sutta* 49). From *Mahāvagga*, another canonical Pāli text, we learn that there were schools to teach the 3 Rs as well as '*Rūpa*' introduction to currency.[28]

*Majjhima-nikāya* speaks of eight professions for house-holders of which *Muddā* (conveyancing), *Ganana* (accountancy) and *Sankha* (appraising) - point to use of writing. *Cullavagga* deals with various methods of voting one of which at least needs writing.[29]

The Jātakas, particularly *Kaṭāhaka*, *Kāma*, *Ruru*, *Kaṇha* and *Kurudhamma-jātakas*, however, provide us with a good lot of information about writing. They refer to writing of letters, of promissory notes, of Royal proclamations, of moral maxims and so on. They mention *phalaka* (board) and *varṇaka* (chalk) as materials of writing. The *Lalitavistara* which was translated into Chinese in 308 A.D. recounts the story of the Buddha. While describing his childhood, we are told that he was sent to a '*lipiśālā*' (Ch.X) along with numerous other children.

He learnt there the 3 Rs under a teacher, Viśvāmitra. Further, we learn that he wrote on a board made of sandal wood and a golden pen (i.e., the pencil had golden cover). The same text gives a list of 64 scripts which the Buddha knew even before schooling (X : 125-19). The list begins with Brāhmī and Kharoṣṭhī. The regional scripts like Vaṅgalipi, Drāviḍa-lipi, Aṅga-lipi, Kanārī-lipi, Dakṣiṇa-lipi; foreign scripts like Cīna-lipi, Darada-lipi, Hūṇa-lipi, find a place there. *Mahāvastu* too mentions Brāhmī and Kharoṣṭhī (1.135.5).[30]

Attention may be drawn to *Kaṭāhaka-jātaka* which speaks of an officer - Bhāṇḍgārika, store-keeper - a designation which necessarily presupposes a regular system of keeping accounts as well as writing - and they could not have evolved all of a sudden.[31]

It is conceded that it is evident on the basis of references that writing was in vogue at the time of *Vinayapiṭaka* and that it was used for official and private purposes. Yet doubt is expressed regarding the adoption of writing to the sacred literature. It is observed : "nowhere do we find the least trace of any reference to manuscripts; much-less of inks or pens or styles or leaves or other writing materials"[32] Whether the sacred literature was available in books or not, there are references to writing materials which establish beyond doubt that there were also 'books' about the time of the Buddha.

The Jaina canonical literature also contribute in this connection. The *Paṇṇavaṇā-sutta* (*c.*168 B.C.) and the *Samavāyaṅga-sutta* (*c.*300 B.C.) give a list of 18 scripts among which Brāhmī, Kharoṣṭhī are found. The *Bhagavatī-sūtra* (5th century B.C.) begins with a salutation to Brāhmī script (*ṇamo bambhīye liviye; ṇamo suāssa*). It is significant to note that *Paṇṇavaṇā-sūtra* describes the 18 scripts as varieties of Brāhmī. *Samavāyaṅga-sūtra* lists 72 *Kalās* (arts) and the list begins with *'leha'* and *'gaṇiya'*. The teacher is called Kalācārya. We also come across *'pūtthaya'* (*pustaka*, book).[33]

The *Rāyapaseṇiya-sutta* describes a book of scripture and speaks of its leaves (*pattagāīm*), the supporting wooden boards (*kambī*), the cord (*dorā*), ink (*masi*), pen (*lekhanī*) and the script (*akkharāīm*). *Kūḍaleha* (codes) is referred to by *Uvāsaga-dasāō* and we also learn about love letters and 'sealed' letters.34

*Tirukkural*, the earliest Tamil work (*c.* 1st century A.D.) opens with the saying that *'a'* is the first of alphabets.[35]

### *Foreign Sources*

Foreign tradition and writers concur with Indian tradition as to the hoary antiquity of the script. A Chinese encyclopaedia of extracts from the *Tripiṭaka*, Fa-wan-shu-lin (A.D. 668) records that three divine powers invented writing : (1) Fan or Brahmā invented Brāhmī, written from left to right, (2) Kia-lu (or Kia-lu-she-ti) invented Kharoṣṭhi, written from right to left and (3) Tsanghich invented Chinese which runs from top to bottom. Of these, the first two were born in India and the third in China and the first is the best of the scripts, the last one is the least important.[36]

Hiuen Tsang, the Chinese traveller in India, (1st half of 7th century) notes that writing in India was invented very early. It is also on record that he got copied 657 Sanskrit books in all and that about twenty scribes worked for him in Kashmir Palace library.[37]

Itsing, who stayed in Nalanda (657-685), we are told, collected 400 texts consisting of 500,000 *ślokas*. Such a large number of books could not have come into existence in just a few centuries.[38]

Alberuni has on records a curious account. The Hindus had a system of writing but it had been lost and forgotten. Consequently, people became illiterate. Then Vyāsa, son of Parāśara, rediscovered their alphabet of fifty letters by the inspiration of god. The writing thus is current from 3103 B.C. (beginning of Kaliyuga).[39]

The account of Greek writers, Nearchos, Megasthenes and Curtius about India, date from 326 B.C. (Alexander's invasion). Their evidence is useful in establishing the existence of written books and in regard to the material used for writing.

Nearchos testifies that paper was being manufactured from cotton and tattered clothes. Curtius observes that the inner bark of certain trees -- evidently birch–bark -- was used for writing. Megasthenes who stayed in Pāṭaliputra, writes about the mile-stones on roads as indicating the distance between two rest-houses. He also mentions written almanacs and Smṛti texts.[40]

*Other Evidences*

Turning to sculpture, an image of Sarasvatī ( 1st century A.D.) from Mathura in Lucknow Museum is *Pustakapāṇi*, i.e. has a book in one of the hands. Attention may be drawn to the images of Brahmā and the sculptures of Patralekhana-kanyā, Māṇikya-vācakar, Sundara-mūrti, Tiruvalluvar and other saints of Tamil Nadu who have a book in their hands.[41]

Thus, we find that the antiquity of writing in India streches back to a very distant period and that there are evidences for existence of books as early as 4th century B.C.

Surely, no one expects a book of those times, to be available as such now. The oldest manuscript that may be available today is not older than a few hundred years. In spite of this fragile nature of the manuscript material and the length of time, we do possess manuscripts which are 1000 years old and some fragments which are even 2000 years old.

*Brāhmī* - ***Invented in 3rd century B.C. ?***

As against the view detailed above, the theory put forth by some historians[42] needs to be noticed here. Nobody can gainsay that there is no concrete evidence of existence of a script before 4th century B.C. The references in Vedic literature are not clear enough. The Buddhist canons too are not of any great value. They are known to have been compiled after the Buddha. Had they known a script, the teachings would have been committed to writing at least towards the end of Buddha's life when his teachings had held the ground. Further, within about four centuries after the Buddha there were at least four Councils[43] held for the codification of the teachings. In the course of codification, it is not clear if any new material was added and if so how much etc. The same is the feature of Jain canons. Thus though these canonical texts do give some information, it is shrouded in doubts of interpolation. In other words, there is no evidence for the existence of writing before the time of Aśoka.

This lack of proof is corroborated by Megasthenes, who nowhere mentions any written record or writing during his stay in Pataliputra. Even the other Greek writers about India also concur in this. If at all, there is a reference to writing, then it is not Brāhmī but to a foreign script that was in vogue in North-Western part only.

The *Arthaśāstra* of Kauṭilya which leaves no doubt about the existence of written communication and documents, is not useful. For, *Arthaśāstra* was not written in the Mauryan Age, but was the product of the Gupta Age.

Putting all these considerations together, it is concluded that there was no script current in the mainland while the North-Western part did have acquaintance with

Ionian and Semitic scripts, before Aśoka. And Aśoka got invented a script which he used as the national script. He got engraved edicts in various parts of his State. His idea was, it is said, that the officers would read it out to the people and explain the significance there of. The officers were trained in the capital in the use of the scripts.

If one chooses to go by concrete evidence alone, this theory of Aśoka's invention deserves appreciation, in the state of our present day knowledge. However, it is possible that we may come across further material like the pottery from Dwaraka to connect Brāhmī with the Indus script.

## Scripts in the Manuscripts Available Now

Whatever may be the origin of Brāhmī, that all the present Indian scripts are the descendants of Brāhmī only is beyond any shadow of doubt.

Since it was known that the manuscripts are subject to easy destruction, a text was preserved through a chain of copies. The structure of a language was scrupulously maintained to preserve the link from the past and the present throughout the length and breadth of India. But, no particular script was insisted upon. Manuscripts were being written or copied from older ones, in the script of the day. However, by 10th century, when the regional scripts had developed fully and independently, a variety of Nāgarī, later called 'Devanāgarī', emerged as a script known commonly in most parts of the country. Manuscripts, however, continued to be copied by and large in the regional scripts.

Thus, the scripts that were current in different regions are found in the manuscripts written in the respective parts. Except a few cases the scripts in the manuscripts available are chronologically near to us. The important scripts of manuscripts may be briefly noticed here :

(1) **Devanāgarī** : This script developed fully by the 10th-11th centuries A.D. and manuscripts also date from the same period. But, Devanāgarī is not confined to any one particular region ; it is not regional. The origin of the name 'Nāgarī-lipi' is variously interpreted. Some argue that it is related

to the Nāgalipi of the *Lalitavistara*. It is shown that, in Tibetan, it is called Kliu-Yeg, the script of the Nagas. Others relate it with the Nāgara-s, the Gujarat Brahmins. The third and simpler explanation of the term as "writing used in cities", "town script", seems more plausible. The words 'Nāgara' and 'Nāgarika' may be compared with this. On this basis, the meaning of Nāgarī could be extended to mean 'cultured' or 'sophisticated'. Another point worthy of note here is that palm leaf manuscripts in Devanāgarī are very rare, may be one in ten thousand (See Nandināgarī). This script is called 'Bālabodha' in Maharashtra and Karnataka (See also Moḍi).

(2) **Grantha** : This script was prevalent in the Tamil Nadu area from about 7th cent. A.D.[44] But manuscripts date from the end of 16th century. It has two varieties :(1) the 'square' hand founds around Tanjore and (2) the 'round' hand of mostly Jains around Arcot and Madras.[45] Grantha ran parallel to Tamil and was used in writing Sanskrit only, hence the name. The term appears in the 14th century.

(3) **Kannaḍa** : One of the early scripts of South India evidenced from about 450 A.D. in Karnataka. Compared to Grantha, Nandināgarī and Telugu, Sanskrit manuscripts in Kannaḍa script are small in number. (See also **Telugu**).

(4) **Maithilī** : Eastern Bihar (Tirhut) and western West Bengal form the location of this script. The Tirhuti variety was used for writing books. There was also a running hand, Kaithi, used for non-literary purposes. The documents date from 15th century.

(5) **Malayālam** : This is confined to Kerala. This script is evidenced late (15th century) in history.

(6) **Moḍi** : This is the running hand of 'Bālabodha', the Devanāgarī of Maharashtra, a survival of Southern Nāgarī. The documents available since 13th century are all non-literary private correspondence and official records. Hence, this need not be reviewed

here. But it may have influenced the Devanāgarī too, at least the Devanāgarī of some schools.

(7) **Nandināgarī** : The Nāgarī in South India developed into what is called 'Nandināgarī'. Why the script was called 'Nandi' is only a matter of conjecture. This is evidenced since the Yadava-Hoysala period (13th century) and the frequency of its use grew during the Vijayanagar period. This script must have developed as a pen-style or stylus-style script and not as a chisel-style one. The absence of the horizontal top-line is suitable to write on palm leaves, otherwise there was the possibility of the leaf splitting due to the line. If Oriya script avoided the top-line by rounding it,[46] Nandināgarī did it in another fashion. The number of manuscripts, including palm leaf, is considerable and is abundant in west half of Karnataka.

(8) **Nepāli or Newāri** : This is current in Nepal and adjoining areas. Manuscripts are available from 12th century. A manuscript dated 1063A.D.deposited in Bodleian Library, Oxford, is said to be the oldest.

(9) **Oriya** : This script current in Orissa has two varieties in accordance with its use : (1) that which was used to write on palm leaf manuscripts, Brāhmaṇi and (2) Karaṇi that which was used for non-literary purposes by Karaṇs. This is related to Vaṅga or Bengali and appears rather late in history.

(10) **Śāradā** : Originally Śāradā appears in about 8th century A.D. The earliest manuscript in this script current in Jammu and Kashmir and North–Eastern Punjab, dates from 11th-12th century.

(11) **Sinhalese** : In Srilanka manuscripts were written in this script. Most of them are Buddhist works.

(12) **Telugu or Āndhra** : This is the script employed in the Andhra Pradesh area. It is not easy to identify Telugu from Kannada in early palm leaves. But it is Telugu by and large. This attitude may be seen in many of the Sanskrit texts printed in Karnataka in the last century and early part of the present; they are in Telugu script. Actually Kannada and

Telugu branch off only around 14th century till which time they were one.

(13) **Tibetan** : It is the script current in Tibet. It has two varieties : dbu-chan is used for literary purposes and printing; dbu-med is for non-literary purposes. Tibetan appears since 7th century A.D. There are several Sanskrit books written in this script. Many of them are Buddhist.

(14) **Tigaḷāri** : This script, employed mostly in the coastal Karnataka - Karwar to Kasargod, is a mixed one. It contains the elements of Malayālam, Grantha and Kannaḍa in order of dominance. There is a large number of manuscripts mostly in private possession; only a fraction has been acquired by the modern libraries. Because this is found in manuscripts only, it has not come to the notice of palaeographers who speak of it as Tuḷu or Tuḷu-Malayālam (Western Grantha). The script has nothing to do with Tuḷu language which is spoken only in and around Mangalore. As we go northwards, the use of the script appears wider and wider. This script is found in manuscripts only and evidenced since 12th century.

(15) **Tuḷu** : A misnomer for Tigaḷāri.

(16) **Vaṅga or Bengali** : This script is current in Bengal (both West and East). It fully developed by 15th century Assamese is a variety of Bengali and Oriya and Maithili are related to this.

*Peculiarities*

Before proceeding further, we may remind ourselves that all the above scripts are sister-scripts being derived from a single source, viz., Brāhmī. This also establishes further that Brāhmī was prevalent all over the country from very ancient times.

It is obvious that the writing in the manuscripts cannot be uniform. Each scribe has his own idiosyncracies, i.e., his own style of writing certain letters at least. Still the script in a manuscript will have all the common features to identify the script. Of course, not all scribes are careful in their writing. The careless ones pose a problem. However, it is curious to find that the scribes of particular schools have developed their own peculiar mode of writing. The Devanāgarī of Dvaita texts on paper, for example, has some specialities of its own. Similarly, the Nāgarī of Jain works differs depending upon the scribe – a hermit (one belonging to Kharataragaccha), a Maravadi-lahiya (scribe) or a Gujarati-lahiya.[47] Such peculiarities of writing in manuscripts could be an interesting study.

The above information about the scripts is mostly based on palaeographic and epigraphic sources. It is pointed out earlier that *Vārāhitantra* speaks of pen-style and other styles of scripts. This classification indeed shows the interest with which those people studied the scripts. The modern palaeographers too distinguish pen-style and chisel-type scripts.[48] The former is found in books and the latter on stone and such material. The style of writing varies in accordance with the type of instrument employed, the choice of which is related to the writing surface on hand. (cf. A child is advised to learn writing with a pencil and pen is recommended at a later stage).

## Notes and References

1. Some of the pioneers in the field are : Charles Wilkins who tried to read (1783-84) earlier scripts and succeeded (1785) in deciphering later Brāhmī. He was followed by Col. Tod who deciphered (1818-27) Gupta script. It was left to Joseph Prinsep to decipher (1837) completely the early Brāhmī. Before these attempts, Firoz Shah Tughlak (14th cent.) who had shifted Aśokan Pillars from Meerut and other places to Delhi, invited scholars to read the writings on it. But they could not decipher it. A second attempt in the direction was of Akbar (16th cent.) and it was also not successful.
2. Aśokan inscriptions are not found south of Karnataka. But, recently, pot-sherds with Tamil-Brāhmī characters have been unearthed from the pre-historic sites in Vembakkoyt-tai village near Sivakasi (Tamil Nadu). *Deccan Herald*, dated 29.6.1986.
3. Dani opines that these variations do not point to regional variations. Dani (1983), p. 48.

4. Fleet (1906); *Ep.Ind.*, 2.25.
5. 1st half of 2nd cent. B.C., acc. to Dani (1983), p. 56.
6. *Ep.Ind.*, 22.1; Fleet (1907).
7. "A unique inscription on a red earthenware jar of the post-Harappan period, recently discovered in the intertidal zone of Dwaraka island has been deciphered by epigraphists.
   "What is interesting is that it is written from left to right as in Aśokan Brāhmī (3rd century B.C.) and unlike in the Indus Seals, where it is from right to left. Four letters are analogous to Brāhmī letters, forging a link between Indus and Brāhmī scripts.
   "The inscription shows the evolution of Indus writing into a simple system and further establishes that writing was in use during the second half of the second millennium B.C., contrary to the belief that there was no writing in this period in India." - *Deccan Herald*, dated 24-6-1985.
8. Cf. Bhandarkar, D.R. (1922).
9. It is rather interesting that the earliest reference to pen and ink in the West is from 7th century (*Encyclopaedia Americana*, 18, p. 241; also 4, p. 225), while writing with ink was known very much earlier in India.
10. Rhys Davids (1881), p. xxii.
11. The reverse form of letters may perhaps be due to the practice of the sculptors who were called upon to engrave for seals. It was known that the impression of a seal would be the reverse of what is engraved on it.
12. See Bhandarkar, D.R. (1922).
13. Diringer (1948), p. 336.
14. S.R. Rao (1978).
15. *'nākariṣyad yadi brahmā likhitam cakṣur uttamam; tatreyam asya lokasya nābhaviśyac chubhā gatiḥ.' Nārada-smṛti.* 4.70.
   *'ṣāṇmāsike tu samaye bhrāntiḥ sañjāyate yataḥ; dhātrā-kṣarāṇi sṛṣṭāni patrārūḍhāny ataḥ purā'* - quoted in *Vyavahāranirṇaya*, p. 81 and *Vyavahāraprakāśa* of Mitramiśra, p. 141.
   *'bhrānteḥ puruṣadharmatvāt lekhyam nirṇāyakam param; anubhūtasya smṛtyartham likhitam nirmitam purā. yatnāc ca brahmaṇā vācā varṇa-svara-vicinhitam'. Śukranītisāra,* 2.291, 297.
   *'gītī śīghrī śiraḥkampī yathā-likhita-pāṭhakah; anartha-jño'lpa-kaṇṭhaś ca ṣaḍ ete pāṭhakādhamāḥ.' Yājñavalkya-śikṣā, Pāṇinīya-śikṣā,* 32, reads b : *'tathā likhita-pāṭhakaḥ'.*
16. *Raghuvaṁśa* 3.28 : *'liper yathāvad grahaṇena vāṅma-yam nadīmukheneva samudram āviśat'* For references to bhūrja, see below.

17. *'Ceṭī - tena hi bhaṇāhi kim nāmı edam akkharam. (nāma-mudrikām darśayati). Vidūṣakaḥ - bhodi, edam akkharam nama putthaye natthi.' Avimāraka,* Act 2, ll. 48-52. Ed. C.R. Devadhar, Pune, 2nd edn., 1951, pp. 119f.
*'...lekhaḥ khalu mām apavahati'. ... tvaryatām lekhaḥ ... Pratijñā-yaugandharāyaṇa,* Act 1, between 3 & 4.
*'Bhaṭa: karmāṇi pustakam āropayati kumāraḥ.' Pañcarātra,* Act 2 after 27. *'Pustakaprāmāṇyāt...vanaukasau (śuka-sāraṇau) gṛhitau.' Abhiṣeka,* Act 4 after 18.
18. *'saṁvatsaram ṛtum...nāma-karmāṇi cābhilikhya vādī... ārthānupūrvān niveśayet; niviṣṭāṁś ca avekṣeta...'; '...prāṅmukham udaṅmukham vā vibhaktopasthānam nibandha-pustaka-sthānam kārayet...tatra adhikara-ṇānām saṅkhyā... nibandha-pustakastham kārayet'. Arthaśāstra,* 3.1.58; 2.25.7
19. *'lekhaka–gaṇaka-sahāyaiḥ siddheḥ ghātāḥ samabhi lekhyāḥ.' Nāṭyaśāstra,* 27.23.
20. *Kāmasūtra* : 3.15 mentions only the number of Kalās. The commentaries give details. Yaśodhara in his com. *Jayamaṅgala* speaks of *lipi-jñānam* as one of them. See also Venkatasubbaiah (1911).
21. Goldstucker (1965), pp. 11 ff; Agarwala (1953), p. 311.
22. *'rāmanāmāṅkitam cedam paśya devy aṅgulīyakam.' Vālmīki-Rāmāyaṇa,* Sundara, 36.2.
23. *'Likhitam sākṣiṇo bhuktiḥ pramāṇam trividham smṛtam'. Vāsiṣṭha-Dharma-sūtra,* 16.10; *Viṣṇu-Dharma-sūtra. '..lekhya-pratyayaḥ'. - Vāsiṣṭha-Dharma-sūtra,* 16.14. See also *Vīramitrodaya, Vyavahāraprakāśa,* under lekhya, vol. II, p. 81 f.
24. *'varṇaḥ, svaraḥ, mātrāḥ, balam, saṁhitā, sandhiḥ' Taittirīya Upaniṣat,* 1.1
*'...svarāḥ-ūṣmāṇah..sparśāḥ', 'sarve svarā ghoṣavanto balavanto vaktavyāḥ.. sarva ūṣmāṇo 'grasta anirastā vivṛtā vaktavyāḥ.. sarve sparśā leśenānabhinihitā vaktavyā..., Chāndogya-Up.,* 2.22. 3, 5.
25. *"imām te vācam vasūyanta āyavo ratham na dhīraḥ svapā atakṣiṣuḥ.." Ṛgveda* 1.130.6ab. Similar is 5.211ab, 5.73.10 and 10.39.14 ab. *"indra brahma kriyamaṇā juṣasva yā te śaviṣṭha navyā akarma vastreva bhadrā sukṛtā vasūyū ratham na dhīraḥ svapā atakṣam." Ṛgveda.* 5.29.15.
26. *Taittirīya-saṁhitā* 7.2.20; *Taittirīya-Brāhmaṇa* 3.8.16.2-4; See also *Śatapatha-Brāhmaṇa* 10.3.1.20. Bhandarkar, D.R. (1922).
27. *'mudrā-lipiḥ śilpa-lipiḥ lipir lekhani-sambhavā; 'guṇḍikā ghuṇasambhūtā lipayaḥ pancadhā smṛtāḥ.' Vārāhitantra.*

*'lekhanyā likhitam viprair mudrābhir aṅkitam ca yat; śilpādi-nirmitam yac ca pāṭhyam dhāryam ca sarvadā'. Khadgamālā-tantra.*
*'...lekha lipi, mudrā-lipi...' Mahāvastu,* 1.135.
Attention may be drawn to Dani (1983), wherein 'pen-style script' and 'stylus script' are spoken of (pp. 52,77, etc).

28. All the inmates of the harem and even thieves were literate : *'antepure likhito hoti... likhitako coro...' Mahāvagga,* Likhitaka-cora-vatthu, I 35, para 93. *'lekham chindati yo evam marati so dhanam vā labhati yaśam vā labhati. saggam vā gacchati ti akkharakkharāya āpatti dukkaṭassa, lekham passitvā marissām ti dukkham vedanam uppādeti'.* The Vibhaṅga makes an exception in favour of learning to write : *'anāpatti lekham pariāpunāti'. Bhikkhuṇo Pātimokkha, Pācittiya,* 49. "There are several passages which confirm in an indisputable manner the existence of the art of writing at the time when the Vinaya texts were put into their present shape." Rhys Davids & Oldenberg (1881) Intd., p.xxxii. At the same time, that some of these lines may go back to the period when these texts originated, too, cannot be disputed.
*'sippam nāma dve sippāni hīnam ca sippam ukkaṭṭham ca sippam... ukkaṭṭham nāma sippam muddā gaṇanā lekha'. Pacittiya* 5.2.15 (*Bhikkhu Vibhaṅga,* p.11).
*'sace kho upāli lekham sikhissati, aṅguliyo dukkhā bhavissanti, sace kho upāli gaṇanam sikkheyya...' Mahāvagga,* p.80.
*'lekhāya samvaṇṇeti nāma lekham chindati'. Pārājika,* 1.3.153.
All the names of the style of writing known in the world were introduced by Bodhisattva. These are the Brāhmī style, the Puṣkarasāri, the Kharoṣṭhi, Yavanāni... *'yac ceha loke saṅkhyā gaṇanam mudrāsthāsthānāni ca sarva eṣā..' Mahāvastu,* 1.135.15; Jones (1949). See also note. 30.
*'bhikkhu hatthacchitram pabbājenti..likhitakam pabbājenti.' Mahāvagga,* p.94.
*'dhanukena pi kīlanti, akkharikāyā pi kīlanti'. Pārājika,* 2.13.198.
*'samaṇa-brāhmaṇā...bhojanāni bhuñjitvā...viharanti...dhanukam akkharikam manesikam...' - Dīgha-Nikāya,* Vol. I, 1.2.14; 2.5.49.

29. Law (1933) 2, pp. 24, 68.

30. *Lalitavistara* was written a few centuries after the Buddha. While it could be conceded that the details of Buddha's life were handed down traditionally, addition of an element of exaggeration cannot be ruled out. If the Buddha as even a child is attributed the knowledge of 64 scripts, it is certain that these scripts were well known before *Lalitavistara* at least.
*'bodhisattvo lipiśālam upānīyate sma...tasmin vidhijña kim atho*

*lipiśāstra mātre. atha bodhi-sattva uragasāra-candanamayam lipiphalakam ādāya viśvāmitrācāryam evam āha - katamām me bho upādhyāya lipim śikṣāpayasi. brāhmī-kharoṣṭhī-puṣkarasārī, aṅgalipim, vaṅgalipim, magadhalipim, māṅgalyalipim, aṅgulīyalipim, śakārilipim, brahmāvali-lipim, pāru ṣyalipim, drāviḍalipim, kirātalipim, dākṣiṇyalipim, ugralipim, saṅkhyālipim, anulomalipim, avamūrdhalipim, daradalipim, khāpyalipim, cīnalipim, lūnalipim, hūṇalipim, madhyākṣaravistāralipim, puṣpalipim, devalipim, nāgalipim, yakṣalipim, gāndharva-lipim, kinnaralipim, mahoragalipim, asuralipim, mṛgacakralipim, vāyasarutalipim, bhaumadevalipim, antarikṣadevalipim, uttarakurudvīpalipim, aparago-dānīlipim, pūrvavidehalipim utkṣepalipim nikṣepalipim vikṣepalipim prakṣepalipim sāgaralipim vajralipim lekhapralekhalipim, anudrutalipim śāstrāvartām-gaṇanāvartalipim utkṣepāvartalipim garuḍa-lipim, nikṣepāvartalipim pādalikhitalipim dviruttarapadasandhi-lipim, yāva-ddaśottara-pada-sandhilipim, madhyahāriṇīlipim,* sar*varuta-saṅgrahaṇīlipim, vidhyanulomavimiśrita-lipim, ṛṣitapastaptām* rocamānām *dharaṇiprekṣiṇilipim, gaganaprekṣiṇīlipim, sarvauṣadhiniṣyandām sarvasārāsaṁgrahaṇīm sarvabhūtarutagrāhaṇīm āsām bho upādhyāya catuṣṣaṣṭilipīnām...' Lalitavistara, Parivarta 10, Lipiśālāsandarśana.*

Hariṣeṇa speaks of 18 *lipis*, one of which is *yavanalipi*. The princes were taught this also. *Bṛhatkathākośa*, 22.4ff.

Incidentally, it may be mentioned that Marathe (1986) has mooted the theory that the names of eight *mātṛs* (*Brāhmī, Māheśvarī*, etc.) are the names of scripts. Brāhmī is well known as the name of script. An inscription is claimed to be in Māheśvarī-lipi. A māheśvarīlipi is mentioned in *Paṇṇavaṇāsutta* (see note 33 below). *'āy vā imā loke saṁjñā brāhmī puṣkarasārā kharoṣṭī yāvanī brahmavāṇī puṣpalipi, kūṭalipi śāktinalipi vyatyastalipi lekhalipi, mudrālipi ukāra-madhura-darada-cīṇa-hūṇābhira, vaṅga, sīphala, tramiḍa-dardura-ramaṭhabhayavaicchetuka-gulmalā- hastadā kasūlā ketukā kusuvā tālikā jajarideṣu akṣarabaddham sarvā eṣā bodhisatvānām nīti.' Mahāvastu*, 1.135.

31. *'seṭṭhiputte lekham sikkhante eva dāso pi ssa phalakam vahamāno gantvā teneva saddhim lekham sikkhi gaṇanam sikkhi...kaṭāhako nāma...bhāṇḍāgarika-kamma...'*
    Kaṭāhakajātaka; *Jātakaṭṭha-kathā*, Volume I, p. 330.
32. Rhys Davids and Oldenberg (1881), Intd., p. xxxiii.
33. Learning of alphabet is included in *Kalāgrahaṇa* and is one of the 72 kalās : the teacher is called Kalācārya (Samāvāyaṅga 11.11.429). We also come across *potthaya* meaning book (b9.33.385). See Sikdar (1964, p. 337) for

other references. *'se kim tam bhāsāriyā ? bhāsāriyā je ṇam addhamāgahāye bhāsāye bhāsimti jatthā vi ya ṇam bambhī-livi pavattayi. bambhīye ṇam livīye aṭṭhārasavihe lekkha-vihāṇe paṇṇatte. tam jahābambhī javaṇāliyā dosāpuriyā, kharoṭṭhī pukkharasāriyā bhogavayiyā pahar-āīyavo ya antakkhariyā akkharpuṭṭhīya veṇaīyā ṇiṇhaīyā aṅkalivī gaṇitalivī gandhavvalivī āyaṁ-salivī māhesarī dāmili poliṇdī se ttām bhāsāriyā.' Paṇṇavaṇā-sutta*, p. 38.

*'bāvattari-kalāvo paṇṇattā tam jahā - lekham gaṇiyam rūvam naṭṭam gīyam vāīyam saragayam pukkharagayam samatālam...' Samavāya*, 62, Sūtra 6, p. 93.

Jain Mahāpurāṇas relate that Ṛṣabhadeva taught first the art of writing (*masi*). Brāhmī is spoken of as daughter of Ṛṣabhadeva. Sikdar (1964), p. 340.

34. The *Rāyapaseṇiya-sutta* (sutra 81) describes a book of scripture and speaks of its leaves (*paṭṭagāīm*), the supporting (?) wooden sheets (*kambī*), the thread (*dora*), ink (*masi*), pen (*lekhani*), letters (*akkharāīm*), etc.
35. *Tirukkural* (1st century A.D.) opening line : 'agara-mudala eluttu'. (In sculpture, Tiruvalluvar, author of this work, holds a book in left-hand.) *Basavapurāṇa* (1369 A.D.) ch.5 mentions Telugu, Kannaḍa, Grantha, Tamil (Dramila), Lāla (Lāṭa, Gujarati) and Persian.
36. Pandey, p. 5. Dasgupta (1958), p. 272; Upādhyāya (1961), p. 237.
37. Mookerji (1947), p. 526.
38. *ibid.* p. 574.
39. Pandey, p. 5f.
40. *ibid.*
41. Sarasvatī in Lucknow Museum (1st century A.D.) and Khajurāho. See the plates (67 & 73) in V.S. Agrawala (1964). Lady writing a letter (Indian Museum, Calcutta, Bhuvaneswar; *c.* 11th century), and white marble Sarasvatī (National Museum, New Delhi, Bikanar *c.* 12th century). Also Sivaramamurti (1952), p.17f.
42. Eg. Goyal (1983).
43. The I council was held soon after the *parinirvāṇa* of Buddha at Rājagṛha. The II after a century later at Vaiśāli. The III during the time of Aśoka at Pāṭalī-putra and the IV at Kuniala-vihāra (Kashmir) patronised by Kaniṣka.
44. P.L. Menariya writes that rajju or grantha-lipi, rekhā-lipi, Citra-lipi and such were used when there was no alphabet, and that rajju or grantha-lipi was current in China and North America. Menariya (1979), p. 86. However, no

evidence is provided. The veracity of his statement appears beyond verification.

45. Vatteluttu and Koleluttu. See Diringer (1948), p. 384f; Burnell, p. 42ff.
46. "The local scribes employing an iron stylus to inscribe the letters were compelled to avoid long, straight, and particularly the characteristic horizontal *mātrā* of the Devanāgarī..." Diringer (1948), p. 366.
47. Jain (1979), p. 90.
48. Dani (1963), pp. 77ff.

# CHAPTER II

# WRITING MATERIALS

In the last chapter, we saw that in India, people were conversant with writing quite early in history and that they wrote their compositions in books. This leads to the consideration of the materials and instruments they used for preparing the books in particular.

*Rāyapaseṇiya-sutta*, a Jain work, describes ten parts or aspects of a 'book'. They are: *patra, kambī, dorā, granthi, lipyāsana, chādana, śṛṇkhalā, masī, lekhanī* and *akṣara*.[1] These are indeed the constituents of a written book. Seven of these, viz., *patra, dorā, granthi, chādana, masī, lekhanī* and *akṣara* are clear. They are in order: the leaves (the written surface), the cord (binding the manuscript), the knot (at one end of the cord), the covering (of cloth), the ink, the pen and the characters (written). The other three (*kambī, lipyāsana* and *śṛṅkhalā*) call for some discussion and may be considered later.

We may first discuss the basic material and then the writing equipments, ink and other instruments.

## (I) MATERIALS

When writing comes to be widely used in a society from domestic correspondence to writing a book on an international topic of perennial interest, selection of suitable material also becomes quite important along with it. For example, daily newspapers are not printed on maplitho paper, nor dictionary is printed on newsprint. In other words, the nature and purpose of a document determines the selection of the material. On the other hand, selection is also conditioned by the easy availability of the material in sufficient quantity. No author/publisher would like his/her book to be printed on paper of varying shades or thickness. This attitude is not something modern. Those who wrote two thousand years ago were also guided by the very same principles. While anything, a leaf, dry or not, for instance, could serve for a brief message intended to last for a short period, a relatively strong material in an uniform size and quality was opted for a book. For those documents which were intended to last "till the existence of the Sun and the Moon", metal or stone was preferred.

People of those days who wanted to have a copy of a work could not afford to insist on this or that kind of material. Works were copied on such material as were easily and readily available around them in required quantities. It is an interesting study to find out the materials employed for writing on by the ancient people.[2] Of course, this has to be gathered from archaeological and literary sources. Though our primary concern is to trace the history of books, all those materials on which writing is found may also be reviewed here. Quite curiously, sometimes, certain works are found copied on those on which we normally do not expect a copy of a work. First, we shall discuss the materials used in the main for copying books and then the others.

**(A) Materials for Writing Books**

Whenever we think of books of ancient India, two materials stand out foremost; (1) Palmleaf and (2) Birchbark. Both of them are evidenced since very early times. Though it is difficult to decide which of them is earlier, it may be possible to surmise that palm leaf or 'some' leaf was the first one. The word *patra* which is being used very commonly for the material, means a 'leaf'. After several attempts of trial and error, perhaps, the palmleaf must have been arrived at as the most suitable, and it was called *'patra'* because it was also a leaf. The Buddhist canonical works employ the term *paṇṇa* (Skt. *parṇa*) which is clearer. Later, the term was extended to include any similar writing material-birch-bark, paper and even a metal sheet (*tāmra-patra*). Of the available bulk of manuscripts, palmleaf very much out-numbers birch-bark. This may also point to the wide use of that leaf.

*'Patra'* as writing material is referred to in early literature. The Buddhist and the Jaina literatures and the *Arthaśāstra* have specific mention of *patra*. *Kaṭāhaka-jātaka*,[3] for instance, reads : paṇṇam gāhetvā...likhitvā... seṭṭhissera muddikayā lāñchetvā...paṇṇam adāsi... paṇṇam vācetvā... ("Taking a 'leaf' (and) writing (on it)... sealed it as the merchant would do...showed the 'leaf'. Having read the 'leaf'...")

*Paṇṇa* (i.e. *parṇa*, leaf) is mentioned here as the material for writing a letter.

We may notice here an interesting episode about banyan leaf (*vaṭa-patra*) being used to copy a book, though recorded in a very recent *kāvya*. Rāmabhadra Dīkṣita was a poet in the Court of King Shahji of Tanjore (17th century). *Patañjali-carita* is one among his numerous *kāvyas*. A Brahmin, Dīkṣita recounts, was taught *Mahābhāṣya* by one of Patañjali's disciples turned to a *brahmarākṣasa* because of the curse of Patañjali. The Brahmin had no anticipation of this, and there were no writing materials near at hand. He is said to have taken down the *Bhāṣya* as taught by the goblin, on the fresh leaves of banyan tree under which the goblin taught him.[4] Later, after returning home, he transferred the text on to palm leaves. Whether this account is an imagination of the poet or part of traditional episodes, it has no other source of corroboration. What we may draw from this here is that materials like banyan leaves were probably employed as a stop-gap arrangement. A similar episode recorded with reference to *Bṛhatkathā* is quite known. Guṇāḍhya resorted to the forest after being defeated in a contest in the royal court. He is reported to have written his book of tales *Bṛhatkathā* on leaves (not specified) with his blood because necessary stationery was not available there.[5] Similarly, we find Śakuntalā writing a message of love to Duṣyanta on a lotus leaf.[6] Thus, any leaf relatively broad served for temporary purposes. Even in the case of books, any kind of leaf[7] was perhaps, employed as a stop-gap arrangement, if necessary, and later transcribed into regularly used material.

### 1. *Palm Leaf (Tālapatra) :*

Three species of palm tree botanically known as –

(1) *Corypha umbraculifera,* (2) *Corypha faliera* and (3) *Borassus flabellifera,* are found in India. The first one grows widely in dry area – Gujarat, Sindh and Rajasthan. The second one is plentiful in humid coastal areas of South India, particularly West coast and in South Mynamwar (Burma). The trees thrive for 40 to 100 years. Infloresence shoots up over 20 feet and signifies the death of the tree. The trees have long tapering leaves with a rib growing opposite to one another on shaft attached to the head of the stem.

Traditionally two kinds of palm leaves are distinguished : (a) *tāla* or *khara tāla* and (b) *talī* or *Śrītāla (Nuṅguppanai* and *Tālippanai* respectives in Tamil). *Tāla* leaves are narrower, thick and yellowish in colour. This variety is abundantly available but easily susceptible to pests.[8] *Śrītāla* leaves are broader, thin, a little brown in colour and cracks develop in them easily. Kauṭilya[9] juxtaposes the words *tāḍa* and *tāḍi,* thus indicating a difference between them probably as noted above. Rājaśekhara[10] also mentions : *tāla* and *tālī* and his observation that stylus is used for writing on *tāla* while a pen is used for *tālī*, endorses, to an extent, the above said description of *khara-tāla* and *śrītāla*. Dr. Sircar[11] identifies tāla or tāḍa as *Borassus* (palmyra) and *tālī* or *tāḍī* as *Corypha* (talipot). Dr. Kaye[12] opines that *Borassus* was probably introduced from Africa while *Corypha* is indigenous and earlier, Hoernle too said that earlier palm leaves were made from *Corypha* (talipot). De Silva[13] notes that palmyra (*Borassus)* was used mostly for letters i.e. temporary purposes and talipot (*Corypha*) for writing books.

#### *Preparation of Palm Leaf*

The palm leaf is subjected to a process of treatment to make it suitable for writing. Mature fresh leaves are first dried and then boiled in water and again dried in shade. The surfaces of the leaves are made smooth by rubbing them with a burnishing stone. They are cut to required size.[14]

R.N. Sampath[15] writes that in South India, the leaves collected are exposed to dry for three days and nights. The sun made them dry and the dew, white. The leaves are gathered during winter.[16]

De Silva[17] describes the preparation of palm leaves as in vogue in Srilanka. Leaf buds about to open are collected from young trees. These buds will be ten to twenty feet long and contain 80 to 100 leaflets. The leaves are separated. They are immersed in cold water and heated on slow fire. As water begins to boil heat is reduced gradually and the leaves are allowed to simmer in water for three to four hours. Then the leaves are dried in shade for three days and nights. The leaves are smoothened by pulling them up and down against a smooth cylindrical wood surface, mostly areca palm. Then they are cut to required sizes. The leaves are tightly pressed and ends and sides are singed with hot iron. It is said burning thus ensures preservation from damp and mould.

Two round holes are punched on the middle points of both halves of the leaves. De Silva quotes a verse that gives directions for punching holes.

> *āyāmena caturbhāgam tribhāgam punar eva ca;*
> *ubhayāḥ sūtra-madhyena tathā kuryāt chidralakṣaṇam.*
>
> (The leaf is folded in three and unfolded; again folded in four and unfolded. The leaf is punched between the creases).

"The Tantras enjoin that the holes should always be punched - never cut with a knife, or produced by burning."[18] Two wooden boards of the same size as the leaves (preferably larger by a few millimetres) and with similar holes are put on either side of the set of leaves. A cotton cord not very thin, passes through the leaf hole of the leaves and the boards; and the bundle is wound round and bound by the same cord.[19] This cord passing through the leaves ensures their order also. The length of the leaves varies from about 4 cms. to 90 cms. and the breadth varies from 2.5 cms. to 8 cms. The written 'book' is usually kept wrapped in a red, sometimes yellow, cloth in North India.

It was noted earlier that the *Rāyapaseṇiyasutta* describes the several parts of a book. The items mentioned there fit into a palm leaf manuscript (See beginning of this chapter).

Usually, letters were incised on palm leaves with a stylus though they could be written with a pen as well. Indeed, there are a few instances of written palm leaves available now. The Jaina canonical works speak of writing on palm leaves with ink.[20]

*Antiquity of Use of Palm Leaf*

Palmleaf was in use at least since about 5th century B.C. 'Paṇṇa' of the Jātakas is presumably palm leaf. The *Arthaśāstra* (quoted earlier) is very explicit in this regard. Hiuen Tsang (7th century A.D.) also mentions its use.

Incidentally it may be noted that the raw leaves were used for various other purposes as well : covering roof tops, making fans and baskets. *Pācittiya* ordains that the bhikkus should not wear footcovering made of talipot.[21]

In earlier times, palm leaf must have been in extensive use than birch bark. For, we find, as early as 1st century A.D., even copper plates used for charters, fashioned like palm leaf, i.e. oblong and narrow. The earliest copper plate of this sort is the Taxila plate of Patika of 21 A.D.[22] We may also mention here that many of the charters of the early Western Ganga Kings too are in this size : 25 cms. x 4.5 cms. 20cms. x 4.5 cms. etc.).

During the third dynasty of Vijayanagar kings (1529-1543), measurements of land, etc., were written in palm leaf registers called *'kavila'*.[23]

Palm leaves were being used as late as the middle of the 20th century. A 19th century palm leaf recording a sale-deed has been recently discovered in Tanjavur by the Epigraphy Department of the Tamil University and another palm leaf manuscript of early 19th century has been discovered in Kanyakumari District.[24] Till recent times, palm leaf was being used in Kerala for writing horoscopes, initial lessons of students, etc.

*Some Early Specimens*

1. The oldest well-preserved palm leaf manuscript is that of *Dhavala*, preserved in Jain Bhandar, Mudbidri. The manuscript contains 1478 leaves written in ink in old Kannada of about 9th century A.D. On either end margins of each side of the leaves, there are artistic drawings of patterns which are different from each other; there are no repetitions.[25] Jaisalmer Jain Bhandar has a copy of *Pañcamīkathā* (1053 A.D.), *Oghaniyutti* (1060 A.D.) and of *Kuvalayamālā* (1082).
2. The Bhandarkar Oriental Research Institute, Pune, is said to possess a Jain work '*Upamiti-bhāva-prapañca-kathā*' (178 folios) of 905-6 A.D.
3. A copy of *Amarakośa-ṭīkā* in the Mysore Oriental Research Institute is dated 1130 A.D.
4. The Hori-uzi Monastery, Japan, has in its collection, two manuscripts of *Prajñāpāramita-Hṛdaya-Sutra* and *Uṣṇīśa-Vijayadhāriṇī* belonging to 6th century A.D.[26] The script shows that its original home was somewhere in Central India. The manuscripts are written with pen.
5. The Cambridge University has a copy of *Parameśvaratantra* and bears the date 252 Harṣa Era, i.e., 858 A.D.
6. A manuscript (written) of *Skānda-Purāṇa* of the 7th century A.D. and of *Laṅkāvatāra-Sūtra* (906-7) are in Durbar Library, Kathmandu.
7. The manuscripts discovered in Kashgar by Macartna and Godfrey are said to date from about 4th century A.D.[27]
8. The manuscript or rather fragments of a manuscript discovered in Turfain during an expedition between 1902 and 1905, are called Turfan manuscripts or more correctly, 'Turfan fragments'.[28] We are told that there were about 160 pieces of palm-leaves recovered from the sites. Dr. H. Lüders strived to put them in an order, and has edited the text thus available therein. They were the fragments of a

drama, *Sāri-puttappakaraṇa* by Aśvaghoṣa, whose date is 2nd century A.D.

*Peculiar Manuscripts*

1. Longest manuscript : The Oriental Research Institute, Mysore, has two manuscripts of 120 cms. in length (1) *Baudhāyana-śrauta-sūtra* and (2) *Vīramāheśvara-ācāra- saṅgraha.* Manuscript of Prameya-Kamala-mārtāṇḍa is 95 cms. in length.
2. Smallest : (1) Oriental Research Institute, Mysore 4 x 2 cms. - *Devībhāgavata* and other ślokas ; (2) Institute of Kannada Studies, Mysore : *Vāsudeva-Nilukade,* 7 x 3 cms., 106 pages, 7 lines and 14 letters per line. There are such miniatures in other libraries also.
3. Single volume : Oriental Research Institute, Mysore: 18 *parvas* of the *Mahābhārata* in one bundle of leaves.
4. Leaves of the manuscript cut to give the appearance of a Śivaliṅga, GOML, Madras.
5. Written palm leaf pieces tied in the form of beads and strung into a rosary. (Kerala Uni. Or. Mss. Library, Tiruvanantapuram).

2. ***Birch Bark (Bhūrja-patra)***

Bhūrja-patra is the inner bark of a tree and not any leaf as the name might indicate. The Bhūrja tree is the Silver birch, botanically identified as *Baetula utiles* or *Baetula bhoj-patra* which is very commonly grown in the Himalayan slopes (above 30,000 feet high) only (from Kashmir to Sikkim). Alberuni calls the tree tuz. It is also called 'Lekhan'[29]. The other uses of this bark are roofing houses, wrapping things, etc.[30] It is popular in North India but not so in South, because of its paucity.

*Preparation*

The inner bark consists of several thin layers (40 to 50 in a strip) These layers are carefully separated. Each layer is as thin as manifold paper. The sheets are white or pinky-white outside and reddish inside. They also have knots and horizontal lenticels parallel to the girth of the tree. The separated sheets are treated with oil and polished with a smooth stone to make them smooth and hard. The sheets are cut to double the required size, usually square and are folded into half. They are kept loose with two wooden boards on either side of a set of leaves as in the case of palm leaf.[31] Sometimes they are stiched as note books and thin leather is used for outer cover.

Letters can only be written on birch bark; it cannot be incised upon and the writing on them is parallel to the lenticels.

*Antiquity*

*Arthaśāstra* recommends a king to have a good stock of bhūrja along with tāla and tālī (*tāli-tāla-bhūrjānām patram*). Curtius, the Greek writer, notes that the people of this country wrote on bark.[32]

*Amarakośa* records that *carmin* and *mṛdutvak* are two other names of bhūrja.[33]

In the Himalayas, Kālidāsa describes in the beginning of his *Kumārasambhava,* the bhūrja-barks which were written with mineral colours and appeared like spotted reddish skin of the elephants, were useful to the Vidyādhara damsels for writing love-letters. In his *Vikramorvaśya,* Kālidāsa testifies that the bark is as thin as a serpent's slough. The Vidūṣka, in that play, fancies a piece of written bark as slough [34]

Alberuni (1030 A.D.) not only speaks of bhūrja-patra as a writing material but also writes in detail about its processing for writing.[35]

With the introduction of paper in about the 12th-13th century, bhūrja-patra lost its place and went out of use in course of time. But, it has been considered holy and sacred formulae and drawings are still written on it and worn in locket as an amulet.[36]

### *Some Specimens*

The earliest available manuscript in birch bark is the *Prākṛt Dhammapada,* also called *Kharoṣṭhī Dhammapada,* because it is written in Kharoṣṭhī characters. It was discovered in Khotan and is ascribed to 2nd or 3rd century A.D. A manuscript of *Saṁyuktāgama-sūtra* is said to belong to 4th century A.D. A manuscript has been discovered in a stūpa of Afghanistan.

The Bower manuscripts of 56 bhūrja-patras dating back to 425 A.D. or earlier, are a set containing a medical treatise, peculiarity being that the sheets are cut to the size of palm leaves. Godfrey collection also consists of manuscripts of bhūrja. Another such collection is the 'Bakshali manuscripts' of 70 leaves and some near scarps written in Śāradā script dealing with Mathematics, the size being 14.5 by 8.9 cms. (longest). It belongs to 8th century A.D. or according to some scholars, 12th century A.D.

The Ādiparva of the *Mahābhārata* in Śāradā script is one of the precious collections of the B.O.R.I., Pune. Bodleian library has a ms(No.1090) of 5th century. India Office Library, London, Oxford University Library (*Ṛgbhāṣya* of Sāyaṇa) Berlin and Vienna Libraries, have birch bark manuscripts among their acquisitions. One can have an idea of birch bark manuscripts (25.5 x 20 cms.; 15th century A.D.) in the photographic reproduction of *Atharvaveda,* deposited in Tūbingen Library, Germany.[37] A few leaves from Taxila written in Brāhmī of about 5th or 6th century and a Buddhist manuscript, *Bhaiṣajya-guru-Vaiḍūrya-prabhā-sūtra* written in Gupta script (5th or 6th century A.D.) had been exhibited in 1964 by the National Archives of India.[38] Mitra wrote that he had with him a piece of birch bark (25 x 20 cms.) containing the whole of *Bhagavadgītā.*[39]

### 3. *Sāñcīpāṭ or Samucipat*

The Aguru or Aloe tree (*Acqulaira agullocha*) is called Sanchi in Assam, and its bark is Sāñcīpāṭ. It is popular mostly in North Eastern part.[40] Bāṇa refers to the pink colour due to the age of books of Subhāṣita, made of aguru bark.[41] The Buddhist work *Āryamañjuśrīmūla-kalpa* speaks of aguru bark as being used for writing *yantras* and *mantras*.[42]

Many manuscripts in Sāñcīpāṭ have been discovered in Assam and preserved in Guwahati University Library, Narayana Handiqui Res. Institute, Guwahati, Chamariya Satha and Kamarupa Anusandhana Samiti. However, none of them is older than 15th or 16th century A.D. A copy of *Sundara-Kāṇḍa* of 15th century is now in Bibliotheque Nationale, Paris. The sheets of Sācī are interspersed with a layer of wood, giving an impression that the writing is on the board itself. Manuscripts of some *parvas* of *Mahābhārata* in Sācī are in Jaipur Maharaja's collection.[43]

Winternitz notices a book written on wooden boards in the Bodleian Library, Oxford. Probably, it is a mistake for bhūrja-patra or Sācīpat with interspersed wooden boards.[44]

*Tūlīpāṭ* is actually paper made in Assam.[45] There are a few manuscripts of the *Rāmāyaṇa* in the Guwahati University Library.

### 4. *Paper*

Paper was invented by Tsai Lun of China in 105 A.D. and was introduced to India by the Moghul rulers. Even earlier, paper had been brought to India by Itsing for copying manuscripts. Whether paper was available even earlier is a matter much discussed. If Nearchos, the Admiral of Alexander's fleet (326 B.C.), who writes that Indians were manufacturing writing paper out of cotton by pounding it, is right, paper manufacture was known to India long before China invented it.[46]

Rajendralal Mitra in his report dated 15/2/1875, comes to the conclusion that paper was in general use in about 10th century. He refers to *Praśasti-prakāśikā*, a treatise on letter-writing, written at the time of King Bhoja of Dhārā. Detailed directions are given for folding the material of letters, for leaving a long space on the left side of such letters as margin, for cutting a portion of the left lower corner, for decorating the front with gold-leaf - all these given in that book apply to paper and not practicable in case of palm-leaf or bhūrja. Another reference to which Mitra draws our attention is a verse in the *Saṁhitā* of Vyāsa, which lays down that a draft of document be written on a wooden board and after correction, be transferred to *patra.* Mitra asks, if 'patra' here meant only leaf, is there any need to have the draft on a board. Therefore, patra is not any cheap leaf but paper which was rather rare. Finally, Mitra argues, "those who manipulated cotton so successfully as to convert it into the finest fabric known to man, would find no difficulty in manufacturing paper out of it".[47]

Ojha also writes that paper was being manufactured since ancient times.[48]

But it is quite surprising, we do not come across a Sanskrit word for paper. *Śaya* is the Sanskrit word for paper (8th century A.D.) as noted in Sanskrit-Chinese lexicon edited by P.C. Bagchi. S.K. Chatterji shows that it is only a Sanskritised form of the Chinese word 'tsie': tsie›che› śaya.[49]

*Kākala*[50], *Kākali* or *Kakala* (Sanskritised form of *Kāgaz*, Ar.), *Śaṇa-patra* are other words in Sanskrit for paper.

During the time of Akbar, Sialkot paper was famous for fine finish. Kashmir was also known for paper manufacture as well as for inks.[51]

It is curious to note that there is a village Kagajipada, 'hamlet of the paper manufacturers' near Vikramapura (the site of the ancient Vikramasilā) in Bihar. A locality of Daulatabad, Satyendra writes, is called 'Kagajpura'.[52]

*Antiquity of Paper Manuscripts*

The earliest paper manuscript now available is from Patna.

It is reported that the world's second oldest Hafiz manuscripts dated 816 A.D., containing a number of *ghazals* has been found in the Khuda Baksh Oriental Library in Patna.[53] A copy of *Dhvanyāloka-locana* in the Rajasthan Oriental Research Institute is dated 1146 A.D.

Among the Sanskrit manuscripts in the Bodleian Library, Winternitz and Keith have noticed one (No. 1091) in North Western Gupta Kuchari script on wooly paper, glazed surface that may belong to a period between 5th and 7th century.[54] A copy of *Dharmābhyudaya* of Udayaprabha, made by the famous Minister Vastupala himself is preserved in Jaina Bhandara, Cambay (dated 1290 VS, i.e., 1234 A.D.)[55] A latest report from Gujarat states that the Jain Derasan Library at Agas, Kheda district, has among its collections, a copy of *Śanta-paīṇṇa* in ten folios, written in about 945-46 A.D.[56] Manuscripts dated 1327-28 A.D. was discovered by Peterson in Anhilwad area. Stein is said to refer to a Kashmir manuscript of *Śatapatha-Brāhmaṇa* as of 1089 A.D.[57]

The paper manuscript in India is usually oblong or square and mostly kept in loose sheets. Scrolls are rare. The British Museum has a scroll of *Bhāgavata-purāṇa*. It measures 18.5 cms. x 166 cms. The paper is very thin and written with small Nāgarī script; contains colour illustrations. It is kept fixed in a box about 30 cms.[58] (13 x 35.5 cms.) in Baroda Oriental Institute. Another illustrated scroll is of the *Mahābhārata*. Similar specimen are also found in certain other libraries like Adyar Library etc.

Tanjore Sarasvati Mahal Library has acquired a miniature manuscript (5 x 3.8 cms.) of *Bhagavadgītā*.

### *(B) Other Materials*

The above mentioned materials were chiefly used for writing books. The other materials can now be reviewed for curiousity. Incidentally, we find certain works written on some of these as well. Besides leaf and bark, the *Vāsudevahiṇḍī* enumerates wood, ivory, iron, copper and silver as materials for writing and sets forth how they were prepared for the purpose.[59] The British Museum contains a fairly representative collection of Asian manuscripts from the point of view of their material like clay, stone, gold, silver, copper, ivory, bark, wood, palm leaf and paper.[60]

The other materials can be divided into two categories: (1) Metals : (a) Copper (b) Gold, (c) Silver, (d) Brass, (e) Bronze, (f) Iron and Tin; and (2) Non-Metals: (g) Stone,

(h) Earthenware (bricks, pots, etc.), (i) Leather, (j) Ivory, (k) Cotton and (l) Wood. Coins are not taken into consideration here.

## *(1) Metals*

**(a) Copper :** Copper is a metal used by man since very early times. In fact, an age is recognised as Chalcolithic in the early history of human race. Hence, it is but natural that it must have been used first for writing among metals. Copper is beaten into thin sheets 6.5 cms. to 76.5. cms in length and 30 cms. to 6.5 cms. in breadth. The Taxila plate and some of the Kadamba and early Western Ganga plates are peculiar in being similar to palm leaf in size.[61] The plates found in North are wider than those found in South. A document consists of several plates three to six or more depending upon the length of the document. They are strung together. A hole is made, usually at the top if breadth is smaller or on the left if oblong. A ring, usually of brass, passes through the hole. The two ends of the ring are fused and royal signet is impressed upon it, so that no plates can be added, or replaced later. The first and the last plates are written on their inner side only, while those in between are written on both sides. Often the four edges are made slightly higher. Obviously, these measures ensure the engraving from rubbing and scratching with each other. A gold-smith usually engraves on a copper plate. The text may be written on the plate first by some one else following which the smith engraves or he may go ahead straight-away. However, the gold-smith is only a scribe, the text being composed by an officer or a poet in the Royal court.[62]

The copper plates are called 'tāmra-paṭa', 'tāmra-paṭṭikā', - patra, – phalaka, -śāsana, śāsana-patra, dāna-patra, etc. The use of copper between 6th and 12th centuries is quite frequent and later the frequency grows in the South.

The contents of writings on copper plates are invariable legal documents, land grants and the like. Some of these can be classed literary as their preamble is usually a panegeric recounting the genealogy and prowess of the doner and some of the compositions are indeed in high flown style. But there are one or two instances of pure literary compositions being engraved on such plates. Hundreds of thick copper plates were discovered in the Saṅkīrtana Bhaṇḍāra inside the temple of Lord Venkateswara in Tirumala-Tirupati, in 1922. These plates are inscribed in Telugu characters with the 12,000 music compositions called 'Saṅkīrtana' in praise of Lord Venkateswara and composed by the Andhra poet Tāllapākam Aṇṇamācārya (c. 1400-1503). *Vāsudeva-hiṇḍī* refers to writing books on copper plates.[63]

The earliest available copper plate is the Sohgaura plate assigned to the pre-Aśokan period on palaeographic grounds. Another interesting feature about this plate is that it is not hammered and engraved but cast on moulds of sand. Hence, the plate is very thick. This is the only instance of the type and was discovered in Gorakhpur. It belongs to the time of Candragupta Maurya (320 B.C.).[64]

Another instance of early plates is the Srivihara plates found in Bhavalpur, Punjab, dating back to 46 B.C. The Taxila plate of Patika, we have already seen, belongs to 1st century A.D. Kaniṣka is said to have got engraved the Buddhist treatises on copper plates.[65]

There are spurious plates as well . For example, there is one copper plate which speaks of itself as being issued by King Janamejaya, the great-grandson of Arjuna of Mahābhārata.[66] However, the script betrays the age of such plates.

**(b) Gold :** Though malleable like copper and therefore, could be hammered into thin sheets, gold is rarely used because of its rarity and prohibitive cost.

In the Jātakas, we find that in those days gold plate (suvaṇṇa-patra) was used to preserve poetic verses of value or moral sayings or to maintain important family records like horoscope and genealogy. Of course, it is a luxury and only wealthy ones could afford this. Sometimes, royal edicts too were issued in gold plates. Reference may be made to the traditional account of Bhāravi's life : The merchant/king who bought the single śloka[67] of the poet from the poet's wife for quite a large sum of money, it is said, got it inscribed on a gold plate and hung it over the door-way of his private apartment. *Naiṣadhīya-carita* speaks of golden Ketakī leaves (kāñcana-ketakasya dalam) for writing.[68] Attention may be drawn to the common parlance: we speak of some great event as worthy of being written on gold.

Writing on gold goes back to quite an early period. Cunningham has discovered in the Gangu stupa near Taxila, a gold plate with votive inscription in Kharoṣṭhi script. Another instance is the set of two gold leaves with some Buddhistic formulae in a script closely akin to Kadamba script of 5th century A.D. discovered at Mauggun village near old Prome, Mynamwar (Burma).[69] Twenty leaves (similar to palm leaf in size) incised on one side only found in a relic chamber in Hmazwa village (near Prome) in Mynamwar is assigned to 5th or 6th century A.D.[70] It is written in early South Indian script, Kannada-Telugu; contains extracts from Vinaya- and Abhidhamma piṭakas. It is reported that a book of seven gold sheets weighing about 2 kgs. and going back to about 1500 years has been found by archaeologists in North Srilanka.[71] sheets (book) are found at Dhaka Dhamdah Tal.[72] In British Museum, there is a roll of gold plate several feet long and an inch broad with a long document written in Malayalam script.[73]

The several kings in the different parts of the country have been issuing from very early times, gold coins with their names or the names of their chosen god or their emblem, etc., imprinted on them.

Nearer our times, the following instance may be worth-noticing. The golden throne in the Mysore palace has above it a white umbrella which is made of gold. Around this umbrella near the edge, is written a hymn of 24 verses in Anuṣṭup invoking prosperity to the ruler who sits under it. Another instance is a garland of 29 gold medallions, each inscribed with a verse of a hymn composed by the donor of the garland, Krishnaraja Odeyar III. The hymn is devoted to Cāmuṇḍeśvarī and the garland (nakṣatra-mālikā) adorns Goddess Cāmuṇḍeśvarī on the hill in Mysore. A similar garland of gold medallions, with 108 names inscribed, decorates Pārvatī in the Nanjuṇḍeśvara temple, Nanjangud, Mysore district.[74]

(c) **Silver** : Though silver is cheaper than gold, still reference to silver as a material for writing is scanty. Only a few instances have been discovered so far. Besides coins in silver, some documents in silver sheets have been recovered from stūpas at Bhattiprolu and at Taxila.[75] Tantrik formulae and yantras - Sūrya-maṇḍala, Ṛṣimaṇḍala, Śrī-cakra and other cakras - are written on silver plates or discs.[76] Jains write their sacred formulae on silver plates. Silver articles and vessels presented to temples and institutions are inscribed with the names of the donors, etc.

(d) **Brass** : Brass is less malleable than any of the above mentioned metals and therefore cannot easily be beaten into thin sheets and letters cannot be incised on it. Hence, it is not employed like copper for plates. But icons and vessels like pots, plates, pillar-covers, decorative *prabhāvalīs* are made of brass. We find pedestal inscriptions, i.e. inscriptions on the pedestals of (sometimes on the back of) icons.[77] The vessels donated to temples and public institutions are inscribed with names of donors, etc. However, there is a solitary instance of brass substituting copper. It is the Gangasandra plate of Cikkasanna Kempa of S.1212 (1290 A.D.).[78]

The earliest writing on brass may be traced to the writing on the vase containing the remains of the Buddha and discovered in the stūpa at Vardek (Afghanisthan).[79] It is assigned to 6th century B.C. A curious instance is a brass plate of the times of Krishnaraja Odeyar-III, called 'Vaṃśāmbuja' exhibited in the Jaganmohan Palace Citraśālā, Mysore. On the side, the names of kings in the genealogy of Mysore Odeyars down to Krishnaraja-III, in order, are given, arranged in the form of petals of a lotus. On the other side, the family of each King, i.e. the name/s of spouse/s and of their children are given in order.[80] As an instance of pillar cover may be given the cover of Garuḍagamba in the temple of Ranganatha in Sakrepatna, Chikkamagalur District, which was caused to be made by

Krishnaraja Odeyar-III as the inscriptions on it shows. A signet ring of the Gupta period has been recovered from Allahabad.

(e) **Bronze** : Bronze, otherwise called 'bell-metal', is rarely used for even utensils. The bells are, however, almost exclusively made of this alloy. On the bells donated to temples and such other institutions, the name etc., of the donors are inscribed. Bronze is regularly used to seal the ring binding copper plates. Sometimes, idols are cast with this. A human head in bronze is recovered from Peshawar; it has letters all around it.[81]

(f) **Iron** : Inspite of iron being very common and cheap, it is not used for utensils or any writing is found on it in any form, because of its susceptibility for oxidation and erosion. However, there are at least four instances of iron pillars standing in the open ground for centuries subject to wind and rain but without a speck of rust on them. Three of these have writing on them too : (1) the famous Meherouli Iron Pillar standing beside the renowned structure, Kutub Minar, in the fort of Raj Pithora in South Delhi. We are told it weighs more than 6 tons and is 653.2. cms. high, has a diameter of 41 cms. at the base and 30.6 cms. at the top. Writing starts about 18.5 cms. from the ground and contains the undated inscription of one king Candra. (2) The pillar at Dhar has Nāgarī and Persian inscriptions around it. The Persian inscription is of Akbar (1591-92 A.D.). (3) Iron pillar in the temple of Acaleśvara on Mount Abu, Rajasthan, is of about 15 th century A.D. It is 50.5 cms. high with a Śaiva trident at its top with writing. (4) The fourth is at Koḍacādri, a peak in the Western Ghats (Shimoga District). On a small plateau at the top are the temples of Kālabhairava and others. In front of the temple of Kālabhairava, is a solid iron pillar about 10 metres high and the square base measures 12 cms. No writing has been found on it.[82]

(f) **Tin** : The use of tin for making vessel or for writing is almost nil. The only instance is a Buddhist manuscript reported to be in the British Museum.[83]

Mysore Archaeological Reports of 1921 (p. 3 and 31)

speaks of a Buddhist image of 1517 A.D., from Nepal. The metallic (not specified) image is of Vajrasatva (= Buddha in Vajrayāna Buddhism) and his śakti Vajrasattvātmikā. There are four lines in Nāgarī and Newari scripts on the back of the pedestal.

### *(2) Non-Metals*

**(g) Stone :** From very early times, stone has been an object for writing upon. The walls of caves have been scratched with pictures inscribed or drawn on them. Ancient people found out that the inscriptions on stone lasts long and therefore incised on them whatever they wanted to perpetuate. Thus King Aśoka got the sayings of the Buddha inscribed on stones. In fact, in one of the edicts, he records that he has taken recourse to this so that it may stay for a long time : *ciraṭṭhitikā hodutti.*[84] The royal proclamations, praśastis, commemorative sayings, exhortations, grants and dedications to temples, forming Agrahāras and other similar matters of public importance are found inscribed on stone.

The forms of stone on which inscriptions occur are slabs, pillars, beams, walls, pavements, pedestals or back of icons, and rocks (i.e. stone in its natural form) with their surface smoothened or not. Early inscriptions are mostly on pillars, beams and lintels.

The edicts of Aśoka which can as well as classed as literary are spread over the length and breadth of the country and are the earliest. Of the later ones, we may note here especially the instances wherein regular literary works are inscribed. Hattigumpha cave inscription, Allahabad pillar inscription (400 A.D.), Mandasor Stone pillar inscription, Talagunda pillar inscription (6th century) are well-known for their literary style.[85]

(1) Musical notations in Pallava Grantha of 7th century A.D. on a rock on the hill, Kudimiya-malai near Pudukottai.[86]

(2) Gwalior Padmanath temple (1085) *Praśasti-Śataka* (112 verses) of Kacchavāha-Vaṁśa; Maṇikaṇṭha wrote this in 1084 A.D.[87]

(3) Two Sanskrit plays - *Harikelināṭaka* of Cāhumāna King Vigraha IV and *Lalitavigraharāja-nāṭaka* of the same King's Court-poet Somadeva are found engraved and partly preserved in Ajmer.[88]

(4) A Jaina work *Unnata-śikhara-purāṇa* (1170 A.D.) in a number of cantos is engraved on a rock near Bijolia in Bhilwada district. It is dated Vik. 1226, i.e. 1169 A.D.[89]

(5) Dhar : Bhojaśālā : (a) A Sanskrit play, *Pārijātamañjarī* of Madana and Bhoja's two *Kūrma-śatakas* on two slabs; (b) Kamal Maula Masjid -- Devanāgarī alphabet and Ākhyāta-Pratyayas (13th century).[90]

(6) The couplet of Mahārāṇa Kumbhakarṇa of Mewad are engraved on stone; some pieces are in Udaipur Museum. *Rājapraśasti-Kāvya* of Raṇa Choda Bhaṭṭa got engraved by Mahārāṇa Rāja Siṁha I on 24 slabs are fixed near Rājasamudra reservoir.[91]

(7) *Niroṣṭhya-Kāvya* and *Siddhodvāha* of Narasiṁha in Hanumakoṇḍa.[92]

(8) "The fifth (Buddhist) Council, according to Orthodox tradition, was held at Mandalay, Upper Burma in 1867-71 under the patronage of King Mindonmin. By this time, the entire Pāli Tripiṭaka had been engraved on 735 marble slabs as follows: Vinaya 111 slabs, Sutta 416 slabs and Abhidhamma 208 slabs around the Kutthodaw Pagoda, Mandalay. These slabs were reinked and copied for the 6th Council, Rangoon, 1954-56."[93]

Even in modern days, the ceremony of laying foundations for buildings is commemorated by inscribing the date etc. and the name of the person laying the foundation. Another instance of modern engraving is found in Tiruvaiyāru where the Saint Tyāgarāja lived and died. In the maṇḍapa over his samādhi, his compositions are carved on marble stones in different scripts and fixed to the wall around.

**Crystal** : There is a solitary instance of a crystal with an inscription. It is a hexagonal crystal discovered in Bhattiprolu stūpa in Kṛṣṇa District, Andhra Pradesh.

It is 3/8 inch each face, record scratched on all six sides. It has a hole through its axis. It is considered as a votive offering made by a woman from Nandapura.[94]

**(h) Earthenware : Bricks :** Bricks are round or square tablets of clay or mud dried and baked sometimes. Letters are to be incised or engraved while they are wet. We have several samples of such tablets in India. Most of the finds are from Uttara Pradesh and are kept at Mathura Museum. Brick tablets from Gopalapura, Gorakhpur District, have Buddhist sūtra on them and dates back to 1st century B.C. on palaeographic grounds.

Another brick from Bhitari, Ghazipur district bears a small inscription, 'Śrī-Kumāra-guptasya'.

An earthen lid discovered in Sanchi stupa and the pottery belonging to the period of Graha Varma of Valabhi (566) are instances where letters are written with ink.[95]

**(i) Leather :** There is a deep contrast between India and other countries so far as leather as a writing material is concerned; whereas it is very rare in India, it is very common in Western Asia, Egypt and Europe. Its rare use for writing may not be due to the consideration of its impurity to touch, for, it was well used for foot-wears, seats and boats. In fact, tiger's skin and deer's skin are even considered holy. The reason for the rarity seems to be that it was not as freely available as palm leaf, etc.

Leather was known to be a material for writing. Perhaps, it was being used as a black-board for drawing plans or to make a draft, or for making calculations in writing almanacs and so on. We find Subandhu (5th century A.D.) acquainted with writing on leather. He writes : "The stars shone like cyphers drawn by the creator finding the world worthless, in the course of evaluating universe, on the ink-black parchment like *(ajinaiva)* dark sky with Moon-Chalk piece".[96] Satyendra quotes from *Devī-Purāṇa*, wherein it is said that a well-decorated bundle of palm leaves wrapped in leather be presented to a worthy person.[97]

St. Petersberg collection from Kashgar is said to include some pieces of leather with Indian scripts. A black piece of parchment is reported to be among the manuscripts in Bṛhajjñāna-kośa at Jaisalmer.[98]

According to S.K. Chatterji, the Sanskrit words *pusta, pustaka, pustikā* - meaning book are the Sanskritised forms of *post*, Pahlavi for parchment.[99] If so, the Indian people had handled manuscripts in parchment and extended the term to include their palm leaf or birch-bark bundles. It may be mentioned in this context that the Sanskrit *pusta* which also means 'doll', may have something to do with hides (*post*).

Satyendra writes that the word '*pustaka*' is not found in Pāṇini, Patañjali, etc., and that it is later than *Amarakośa*. But, attention may be drawn to *Avimāraka*, one of the plays of Bhāsa, where the word occurs. Going back we find 'potthaya' prakrit form of *pustaka* in Buddhist and Jain canons. *Arthaśāstra* also knows about pustaka, books or documents.[100]

**(j) Ivory** : Though very thin plates can be made out of ivory and though it is well suited for fine calligraphy, we have no specimens, obviously because of the extreme paucity of the material. However, Orissa State Museum at Bhuvanesvar has acquired recently a set of ivory sheets on which the *Gītagovinda* is engraved.

**Shells** : There are mantras written on tortoise shells and conch shells discovered in Srikakulam district.[101]

**(k) Cotton** : (i) *Cloth* : Cotton-cloth was often used for writing. However, books are not found copied on cloth because it is not durable : it easily gets infested. It is obvious that cloth cannot be used as such for writing. To make the surface smooth, a layer of rice or wheat pulp was spread on it, dried and polished with a smooth stone. It is called paṭa, paṭikā or kārpāsika-paṭa. The Smṛtis refer to writing on cotton-cloth. *Yājñavalkya-Smṛti* speaks of charters on a copper plate or a paṭa which Vijñāneśvara explains as kārpāsapaṭa. *Śrīkaṇṭhacarita* speaks of paṭṭaka.[102]

Sircar informs that a stone inscription of about the first quarter of the 8th Century A.D., refers to itself as *kraya-cīrikā*, where 'cīrikā' means cloth. The earliest mention of paṭa is however to be found in the Nasik inscription of Andhra period.[103]

Hariṣeṇa (932 A.D) writes about paintings on cloth. Bāṇa refers to writing on cloth in his *Harṣacarita* : A messenger from King Harṣa's court brought Bāṇa a 'letter' on cloth which he had tied with his turban. In his *Kādambarī* Bāṇa refers to writing on *valkala*.(bark-garment) : Puṇḍarīka, who fell in love with Mahāśvetā sends his message of love to her writing it on a piece of his garment. We find in Bhaṭṭanārāyaṇa's *Veṇīsaṁhāra*, Karṇa sending a message from the battle-field to his master Duryodhana and he writes on a piece of silk from his turban.[104]

Peterson found a copy of *Dharmavidhi* of Śrī-Prabhasūri, with Udayasiṁha's commentary, written on 38 cms. broad cloth. There are 93 leaves of it and is dated 1361-62 A.D. The copy is in Patan Śāstrabhaṇḍar.[105]

Sarvatobhadra and other Maṇḍalas and sketches of Ghaṭa-sthāpanā, etc., are drawn on cloth sheets. They are called Paṭa-citras. Ojha writes that a class of people in Rajasthan prepare almanacs on long pieces of cloth.[106]

The Prince of Wales Museum, Bombay, has collected a few Paṭa-citras from Nepal. There is a 13th century Maṇḍala and another legend of Avalokiteśvara dated 1617 A.D. Both these have writing in Nāgarī as well as diagrams or pictures in colour. L.D. Institute, Ahmadabad, too has several Paṭacitras.

Sketches of the deities of Ugraratha-Śāntiprayoga are drawn on one side of a long piece of cloth with a breadth of about 30 cms. A thin wooden roller is pasted at one end. It is kept rolled on it to facilitate reference. A colour painting of Līlāśuka, Parrot of Goddess Mīnākṣi is made on cloth of size 89 x 119 cms. Both these are of 17th century and are in the Oriental Research Institute, Mysore.

(ii) *Kaḍita* : A paste of powder of fried tamarind seeds mixed with powdered charcoal is smeared on both sides of cloth, dried and polished with a smooth stone. This appears black like a slate, and could be used as such. The cloth used for this is about 22 to 30 cms. in breadth and length is indefinite. It is folded alternatively so that the size appears as a square, and is used like a bound-book. One side could be completed as one goes forward and then reversed when the other side comes up.[107] This is called 'Kaḍata' or 'Kaḍita' (Kannada). Chalk or pot-stone pencil was used to write on this. It was used in offices of administration as ledgers to maintain accounts or any other official record. It was used so regularly that 'Kadita' has come to mean an "office record, file".

The earliest Kaḍita is of about 1250 A.D. Kaḍitas so far discovered are from Karnataka only. However, the Siamese (Thains) have precisely the same; the Betaks of Sumatra contain merchants' accounts.[108]

Most of the Kaḍitas discovered are from the Śringeri Maṭha. Except a few which contain copies of inscriptions on stone and copper plate and matters of importance, relating the Sringeri Matha and its Svāmis, all other bundles contain the accounts of the Maṭha.[109]

Another Kaḍita has been recently discovered in the Bungalow of Diwan Purnaiah, minister of Tippu and regent of Krishnaraja Odeyar III, at Yelanduru, Mysore district.[110]

**(I) Wood** : (i) *Board* : Wooden board is 'phalaka'. It must have been used for temporary writing -- learning alphabets or drawing sketches or making drafts. References to it are available in literature. The earliest mention is in *Vinayapiṭaka*. Kaṭāhaka-jātaka refers to boards used for learning alphabets. In *Lalitavistara*, we read that Gautama, the Buddha as an young boy used a sandal wood board for learning alphabets.[111] The Nasik inscription records the use of 'phalakas' for writing agreements of loans in the guild-halls.[112] *Kātyāyana-Smṛti* prescribes the plaint to be written on a board with chalk and it is called 'pāṇḍulekha' Daṇḍi presents Apahāra-Varma as sending his lady-love a message of love written on boards.[113]

Bodleian Library, Oxford, is said to possess manuscripts of boards from Assam. Perhaps it is a mistake for sācipot sheets inter-laid by boards. See above under Sāncipat.

R.L. Mitra writes: " In the śāstras, tablets of wood and metal have been recommended as materials for writing upon... Wooden tablets are confined to petty traders' account-books in Bengal; but in North-Western provinces, poor people have some religious books written with chalk on blackened boards."[114]

(ii) *Wooden blocks* : The following extracts from report in MLBD News-letter Oct. 1984, p.9f. which is self-explanatory, is worth quoting in this regard[115] :

> The Tripitaka Koreana is an invaluable source of Buddhist studies. Because of its authoritative qualities, Buddhist scholars, the world over have relied heavily on these. They have been kept for centuries in the ancient Buddhist temple of Herein-sa. The Tripitaka consists of 81,268 wooden blocks prepared in the first half of the 13th century and preserved in perfect condition to this day. The engraving work was completed in 16 years by thousands of devout monks. Each block is 67cms. long and 23 cms. wide. The corners are metal bound to protect them from cracking. To ensure that the blocks were preserved for centuries, they were soaked in sea for three years before being carved. The salt in wood is believed to repel insects and the lacquer coating ensures that they remain worm-proof.

(iii) *Bamboo Chips* : Another item of wood used for writing is the bamboo chips (śalākā). Vinayapiṭaka prohibits the monks from incising on bamboo chips. Buddhist monks are also said to have used bamboo chips with some marks or letters as identification slips.[116]

"An old manuscript of the ancient epic 'Rāmāyaṇa' has been found in a house in a remote tribal village of Tripura. The epic was written on very thin and polished "bamboo plates" in indelible vegetable ink, indigenously manufactured by the tribals themselves."[117]

## (II) WRITING INSTRUMENTS

We can distinguish the instruments into three types :

(i) Those with hard and sharp tips to incise; (ii) Those with a soft and smooth tips to write and (iii) Brush or such material to paint.

The term 'lekhanī' however, stands for any writing instrument and is as old as the *Mahābhārata* and the *Rāmāyaṇa*. Even so, the verb 'likhati' refers to scratching, engraving, writing and includes painting too.

(i) The stylus for incising on palm leaves is called 'kaṇṭaka' 'loha-kaṇṭaka'[118] or 'śalākā'[119]. It is a rod made of iron about 10-30 cms. in length and with the thickness of a pencil. It tapers to one end and has a sharp tip. The other end is made flat and sometimes decorated with jingles.

De Silva observes that the style was made of gold, silver, copper or brass and was plain or ornamented. It was tipped with a steel point which was sharpened from time to time on an oiled stone. The point was of four varieties beside the fine point and the length of the style also varied. The choice depended on the type of work on hand - 10 to 20 lines per page. The four points were : chatra (sun shade), patra (leaf), nala (tube), and gaṇḍa (ball). These points in order, were four, two, three aṅgulas and one aṅgula in length and the lekhanīya (writing length) was ten aṅgulas.[120]

(ii) The quill of porcupine or bamboo twig or lālada kaḍḍi - a kind of reed (thin bamboo) is used as pen to write on birch-bark. It is called Kuñca or Vartikā. Mitra writes that rich house-holders in Bengal employ the Vṛṇāla or Khakra reed that North-West provinces the reed or lalamus (kalam) is generally used.[121]

Kuñcika, Masikuñcika, Tūlī or Tūlikā or Dūṣika or Varti

is a brush. Brushes are made of reeds, wood, iron and fibres and hairs.

Varṇaka or Varṇikā is a small colour stick, usually white -- a pencil -- to draw letters on a board. Subandhu, Hariṣeṇa and Śrīharṣa employ a term 'khaṭinī' in the sense of chalk.[122] Manaḥśilā -- naturally available soft stones like the pot-stone for writing. Varṇa-Vartikā stands for coloured pencil. The affluent had golden coverings for the pens/pencils.

*The following terms may also be noted here*

(a) akṣara-tūlikā (reed/pen); akṣara-bhūmikā (tablet/board).[123]

(b) akṣara-mudrā; akṣara-muṣṭikā.[124]

(c) kācana/kācanaka (string/tape which ties parcel/bundle of papers/leaves of manuscripts); Kācanakin (manuscript writing) : Kacela (storing) cover keeping together leaves of manuscript; dūṣika (brush); pratipustaka (copy of a original ms.)[125]

(d) khaṭidala, khaṭimdala.[126]

(e) kuci (citralekhanikā).[127]

## III. OTHER INSTRUMENTS AND MATERIALS

Instruments like ruler and compasses or bow pen are used to draw lines and circles while writing patterns and designs. For drawing parallel lines on paper and birch-bark, a board is fixed with strings horizontally at equal distances : Paper to be ruled is placed over it and rubbed with a piece of cotton. This is called Rekhāpaṭṭi or Samāsapaṭi. Burnishing stone and conch or shell is useful in polishing. Cinture is employed to bore holes in palm leaves. Knife is also part of the kit.

The pens are kept in a box with or without cover. Sometimes, an ink-pot will have an attached pen-holder. The box to keep the ink-pot/s is often decorated.

The manuscripts are also kept in decorated boxes.

While reading, the manuscript is kept on a stand, a sort of low stool or frame called 'Vyāsapīṭha' ('lipyāsana' of Rāyapaseṇiya-sutta ). Bāṇa calls it Śaraśalākā-yantra.[128] "... a frame about eighteen inches in height somewhat resembling an artist's easel..." being employed in Siam for keeping manuscripts is referred to by Schyuler.[129]

Kambī or Kamba noted earlier, is a kind of ruler, Sircar writes, to keep the lines of writing straight or to track the lines while reading.[130] The term is found in Rāyapaseṇiya-sutta.

The word 'Kambī' means a 'strip' and therefore, it may be the strip of wood on either side of the bundle, as the commentator interprets, *pṛṣṭhaka-dvaya*. But, Satyendra observes that kambī is a sufficiently long strip of some metal, ivory, wood or bamboo useful in tracking the lines while reading a manuscript. Though this is plausible as Sircar also notes, the end-board is more an integral part of a book than the 'reading strip'. Further, it must be noted that word *'kambiāo'* is not in singular number. There need not be more than one reading strip for one book and this supports the interpretation of the commentator.

Chisel and hammer and such materials are used in inscribing on stones. But, these are not exclusive writing instruments.

Rāyapaseṇiyasutta mentions 'lipyāsana' and 'śṛṅkhalā' which need some consideration.

**Lipyāsana** : The commentator's interpretation is 'ink-pot'. But the analysis which is obvious enough, viz., lipi-āsana, might prompt one to surmise that this term refers to the material to write on. In fact, Satyendra takes it in the same sense. But such an understanding comes into conflict with *'patra'* in the context in which both the terms appear. When the basic material for writing is specifically mentioned (*patra*), I think repeating the same in general terms does not arise. The idea of ink-pot too does not appear apt, though it is possible. Probably, lipyāsana refers to the 'writing desk' or the 'book-stand' called *'Vyāsapīṭha'*, just as *'lipi-sajjā'* means stationery. Also compare *akṣara-bhūmikā*.

Śṛṅkhalā is chain related to the ink-pot according to the commentary. But, its purpose is not known. Probably the lid was attached to the ink-pot with a chain. Or was the pen attached to the ink-pot ? I do not think śṛṅkhalā has anything to do with the gingles with which pens are often decorated.

## (IV) INK

For writing or to make incised letter on a palm leaf appear clear, a dye is necessary. The dye or ink is called 'masi' or masī' or 'maṣi'. The lexicons record a few other words : Mela, Masijala, Patrāñjana. Of these patrāñjana, as the word itself indicates, is a paste used to blacken the letters incised on a palm leaf. After incising a palm leaf, the paste is completely smeared over the leaf and then wiped. The paste settles into the grooves and the letters appear clearly. The other words like Masijala show that it is liquid used to write with. Ink was stored in pots called Masipātra, Masibhāṇḍa, Masikupikā, Melananda, Melandhu and Melandhuka, Masimallikā.[131] The pots were made of gold sometimes. Shells were also used.[132]

The earliest reference to ink is found in Gṛhya-sūtras wherein the word 'masī' occurs frequently. The early orientalists, Benfey and Weber, derived the term 'melā' for ink, from the Greek *melas* thereby showing that ink was borrowed from the Greeks. But, later research has shown that ink was indigenously developed. Buhler tries to derive *melā* from *maila*, dirt. But the more plausible derivation is from the root *mel* 'to mix'.[133]

The use of ink is evidenced from the 5th century B.C. Inside the lids of each of the two relic-vases discovered at Sanchi, a letter is written with ink. Another specimen is again a relic-vase from Andher (2nd century B.C.). The Greek writers, Nearchos and Curtius (4th century B.C.), have written that Indians wrote on paper and cotton. The Jain canon speaks of *masi*.

The earliest available complete manuscript written with ink is the Kharoṣṭhī Dhammapada (1st century A.D.) discovered in Khotan.

## Coloured Inks

The coloured paintings and the painted inscriptions in the caves of Ajanta show the skill of those people in preparing and using coloured inks in that early age. Though ink of different colours were known, only black ink was used for writing books. Of those colours, red and yellow are used in books. The yellow is used chiefly for erasures. The margin line on either side of the page, daṇḍa marking the end of ślokas, close of chapters or sections are in red ink. Usually, Jain writers are fond of employing varieties of colours.

Sometimes, gold and silver inks are also used for borders of leaves.[134]

## Types of Inks

We have evidence to show that two types of ink were employed : (i) delible and (ii) indelible. Delible ink was for ordinary day-to-day purposes. Indelible ink was used for writing manuscripts and documents. Jonarāja cites an interesting anecdote which shows his cunning but unintelligent uncle who effected a correction with the ordinary ink in the document and thus depriving his ward of his legitimate share of property, and the clever judge who ordered the document to be washed and thereby exposing the true state of affairs and uniting the ward with his legitimate share.[135]

As an alternative to regular ink or as an expedient, fresh leaf juices were used. 'Tamāla-rasa' (juice of tamāla leaf) and 'alaktaka-rasa' (juice of *alaktaka* leaf red) are referred to by Bāṇa while Bhavabhūti refers to the former.[136]

A reference may be made to the instance of writing in blood. Writing one's vow or name in one's own blood shows the determination of the writer. When one wanted to write in a place where ink would not be available and if the urge is compelling, one wrote with one's blood. We are told that Guṇāḍhya wrote his *Bṛhatkathā* in his own blood. Bhaṭṭa-Nārāyaṇa's Karṇa writes with his own blood a message to his master.

*Preparation*

Various recipes for preparing ink are given in a few works. Mostly, it is passed on in tradition.[137] The ordinary variety of ink is prepared by mixing powdered charcoal with gum and some other sticky substance like sugar and dissolved in water which determines the colour of the ink. The permanent variety is prepared in various ways. The procedure involves boiling soot or charcoal of certain plants or nuts with oils like almond oil or sesamum oil.

One or two recipes may be detailed. The charcoal of pepul tree is baked in water with gum and collyrium from a sesamum oil lamp is mixed with this. Thus, indelible ink is prepared. Ordinary ink is only a mixture of collyrium or soot, gum and water.

Charcoal of almond shells is baked in cow's urine. Such ink was used to write on birch-bark.

Coloured inks are prepared in the same way or natural colours available are used. Śilājit, or Dhāturasa, herbal juice like alaktakarasa are freely referred to in Sanskrit works in regard to painting with colours. Alaktaka or Hiṅgalu was used for red colour and Haritāla for yellow.

There are many paper manuscripts with miniature paintings; for example: *Gītagovinda, Śivamahimna-stotra, Caura-pañcaśikā* (all printed). Another instance of water colour painting is *Śrītattvanidhi*, a work of the early 19th century produced by the Mysore Citrakala School of Arts. It is written on both sides of foolscap sheets of paper. It contains nearly 500 pages of coloured illustrations and is preserved in the Mysore Oriental Research Institute (See also ch.3, under illustration and decoration).

The oldest known are the Devībhāgavata miniatures. The paper is in the size 19 x 11.5 cms., picture panel at the right hand side 7. 5 x 11 cms. and the writing 14 lines per page.[138]

Only Jaina and Buddha miniatures on palm leaf (1150-1400) are reported and no brahmanical mss. Paper appears after 1400.[139]

## Notes and References

1. *'tassa ṇam potthaya–rayaṇassa imeyārūve vaṇṇāvāse paṇṇatte, tam jahā : rayanāmayāyī pattagāyim riṭṭamayīyo kambiyāvo,*

*tavanijjamaye dore, nānā-maṇimaye ganṭhī, veruliyāmaye lippāsaṇe, riṭṭāmaye chādane, tavaṇijja-mayī saṅkalā, riṭṭāmayī masī, vayirāmayī lehanī, riṭṭamayāyim akkharāyim, dhammiye satthe..' Rāyapaseṇiya-sutta,* p. 550f.

2. The material written on may be called in general, lekhya-vastu. In case of painting, the word 'bhitti' is generally used. The other materials may be called 'lekhana-sādhana or lipi-sādhana' or 'lipi–sambhāra' viz. instrument, ink, etc. We find the use of the term Upādāna-sambhāra: *nirupādānasambhāram abhittāveva tanvate, jagac citram namas tasmai kalāślāghyāya śūline.* (quotation in *Kāvyaprakāśa* 4, ud. 50. The stationery may be termed 'lipi-sajjā' or 'lekhana-sāmagrī'.
3. Kaṭāhaka-jātaka, see note 31, ch.1; Sivaramamurti (1952), p. 18. Also cf. *Abhijñāna-Śākuntalam: amātyo vijñāpayati arthajātasya gaṇanā-bahulatayā ekam eva paurakāryam pratyavekṣitam. ted devo patrāropitam pratyakṣīkarotu.* (after 6.21).
4. *'apacita-vaṭapatrajālagarbhe nakhaśikhareṇa dṛḍham lilekha tāvat.' Patañjali–carita,* 5.33.
5. *'tathaiva ca guṇāḍhyena paiśācyā bhāṣayā tayā; nibaddhā saptabhir varṣair grantha-lakṣāṇi sapta sa; maitām vidyādharā hārṣur iti tām ātmaśoṇitaiḥ; aṭavyām maṣy abhāvāc ca lilekha sa mahākaviḥ.' Kathāsaritsāgara,* 8.2-3 Bihar Rastrabhasa Parisad, Patna, 1960 (2nd edn. 1974), Vol. I.
6. *etasmin śukodara-sukumāre nalinīpatre patracheda-bhaktya nakhair nikṣipta-varṇam kuru.' Abhijñāna-Śākuntalam,* 3, after V.13.
7. *'bhūrje vā tejapatre va tathā vā tālapatrake;*<br>*vināgurum ca deveśi pustake kārayet priye.*<br>*sambhave svarṇapatre ca tāmrapatre ca Śāṅkari;*<br>*anyavṛkṣatvaci devi tathā ketakipatrake.*<br>*mṛttāmra-patra raupye vā vaṭapatre vārānane;*<br>*anyapatre vā sudale likhitvā yaḥ samabhyaset.'*<br>*Yoginī-tantra,* p. 184.
8. *'tāḍapatratruṭir jajñe śalabhebhyaḥ.' Prabhāvaka carita,* p. 338.
9. *'tāḍi-tāla-bhūrjānām patram.' Arthaśāstra,* 2.17.
10. *sa-lekhanikā-maṣībhājanāni tāli-patrāṇi bhūrja-tvaco vā; sa-loha-kaṇṭakāni tāla-patrāṇi.' Kāvyamīmāṁsā, p. 58.*<br>*'tālyām dṛdhadalā tāḍi patratālī vārāṅganā;*<br>*patrāli phalapākāntā tālādyāḥ syuḥ tṛṇadrumāḥ*<br>*Vaijayantī,* p. 63.
11. Sircar (1965), p. 61.
12. Kaye (1927), p. 9.

13. De Silva (1938), p. xiii.
14. Two stanzas traditionally handed down, give the features of the leaf that is fit and not fit for writing: *tāḍapatram dṛḍham saumyam ṛju sāgram dvidhā-kṛtam; mṛdulam yat praśastam tan matam lekhā-vilekhane.karkaśam kalmasam vakram hīnāgram sphuṭitam yugam; tālapatram na tat śreṣṭham matam lekhā-vilekhane.*
(palm leaf which is not cleft, is clean (or smooth) and straight, having ends (not broken), separated from the rib, soft, is best for writing. Palm leaf which is hard, un-clean (or rough), not straight, without ends (i.e. broken), cleft, not separated from the rib, is unfit for writing).
15. Sampath (1975).
16. M.Schuyler (1908) describes the making of palm leaf manuscripts in Siam. It is very much similar to the process in India :
"...The first operation in converting the leaves into the finished manuscript is to divide them by cutting out the midrib, thus making two leaves of each leaf of the tree. These leaves are then made up into bundles of some hundred pieces each and are then placed between boards tightly tied up and wedged in a press. While still there the edges of the leaves are trimmed smoothly with a semi-circular knife which is in a handle some two feet long. After sanding the leaves to give them a smooth surface for writing..."
17. De Silva (1938), p. xiv.
18. Mitra: Report, 1875, Gough, p. 20.
19. Segal (1979) recommends silk/nylon cord.
20. Sikdar (1964), p. 338.
21. Law (1933) 2, p. 63.
22. Discovered in the middle of the ruins near Taxila Shah-Dheri, deposited in the Library of R.A.S. (*Ep.Ind.* 4.5). The Bower manuscript (birch bark) have the sizes: 228x50 mm. to 290x63 mm. For Western Ganga plates, see *Mysore Archaeological Reports* 12, p. 2 (220 x 63 mm.), ibid. 14, pl. 1 (202 x 37 mm.). Kalwan copper plate measures 223 x 64 mm.: *Ep. Ind.* 21.39.
23. Ramayya, N.V., Madras 1935, p. 197; quoted by Gode (1943), p. 18.
24. "A 19th century palm leaf with treasury seal recording the sale of boy has been discovered recently by the Epigraphy Department of the Tamil University here. (Thanjavur)." *Deccan Herald*, dated 26-9-1982.

"A palm leaf manuscript throwing light on the British army entry into Travancore State has been found among old records preserved in a house in Kulaśekarapuram village of Kanyakumari district." *Deccan Herald*, dated 29-11-1986.

25. A microfilm copy of *Dhavala* manuscripts is in the Oriental Research Institute, Mysore University.
26. Hori-uzi manuscript is not earlier than 700 A.D. according to Dani (1963), p. 154. See also Shashi Bala (1980).
27. Hoernle (1897).
28. Lüders (1911)
29. Satyendra (1978), p. 129; Sircar (1965), p. 64; Sampath (1975).
30. Kaye (1927). Bāṇa: *Harṣacarita*, p. 241 "*:..sthāṇava-vraṇa-vyathita-gulpha-baddha-bhūrjatvacā...*"
31. Kaye (1927).
32. Pandey, p. 67.
33. *Amara-kośa* 2.4.46; '*bhūrja-patre bhujo bhūrjo mṛdut-vak carmi-carmikau.*' *Vaijayantī-kośa*, p. 48.
34. *bhūrja-tvacaḥ kuñjara-bindu śoṇāḥ, vrajanti vidyādhara-sundarīṇām anaṅga-lekhakriyayopayogam'*. *Kumārasambhava*, 1.17.

    '*bhujaṅganirmoka iva bhūrjapatragato' yam akṣara-vinyāsaḥ'*. *Vikramorvaśīyam*, after 1.11.

    '*bhūrjatvak-komalam'*. Bāṇa, *Harṣacarita*, p.217.

    Abhinavagupta refers to *bhūrja* as *valkala*, the inner thin bark of trees, as distinguished from *cīra* which is narrow and thick: '*cīram iti avitatā sthūlā ca vṛkṣa-tvak, valkalam ca tad-viparītam yathā bhūrja-tvak*'. *Nāṭyaśātra Abhinavabhāratī* 21.141, (GOS), vol. II, p. 130.
35. Sachau 1.171; Pandey, p. 67.
36. *Yoginī-Tantra*, See note 7. '*mantra...bhūrjapatre gorocanayā likhitavyam*'. *Āryamañjuśrīmūla-kalpa*, p.50. Attention may here be drawn to the rather curious report that no Jaina work written on birch-bark has been found. Jain (1979), p. 90.
37. Bloomfield, M. and Garbe, R.: *Atharva-veda*, Baltimore, 1901. The birch bark codex of *Atharvaveda* (Paippalāda) deposited in the Tübingen Library is reproduced chromo-photographically.
38. Satyendra, p. 147.
39. Mitra: q.Gough, p. 17.
40. Sircar (1965), p. 65.

41. *"agaru-valkala-kalpita-sañcayāni ca subhāṣita-bhāñji pustakāni."* Bāṇa : *Harṣacarita*, p.217. cf. *Yoginī-tantra* (note 7).
42. Pandey, p. 71.
43. Satyendra, p. 151.
44. Satyendra, p. 148.
45. *ibid.*
46. Pandey, Gode (1952)
47. Gough, p.16: Mitra's Report dtd: 15.2.1875 to J. Waterhouse, Secretary to Asiatic Society of Bengal.
48. Ojha, p. 144f. It is reported that P.G.Gosavi of Hand-made Paper Institute, Pune, is of the opinion that paper manufacturing could be traced in India to the 2nd century B.C. and even earlier. (*Deccan Herald*, 8.2.1986). See also Menariya (1979), p. 85.
49. Sircar (1965), p. 68.
50. *Prabhāvaka-carita* mentions Kākala as the name of a Kāyastha (*'kākalo nāma kāyasthaḥ'*). śl.112; p. 303.
51. See Gode (1943) and (1944) bed; Menariya (1979), p. 85.
52. Satyendra, p. 149.
53. *Deccan Herald*, 23.7.1987.
54. Palaeographical Index of Dated Mss.etc. Winternitz and Keith (1905).
55. Sandesara (1953), p. 39.
56. *Deccan Herald*, 4.3.1986.
57. Sircar (1965), p. 68.
58. Francis, F. (1975), p. 249.
A fragment of a paper scroll is with Vidwan R.G. Malagi of Oriental Research Institute, Mysore; contains *Bhagavadgītā* chs. 7.19 to 14.9 written on both sides in Telugu script. It measures 5.3 x 60 cms. Perhaps only 4 cms. of length containing the part of the text is lost.
59. Sikdar (1964), p. 338.
60. Francis F. (1975).
61. See note 22 above.
62. *'mṛdulekhā-vilāsam cāmarāja balahadal bareduda biruda rūvāri-tilaka gaṅgācāri kaṇḍarisida.'* (Gangāchāri, the arch-engraver, engraved what was written with chalk by Chamaraja, the calligraphist). - Malliṣeṇa's epitaph. *'baredu kaṇḍarisida'* (...wrote and engraved'.) - S.B.77 Chikkabeṭṭa, *Ep.Car.*2.
63. Two cart loads of copper plates containing songs of Tallapāka Vārīyar discovered in 1904; also listed by Sewell : *List of Antiquities*, vol.1, p.153.*yiyareṇa tāmbapattesu taṇubheṣu rāyalakkhaṇam raeūṇam nihālāraseṇam timmeūṇa tambabhāyaṇe pothavo pakkhito nikkhito nayarabāhim*

*dubbābeḍhamajjhe' Vāsudeva-hiṇḍi,* p.189. See also Burnell, p.86.; Hoerning (1883).

64. *Ep. Ind.,* 2.2.1; (Fleet 1907).
65. "King Kaniska had the treatises, when finished, written on copper plates and enclosed these in stone boxes, which he deposited in tope made for the purpose." Walters (1961), p. 271.
66. *Ep.Car.* (Rice) 8 pt. ii, pp. 79f. Sb 183. Kuppagadde copper plate.
67. *'sahasā-vidadhīta na kriyām avivekaḥ param āpadām padam; vṛṇute hi vimṛśya-kāriṇam guṇalubdhāḥ svayam eva sampadaḥ.'*Bhāravi, *Kirātārjunīyam,* 1.59.
68. *'dalodare kāñcana–ketakasya kṣaṇān masībhāvuka-varṇarekhām; tasyaiva yatra svam anaṅga-lekham lilekha bhaimī nakha-lekhanībhiḥ.' Naiṣadhīyacarita,* 6.63.
69. *Ep.Ind.* 5.11; Law (1933) 2, pp. 668, 670; Pandey, p. 78. The two gold leaves are in the size 6 "x 7 " and twenty lines are written on one side of each; discovered in 1877.
70. Archaeological Survey of India *Annual Report* 1926-27, p. 200. The bunch of twenty gold leaves enclosed within two gold leaves were discovered in 1926-27.
71. *Sādhvi,* (Local Newspaper), 30.12.1982.
72. Sircar, (1965), p. 78; Satyendra, p. 137.
73. Catalogue of Malayalam books in the British Museum. For other instances see Hoerning (1883).
74. *Ep.Car.* 5, pp. 261ff, 285ff: Mysore 97 and 157; See also pp. 204 ff.
75. Marshall (1914), p. 975.
76. cf. *Yoginī-tantra;* see note 7 ; above.
77. Panel containing 24 Tīrthaṅkaras, Nahar Museum, Calcutta; *Mysore Archaeological Reports,* 1941, No. 49, p. 249.
78. *Ep.Car.* 10, Gd.22, p. 233.
79. Narasimhachar (1964), p. 33.
80. *Ep.Car.* 5, pp. 161ff, Mysore 26.
81. *Mysore Archaeological Reports,* 1928.
82. *Corpus Inscriptionum Indicarum,* Vol. 3 No. 32, Part XXI; A, p. 139. (2) and (3) Satyendra, p. 137, (4) *Deccan Herald,* 2.2.1983.
83. Hoerning (1883).
84. *'lekhitā cira ṭṭhitikā hotu'.* Upadhyaya (1961), p. 240.
85. Hattigumpha cave Inscription. *Ep.Ind.,* 20,7. Allahabad and Mandasor Pillar Inscriptions: *Corpus Inscriptionum Indicarum* Vol. 3. Talagunda pillar Inscription of Kakustha-varman: *Ep.Ind.,* 8.5 : Very hard granite octogonal staff tapering

upwards, 6-1/7ft. high; 7" face, written in box-headed Kadamba script (1st half of 6th century).

86. *Ep.Ind.*, 5.12.28. A song is found in Bantvala Inscription of 1886 A.D. *Ep.Ind.*, 33.55.
87. Satyendra, p.137.
88. Kielhorn (1891)
89. Ojha, p. 150, Narasimhachar (1964), p. 35. Satyendra, p. 131, 140.
90. 'Dhar Praśasti of Arjunavarman'. *Pārijātamañjarī* or *Vijayaśrī-Nāṭikā* by Madana. (*Ep. Ind.*, 8.9.); discovered in 1903; slab fixed in wall with written face inside. Black stone 1722 x 1520 mm. ; 82 lines, 76+ verses.
Two Prakrit poems at Dhar. 2 *Kūrmaśataka* poems: 109 āryā verses each, 83 lines, black stone, same place as the preceding. (*Ep.Ind.*, 8.25). Ākhyātapratyayas : *Ep.Ind.* 31.4.
91. *Ep. Ind.*, 29.34; Satyendra, p. 132; Menariya (1979), p. 85.
92. 'Hanumakonda Niroṣṭhyakāvya'. (*Ep.Ind.*, 36.27) Author: Nṛsiṁha 12th cent. On a rock on the hill Siddeśvaranigutta, Hanumakonda, near Warangal. Written portion: 2026 x 1038 mm. 26 lines; incomplete, 37 anuṣṭup verses.
*Siddhodvāha of Nṛsiṁha*. Ed. P.V.Parabrahma Sastri. Govt. of Andhra Pradesh; Hyderabad, 1968. 30 p. on a huge boulder on a hillock Ururgutta, Warangal, written panel 4.5 x 2 metres; 3 vertical sections, 154 lines (48+52+54), Telugu script.
93. *Suttanikāya*, Bihar Govt., Vol. I, Intd. p. viii. Norman, (1983), p. 12f. Two more instances of literary pieces in stone may be mentioned: (1) *Sūryaśataka* of Mayūra - inscribed on a pillar in the Sūrya-maṇḍapa (now broken), Kacchapeśvara temple, Kañci; written in early Cola script of 10th cent. A.D. Sivaramamurti (1952), p.1. (2) "In another place, a few gaṇas re: prosody-*nṛsiṁhoktagaṇāḥ* - engraved on a stone pillar." P.V. Parabrahma Sastri (Ed): *Siddhodvāha*, Intd.
94. *Ep.Ind.*, 2.25.
95. *Ep. Ind.*, 2.20, *Corpus Inscriptionum Indicarum* vol. 3, Nos. 13 (p. 260), 27(p. 294), 42 (p. 329) etc. for clay seals. Three more instances may be cited: In the stūpa mound in Nalanda site, Bihar Sheriff Taluk, Patna district, broken pieces of terracotta are found; these frequently contain part of Nidāna-sūtra or Pratītyasamutpāda-sūtra. *Ep.Ind.*, 21.32 is about a fragment of a brick with script of 6th cent.A.D. Also see *Ep. Ind.*, 24.5. Another terracotta fragment is

discovered; it is engraved on both sides. Clay seals, votive tablets (with *'ye dhamma'* etc.) in early Chalukyan script are recovered from Sankaram, Visakhapatnam district.

96. *'...viśvam gaṇayato dhātuḥ śaśikaṭhiri-khaṇḍena tamomaśīśyāme ajina iva viyati saṁsārasya atiśūnyatvāt śūnya-bindava iva vilikhitāḥ...tārā vyarājanta.' Vāsavadattā*, p.168.

97. *"śū-tāḍapatrake śaste same patrasusañcite; vicitra-kañcikā-pārśve carmaṇā sampuṭikṛte'. Devīpurāṇa.* Satyendra, p.142.

98. Pandey, p. 75. Menariya writes that it is mentioned that *Bṛhatkathā* was written on leather only. Menariya (1979), p. 85. In Adyar Library, a scroll of sheep skin with Hebrew characters is preserved. There is a reference to Avesta on ox hides written with liquid gold. Dasgupta (1958), p. 279.

Strabo refers to government documents on parchment from India to Augustus Ceaser (died A.D. 14). Smith,V. (1902).

99. Dasgupta (1958), p. 278 (following Gauthiot).

100. See note 17, 18 and 34 ch.1.

101. Sircar (1965), p. 74. cf. *"...Kuśala-śilpi-lokollikhi-tānām ca śūkti-śaṅkha-galvarka pramukhānām pānabhājanānām nicayān..." Harṣacarita*, p. 217. A Brāhmi record on conch shell is recovered from Salihundam. *Ep.Ind.* 28.25. An ivory seal with Mauryan Brāhmi writing is found at Rupar near Ambala. Sharma, Y.D. (1953), p. 123 pl. 48A.

102. *'pate vā tāmrapaṭe vā svamudropacinhitam'. Yājña-valkya-smṛti*, 1.318. See also Sircar (1965), p .66. *'paṭṭikā-likhita-durgā-stotreṇa.'* Bāṇa : Kādamābarī p.338. *"vyomapaṭṭakatale nirargala-paṅktayo bali-bhujām virejire; udyad-antaka-nideśa-śāsanam kalpayantya iva varṇarājayaḥ.'* Maṅkha: *Śrīkaṇṭha-carita*, 22.37; *'ājñā ca paṭṭaka-tale likhitā bhavati'*. Jonarāja thereon. *"...saṅkhyā-lekhya-paṭṭikām iva kuberakośasya..."* Bāṇa: *Harṣacarita*, p. 252.

103. *'saṅkṣiptā kraya-cirikā' Ep.Ind.*, 26.32, p. 246. Sircar (1965), p. 66; Gode (1952). *"...lekha-garbhayā nīlirāga-mecaka-rucā cīra-cīrikayā racitamuṇḍa-mālakam..."* Bāṇa: *Harṣacarita*, p.151. *Cīrikā* in *Bṛhat-kathākośa* means hem og garment. Upadhye, A.N. (1943). *'likhitvā kuṅkumenāśu svalpa-sambhāra-cīrikām.'* Kṣemendra : *Narmamālā*, 2.116.

104. *"celanopari; celanārūpasaṁyuktam likhita-paṭam ādarāt." Bṛhatkathākośa*, 55. 193. *Viṣṇucitrapaṭam...* ib. 108.48. "(paṭa, also paṭṭa). *"...ati-nibiḍa-sūtrabandha-nimnitāntarāla-kṛta-lekha-vyavacchedaya lekhamālikayā parikalita-mūrdhānam*

*praviśantam lekhahārakam adrākṣit.*" Bāṇa : *Harṣacarita*, p.52. "...*tamāla-pādapāt pallavam ādāya niṣpīdya śilātale tena gandhagaja-mada-surabhi-parimalena rasenottarīya-valkalaikadeśād vipāṭya paṭṭikām svahastakamala-kaniṣṭhikā-nakha-śikhareṇa abhilikhya iyam patrikā*..." Bāṇa : *Kādambarī*, p. 236. Attention may be drawn to *Āryamañjuśrīmūlakalpa* which speaks of atasī-valkala : *'ātasye valkale caiva śuddhe tantuvivarjite.'* (p. 131).
*'tato'panīya śīrṣasthānāt paṭṭikām śarīra-saṅgalitaiḥ śoṇitabindubhiḥ lipta-mukham bāṇam kṛtvā abhilikhya preṣito devasya sandeśaḥ. (paṭṭikām arpayati). Veṇīsaṁhāra*, 4 betn. 11 & 12 Ed. G.V.Devasthali, Bombay, 1953, p.121.

105. Jain (1979), p. 90.
106. Ojha, p. 146.
107. This 'never-ending' nature of 'kaḍita' has given rise to the use of the word in Kannada in a sarcastic way. When a person begins to relate something in minute details not liked by the hearers, the person is spoken of as having opened the 'kaḍita' ("*tegeda kaḍita*"). The person may also be admonished to close down the kaḍita (*'kaṭṭu ninna kaḍita'*).
108. Burnell, p. 87.
109. *Mysore Archaeological Report* 1919.
110. *Deccan Herald*, 9.11.1987. A set of 230 volumes is with Karnataka State Archives, Mysore Branch.
111. "...*uragasāra-candanamayam lipi-phalakam ādāya*.." *Lalitavistara*, 10. "*seṭṭiputte lekham sikkhante eva dāsopissa phalakam vahamāno gatvā teneva saddhim lekhāni sikkhi, gaṇanam sikkhi.* Kaṭāhaka-jātaka, *Jātakaṭṭha-Kathā*, 1. p. 330.
112. Nasik Inscription, No.7, *Archaeological Survey of Western India*, Report 4.102.
113. "*pāṇḍulekhena phalake, tataḥ patram viśodhayet*". *Kātyāyana-smṛti*, q.by Mādhava (Burnell, p .87). "*pāṇḍulekhena phalake bhūmau vā prathamam likhet; nyūnādhikam tu saṁśodhya paścāt patre niveśayet.*" Vyāsa.
"*phalakādau tato mantrī mantram tatra samuddharet'*. *Yogini-tantra*, p.183. "...*nāgadanta-niryāsa-kalka-varṇitam phalakam ādāya maṇisamudgakāt varṇavar-tikām uddhṛtya tām...ālikham.*" *Daśakumāra-carita*, ucchvāsa 2, p.132. *'hṛdaya-phalake saṅkalpa-tūlikayā citritām iva...*, *Vāsavadattā*, p. 84. "..*likhitāneka-lekhya-phalaka-sampuṭān*..." Bāṇa: *Harṣacarita*, p. 217. Alaka on *Haravijaya*, 30.15: - *'phalakeṣu vartikām ādāyam'*. *Kāvyamīmāṁsā*, p. 58: *'sa-phalaka-khaṭikā-samudgakaḥ.'*
114. See Gough, p. 18.

115. Attention may be drawn here to (1) Burnell's find that in Burma, "Buddhist rituals are often written on slips of wood covered with gold or silver lacquer, the letters being black" specimens of which are in British Museum (Burnell, p. 87) Also Hoerning (1883). (2) the wooden pillar buried in the bed of a tank at Kirari, Chattisgarh division, Rajasthan, has Brāhmī characters of 2nd c.A.D.; mentions official designations and names of officers. *Ep.Ind.*, 18.19. Sircar (1965), p. 69.
"M.A.Stein in 1900 dug up out of the sands in the deserts of Taklamakan near Khotan, five hundred small tablets of wood covered with writing, which reach back to the fourth century and are perhaps older still." Winternitz (1926), p. 33.

116. Burnouf (*Historie du Boudisme*, p. 259, note) is said to have written that the Buddhist monks used bamboo chips called 'śalākā' as passport. Pandey, p. 73; Buhler, p. 5, 93; Sircar (1965), p. 69. But the *Pali-English Dictionary* of Childers (London 1909, p. 425) nor the *Buddhist Hybrid Sanskrit Grammar and Dictionary* of Edgerton (New Haven 1953, p.524) records the sense of passport to *śalākā*. It is described as 'chips of wood, bark, bamboo, talipot leaf or other similar material'. Śalākā was only an identification 'card' for receiving food, etc., a ticket for food .cf. *"vaṁśenaivollikhed varṇam"*. *Yogini-Tantra*, p. 183. Subramaniam (1957) speaks of a bamboo piece incised with a style on the outer enamel between joints. (p. 221).

117. *MLBD News Letter*, Oct. 1987, p. 6.

118. Rajaśekhara writes about the kit of an author: *'...cārvakṣaraḥ nānālipijñaḥ. tasya sampuṭikā-* 1) *sa-phalaka-khatikā-samudgakaḥ*, (2) *sa-lekhanīka-masībhājanāni tāḍipatrāṇi bhūrjatvaco vā*, (3) *sa-lohakaṇṭakāani tāladalāni*; (4) *susammṛṣṭā bhitta-yaḥ satatasannihitāḥ syuḥ.' Kāvya-mīmāṁsā*, p.58.

119. Śalākā, also called sūcī may be of copper, gold, silver or bronze; length being 8, 10 or 4 aṅgulas. *Yoginī-Tantra*, p.183-4: *"...lekhanyā sumanoharam svarṇa-yaṣṭyā aṣṭaṅgulyaḥ kaniṣṭhyāḥ pramāṇataḥ..."* ib., p.15. cf. "The pen or rather stylus is a needle point like the needle of a sewing machine inserted in a wooden handle like an enormous cigar about eight inches in length". Schuyler (1908).

120. De Silva (1938), Intd., p. xiv.

121. Mitra also notes that crow quills were used for writing very small characters for amulets but never for ordinary manuscripts. See Gough, p.18, cf. *'bṛhannālasya sūcyā vā...*

*Yoginī-Tantra*, p.183. Sircar observes that Kalama is recorded as a Sanskrit word in the Sanskrit-Chinese lexicon of 8th century. He also notes that a pen made of reed or bamboo is called Iṣīkā or Iṣikā. Sircar (1965), p. 82.

122. *'tūlikā varṇavartikā'. Amarakośa*, 3.10; 3.25 *'lekhanī tūlikā kūrcī.' Vaijayantī*, p.137. *'unmīlitam tūlikayeva citram.' Kūmārasambhava* 1.32; *'tūlikā kaṭhikā lekhya-kūrcikā: iti viśvaḥ.'* Mallinātha there on. *'vartikām ānaya.' Abhijñāna-Śākuntala*, after 6.14. *'aruṇadhātuvarti-phalakeṣu likhantīm.'*– Bhavabhūti: *Mālatīmādhava*, 5.144. *"udbhinna-ratna-kiraṇāruṇa–dhatuvarti-preṅkhat-phaṇāguli-bhujaṅgama-bhogah-astam; roṣādivānadhi-gataprasāram valantīs sotkhaṇṭham ūrmi-phalakeṣu nadīr likhantam." "aruṇa-dhatumayī vartis tūlikā.., yo hy utkaṇṭhitaḥ sa vinodāya phalakeṣu vartikām ādāya priyām likhati."* Ratnākara: *Haravijaya*, 30.15 and Alaka thereon. *"ālātalekhāluḥ udghāṭinī kuñcikā (candra)." Anargharāghava*, 7.83.

A painter's box is vartikā-karaṇḍa. *'khaṭikā karaṇī haimī parato ratna-mūṭikā; sindūrādyā rajobhedo pañca-raṅgaka-sūtrakam.' Narmamālā*. 3.2.

*"dvikuṇḍalī vṛttasamāptilipyāḥ karāṅgulī kāñcana-lekhanīnām; kaiśyam masīnām smitabhā kaṭhinyāḥ, kāye yadīye niramāyi sāraiḥ."* -Śrīharṣa : *Naiṣadhīyacarita*, 10-87; Mallinātha cites Viśva: *'khaṭikā tu kaṭhini.' 'śukladhātau pākaśuklā kaṭhini kakkhatī khaṭī.' Vaijayanti*, p.42. *'yāval likhati tām bhūmau khaṭikayā ghanam.'* Hariṣena : *Bṛhatkathākośa*, 57.452. *Lalitavistara* 10....*śaśikhaṭinī-khaṇḍena...' Vāsavadattā*, p.38.

123. *Jayamaṅgalā* Com. On *Kāmasūtra, 3.15.*

124. Ravigupta: *Candraprabha-vijaya-kāvya.*

125. Monier-Williams: *Sanskrit-English Dictionary.*

126. *Prabhāvaka-carita*, p.273.

127. *Uṇādisūtra. 5.* 31.

128. Though it is not possible to say how śarayantra looked like, it may be surmised that it was something which could be manipulated i.e., folded and spread, because it was called *yantra. 'sandhyā-raktāṁśuka-viṣama-prarūḍha-bisalatā-śara–yantrānugata-śata–patra-pustaka-sanāthe...' Vāsavadattā*, p. 200 f.

129. Schuyler (1908).

130. Sircar (1965), p. 82. 'Kambi f. a shoot or branch or joint of a bamboo, L.' Monier-Williams: *Skt.Eng. Dictionary.*

131. *"Melānando masighaṭī melāmbu malināmbu ca; melā (maṇir na-santasya lekhanyā) kaṇikoddhṛtā". Vaijayantī*, p.138; *"melā masijalam patrāñjanam ca syān masir dvayoḥ."Trikāṇḍaśeṣa* q.on *Amarakośa* 3.5-10. *"Yatnād anviṣya kā grāhyā lekhakaiḥ*

*masi-mallikā; ghanāndhakāra-niśśaṅkam modate kena bandhakī. (Nārikeraja).*" Dharmadāsa: *Vidagdhamukha-maṇḍana,* 3.29. '*hiraṇmayam śāsanalekhahetoḥ sajjam masībhāṇḍam iva smarasya*'. *Śrīkaṇṭha-carita* 6.51; Jonarāja thereon: '*masībhāṇḍam kajjalarasapātram*" (25.28); '*lekhanī lekhana-kāṇḍam*' (10.19).

"*asitagirisamam syāt kajjalam sindhu-pātram, sura-taruvara-śākhā lekhanī, patram urvī; likhati yadi gṛhītvā śāradā sarvakālam tad api tava guṇānām īśa pāram na yāti.*" Puṣpadanta: *Mahimnastava,* 32. '*tvat kṛte yā*'– *nayā vedanānubhūtā sā yadi nabhaḥ patrāyate, sāgaro melanandāyate brahmā lipikarāyate bhujagapatir vā kathakāyate tadā kim api katham apy anekair yugasahasrair abhilikhyeta kathyeta vā,*' *Vāsavadattā,* p. 211.

"'*kāyastha iti laghvī mātrā, tathāpi na yuktam prākṛtam rūpam avajñātum...masībhājanam patram ca upanaya...śrotriyākṣarāṇi prayatna-likhitāny api niyatam asphuṭāni bhavanti. ...adatta-bāhyanāmānam lekham śakaṭadāsena lekhayitvā mām upatiṣṭhasva.*" Viśākhadatta: *Mudrā-rākṣasa,* 1. betn. 19-20. '*madanagaṇana-sthāne lekhya-prapañcam udañcayann iva kila bṛhat patra-nyasta-dvirepha-maṣikaṇaiah; kuṭilalipibhiḥ kam kāyastham nanāma visūtryan vyadhita virahi-prāṇeśv āyavyayāvadhikam madhuḥ.* Maṅkha: *Śrīkaṇṭha-carita* q. Ruyyaka: *Alaṅkārasarvasva* on Samāsokti. '*Lipyakṣarāṇām masi-bindurūpāṇām*', Jayaratha on Citra. ib.

132. '..*harita-patrarasāṅgāra-masi-malina-śambūka-vāhinā.*" Bāṇa: *Kādambarī,* p. 338.
133. Pandey, p. 83f.
134. Pandey, p. 86. Hemādri: Dānakhaṇḍa, 3.549 ff. "*marakata-śakala-kalita-kaladhauta-liper iva ratijaya-lekham*'– *Gītagovinda* 8. Kaladhauta-lipiḥ : illumination of a manuscript with gold; characters written in gold (V.S.Apte).
135. "*vikrītam prasthadaśakam iti varṇān alekhayat. tasmin rājñi vicārajñe monarājasya nandanaḥ; balādhṛtam bhuvam rāja-sabhāyām aham ākṣipam. pratyar thibhir athānītam bhūrjam rājājñayā nṛpaḥ; yukti-jñaḥ salilasyāntar vācayitvākṣipat tataḥ. naṣṭeṣu navavarneṣu purāṇeṣu sthireṣv atha; bhūprastham ekam vikrītam iti sabhyān avācayat.*" Jonarāja: *Rājataraṅgiṇī,* vv.804 ff.
136. "*dhūma-raktālaktakākṣara-tālapatra-kuhaka-tantra-mantra-pust-ikā-saṅgrāhiṇā...paṭṭikā-likhita-durgāstotreṇa...*" Bāṇa: *Kādambarī,* p. 338.

"*yaḥ paraśurāmasya yuṣmābhiḥ vartāharaḥ preṣitaḥ tenaitat*

*tamāla-rasa-vinyastākṣaram tālipatram upānītam.*" Bhavabhūti: *Mahāvīracarita*, p. 50 (NSP). '*tamāla-pādapāt pallavam ādāya niṣpīḍya śilātale*..' *Kādambarī*, p.236.

137. Burnell, p. 93; Pandey, p. 85; Ojha, p. 154f, Gough p. 18f; Satyendra, p. 54ff. Gode (1946). Along with liquid inks, ink tablets were also in vogue. cf. '...*maṣarāśi-praviṣṭeva masiguṭikā*...' *Mṛcchakaṭika*, 1. before 33.
138. Francis (1975)
139. Satyendra, p. 160.

## CHAPTER III

# COLLECTION OF MANUSCRIPTS

Before the middle of the last century, collection of manuscripts had no special significance. It was just acquiring books to a library private or of an institution. Universities like Taxila, Nalanda, Valabhi had huge libraries. Particularly, Nalanda which flourished from 4th century A.D. to 1205 A.D. when it was destroyed, had a rich library containing countless books. It had a library complex called 'Dharmagañja' of three buildings : *Ratnasāgara, Ratnodadhi* and *Ratnagañjaka*. Of these, Ratnodadhi had nine storeys and housed the sacred scripture.[1] The Chinese scholar Itsing stayed in Nalanda (675-685 A.D.) and collected copies of about 400 texts consisting of 500,000 ślokas.[2] Another Chinese scholar who came earlier, Hiuen Tsang, visited Kashmir Palace Library and twenty scribes had been employed to copy the books selected by him. He mentions libraries and reading rooms in the Jetavanavihāra. The libraries were richly furnished with Buddhist literature as well as Vedic and other non-Buddhist literature and all treatises on the art and science of those times.[3] An inscription of Guhasena of 559 A.D. records a grant made for acquiring books and looking after them in the monastery at Valabhi where a University flourished between 475 and 775 A.D. under the Maitrakas.[4]

The kings and chieftains had their palace libraries.[5] Wealthy persons also maintained libraries of their own. We learn that Kumārapāladeva had established twenty-one libraries (Bhaṇḍars) in Gujarat. Vastupāla, Kumārapāla's minister, was a great patron of learning. He established libraries in Anhilwad, Stambha-tirtha (Cambay) and Bhṛgukaccha (Bharuch) at a cost of eighteen crores.[6] Akbar's Imperial Library (Kitab-Khānā) at Agra had 24,000 volumes, as reported by the Spanish priest who visited it in 1641.[7]

An inscription dated 1442 A.D. Pagan (Mynamwar) lists 295 works donated to Buddhist order by a governor and his wife.[8]

But, as printing was introduced and the new mode of education was gaining ground under the British rule, personal attention towards 'books' i.e. manuscripts, began to diminish.

As early as 1780, a few British officers posted to their work in India got acquainted with Sanskrit language and literature. They took interest in Indian culture and collected privately, books and curious items like sculptures, inscriptions, epigraphs, etc. One of them, Sir William Jones, established an institution - The Asiatic Society of Bengal - in 1781 to collect manuscripts and other antiquarian articles and publish manuscripts and other studies. Jones had a collection of his own. Sir Robert Chambers (1774-1779) had a unique collection of manuscripts. He was a friend of Sir William Jones and also sometimes President of the Asiatic Society of Bengal. The Prussian Government purchased his collection and deposited them in the Imperial Library, Berlin. In 1807, Sir Jones and Lady Jones presented their collection to the Royal Asiatic Society. Mackenzie, who came to India in 1782, was an Officer in the Survey Office. Between 1796 and 1806, he was posted to survey South India. During this period, he collected manuscripts and other items of antiquarian interest. His collection was so valuable that the East India Company purchased it for £ 10,000 and deposited it in the India Office Library, London. Some manuscripts collected by Mackenzie are also deposited in the Government Oriental Manuscripts Library, Madras.

Bühler who worked in India and Aufrecht who worked in Germany and England, gave their collections of manuscripts to India Office Library, London, in 1888 and 1904, respectively.

In the latter half of 19th century, the then Government of India took an active part and allocated funds for collection of manuscripts.

In May 1868, Pandit Radhakrishna of Lahore wrote to the then viceroy, Sir John Lawrence, welcoming the orders of the Government "for collecting the catalogues of Sanskrit, Arabic and Persian books in existence in many parts of India" and suggested "the compilation of a catalogue of all the Sanskrit manuscripts in the libraries of India and Europe". Whitely Stokes, Secretary to the Council of the Governor-General for making laws and regulations, submitted a note on August 6, 1868, under instructions. His note was favourable and advocated the necessity of collecting and preserving the manuscripts. Further, he drew up a scheme for the same. He showed how the scheme is beneficial to the administration including the political plane. However, the last paragraph is worth-quoting, as it presents a true state of affairs so far as manuscripts are concerned :

> But whatever may be done, I trust that no time may be lost in doing something. The climate and the white-ants of India are awful destroyers of manuscripts. The old race of Sastris is dying out; the younger natives are losing their interest in the study and preservation of their national literature; and it is safe to say that in another generation, unless the Government bestir itself at once, much of value that is now procurable will have disappeared for ever.

The Governemnt of India resolved in November 1868 accepting the scheme of Whitely Stokes and ordered on 3rd November 1868 that the Resolutions "in regard to the discovery and preservation of the records of ancient Sanskrit literature be forwarded to all provincial governments and the then native states." Accordingly, scholars were deputed to tour in search of manuscripts, to make a list of manuscripts available and to purchase more important of them.[9]

The Government of India published (1878) the reports of scholars on the search of manuscripts during the first ten years. The contribution of Buhler and Kielhorn stand out in the matter of bulk. The names of some of the scholars who worked in this period are : R.L. Mitra (Bengal), R.T.H. Griffith (North-Western Province), Bühler (Gujarat,

Rajaputana, Kashmir), Kielhorn (Bombay), Burnell (Tanjore), Oppert (Madras), G.B. Malleson (Gaurdian to His Highness the Maharaja of Mysore-- Sarasvathi Bhandara, Mysore Palace Library), Visnu Sastri (Central Provinces), Devi Prasad (Oudh).

Two years before the Government of India resolved to compile catalogues of Sanskrit manuscripts, i.e. in November 1866, Government of Bombay spared some money to Bühler with which he had collected many manuscripts.

Following Bühler and Kielhorn, scholars like R.G. Bhandarkar, P.Peterson, K.Kunte and many others covered Western India, Bombay, Gujarat, Rajasthan, Punjab, Kashmir and the then Central Provinces. Their reports have been published from time to time (1869-1906).

Rajendra Lal Mitra worked in Bengal. His Reports (1-11) (Notices of Sanskrit manuscripts) were published from 1871 to 1895. This was continued by Haraprasada Sastri till 1906 (Second series).(Reprinted by Sharada Prakashan 1990 )

In the South, A.C. Burnell compiled the Catalogue of Tanjore Saraswati Mahal Library. He was followed by Oppert (Reports, 1880-1885), B.L. Rice (Mysore and Coorg 1884) and E. Hultzsch (Reports 1895-1899).

**Discoveries of Manuscripts in Central Asia**

In 1895, G.Macartney, who was a special assistant for Chinese Affairs at Kashgar, discovered six sets of Sanskrit manuscripts picked up from the ground at Kük Gumbaz. It was a kind of soft paper of darkish colour. Hoernle ascribed them to 2nd century A.D.

During 1909 and 1915, there were two expedition to Central Asia for discovery of antiquities. Of the items collected, there were also manuscripts or fragments thereof.

In the last century there were at least 60 Collectors (Indian and foreign) and their collections named after them are deposited in various libraries round the world.

**Major Manuscripts Libraries :** ***India***

We may now briefly acquaint ourselves with the major Manuscripts Libraries of today in India.[10]

The Saraswati Bhavan Library of the Government Sanskrit College, Benaras (now, Sampurnanand Sanskrit University) is the earliest modern Manuscripts Library in India. It was established in 1791. It had a Journal, *Paṇḍita Patrikā*, in which Sanskrit works were printed serially. Later, books were issued in the series Princess of Wales Sarasvati Bhavana Sanskrit Series.

Maharaja Serfoji of Tanjore (1798-1832) established a Library in the modern sense. The Madras Government recognised it as a Library in 1918. Tanjor Palace Library was its nucleus.

1857 saw the establishment of Ranvir Sanskrit Residential Institute in Jammu.

The Government Oriental Manuscripts Library (GOML), Madras, has been taking care of manuscripts from 1870. The Adyar Library and Research Centre was found in Madras in the year 1886.

The Government of His Highness the Maharaja Chamaraja Odeyar, Mysore, established in 1891 the Government Oriental Library in Mysore which included then the Archaeological Section also. Pt. A. Mahadeva Sastri was its first Curator. He was followed by Dr. R. Shama Sastri of *Arthaśastra* fame. Publication work was also started quite early, i.e. in 1893. With the establishment of the University of Mysore in 1916, the administration of the Library was transferred to the University. In 1943, the Library was recognised as Oriental Research Institute. In 1966, the Kannada manuscripts were transferred to the newly established (1964) Institute of Kannada Studies of the University.

In 1893, the Central Library, Baroda, started a section for Sanskrit manuscripts. By 1927, this section developed so as to be rechristened Sayaji Rao Gaekwad Oriental Institute. Many rare texts have been published.

The manuscripts collected by the Government of Bombay were made in 1917 the nucleus of the world-famous Bhandarkar Oriental Research Institute named after the great savant R.G. Bhandarkar. It has since been a wellknown International centre for Sanskrit studies.

Maharaja Svati Tirunal Rama Varma (1812-1827) developed the Maharaja's Palace Library in Tiruvanantapuram (Kerala). The Curator's Office established a library of manuscripts collected. These two were amalgamated into the Oriental Manuscripts Library ushered in by the Kerala University (1937).

Sri Venkateswara University established an Oriental Research Institute in 1939.

The Kuppuswami Sastri Research Institute, Madras, takes its name from the renowned scholar Mahamahopadhyaya S. Kuppuswami Sastri of Madras. It came into existence in 1944.

There are many more Universities, Institutions, Maths, Jain Bhandaras, where Sanskrit manuscripts have been collected. There are more than 300 libraries, small and big, all over India. A list is given in the Appendix.

*Abroad*

Of 77 libraries in countries outside India, the most important are[11] :

| | | |
|---|---|---|
| Denmark : | 1. | Royal Library, Copenhagen. |
| France : | 2. | Bibliotheque Nationale, Paris. |
| Germany : | 3. | Preussiche States bibliothek, Berlin. |
| | 4. | Universitats bibliothek, Leipzig. |
| | 5. | Staats bibliothek, Marburg. |
| | 6. | Bayerishe Staats bibliothek, Muenchen. |
| | 7. | Universitats bibliothek, Tuebingen. |
| Great | 8. | British Library, London. |
| Britain : | 9. | India Office Library, London. |
| | 10. | Royal Asiatic Society, London. |
| | 11. | Bodleian Library, Oxford. |

| | | |
|---|---|---|
| | 12. | India Institute, Oxford. |
| | 13. | Cambridge University Library, Cambridge. |
| Nepal : | 14. | Darbar Library, Kathamandu. |
| Pakistan : | 15. | Punjab University Library, Lahore. |
| Sri Lanka : | 16. | Museum Library, Colombo. |
| USSR : | 17. | Aziatasij Muzej Imperat, Akademii Nauk Petrograd. |

We learn from Pandurangi's book[12] that hundreds of manuscripts are yet to be catalogued in Bodleian Library and Libraries in Germany. It is fervently hoped that scholars will consider it and will see that they are catalogued early. Since most of these manuscripts were the early collections of European Indologists, the collection might be of rare manuscripts. Who knows, there may lie a manuscript of a work known only in name or a better manuscript that solves the textual problem of works like Nāṭya-Śāstra ?

Though sufficient effort has been put forth in putting together the available manuscript material in institutions wherein they could be looked after, there are still manuscripts lying in private custody here and there, and there can be no complacency in regard to their collection on the part of the Manuscripts Libraries. However, the work of organising or co-ordinating the activities of the various institutions -- government as well as aided and private - dealing with manuscripts both in India and abroad, is yet to be undertaken. Prof. M.V. Sitaramaiah[13] has rightly given a call for establishing a Central Manuscripts Library wherein the microfilms of all the Indian manuscripts may be preserved along with the manuscripts which may be made over to it. This indeed is a laudable idea but involves huge expenditure. Further, it may give rise to certain problems : whether 'all manuscripts' means 'all copies' irrespective of value - several copies of *vratas* for instance should be made etc. But, to begin with, there could be a Central Manuscript Service from which scholars can get information on and/or microfilm copy of a needed Indian manuscript in whichever library it may be. This institution will thus be able to consolidate and co-ordinate the work going on in the field of manuscript studies around the world. We may look forward to the B.M. Shri Memorial Foundation of which Prof. Sitaramaiah was one of the founders, to give a lead in this direction.

In this connection, the programme of work of Indira Gandhi National Centre for the Arts, Department of Arts, New Delhi, must be noted. One of the main aims of the Centre is to serve as a major resource centre for arts - written, oral and visual (Kalanidhi). It is to serve as a reference library of national importance (such as bibliographical, reference, referral, document, supply etc.) in all branches of humanities and arts.[14]

Inspite of the fact that all our universities having facilities for research in Sanskrit have established Manuscript Libraries, yet there does not appear to be a clear idea about the nature of a Manuscript Library in the minds of the administrators. Before closing this chapter, it may be worthwhile to cast a glance on what the library-pundits write on a modern manuscript library[15] even though there is fundamental difference as regards the concept of a manuscript. Manuscript means anything written in hand; it may be personal correspondence, marginal notes on some printed material, written essay and so on. But, it is not necessarily limited to books only, as it is understood in this book. However, the difference may be overlooked for a moment, as the principles can very well be adapted to any type of Manuscripts Library.

Manuscripts Library is to be distinguished from an archive and a museum. An archive preserves the permanent records of a government institution; the records which are of historical importance of an institution are preserved for future use primarily of that institution. Its service to scholars is only incidental.

A museum may collect materials from various sources. Though the choice of materials is not restricted to any particular item and it may be anything from pieces of pottery to a throne, still, there are museums devoted to one particular field of knowledge. The general public are benefitted by a museum. The Manuscripts Library acquires manuscripts and very rare books from any source, preserves them and provides its services to the scholars and students.

A Manuscript Library should be an independent institution, and it is "not to be part of a large general library system", for manuscripts cannot be looked after as printed books and cannot and should not be handled as printed books; the staff needs to be trained in manuscript care. The person responsible for manuscript-care "should know how to do research himself/herself so that he/she can appreciate the problems of visiting scholars". Not only that, the person "must know the special techniques of caring and cataloguing". If this requirement cannot be provided, one should refrain from establishing a manuscript library.

The primary function of a manuscript library is to serve scholarship; therefore it must provide adequate working space, decent lighting and reasonable schedule of working hours, adequate aids to find the desired material from among the collection and publish and information about its collection. No manuscript library deserves to exist if it is unable to inform scholars of its resources. It must provide duplicating and reproductive services and should not discriminate among its users.

## Notes and References

1. Sankalia (1972), pp.72f & 244. Upadhyaya (1961), p.156f.
2. Mookherjee (1947), p. 574.
3. Watters (1961), p. 386.
4. *'saddharmasya pustakopacaryārtham'* - *South Indian Epigraphy*, 7, p. 67. Upadhyaya (1961), p. 66. *'...bali-caru-satra-cīvara-piṇḍapāta ...bheṣajyadyārthamdharma-ratnasya lekhanādyartham vihārasya ca khaṇḍa-sphuṭita-samādhānār-tham...'* Nalanda plates of Devapaladeva, *Ep.Ind.*, 17, 17, p. 322.
5. King Siddharaja procured for Hemacandra all grammar texts available from different parts of the country, to facilitate Hemacandra to write his *Siddha-hema-śabdānuśāsana*. After the grammar text was ready, the king got several copies made of it and sent them to various parts. Kashmir received twenty copies. Sandesara (1953), p. 11.
6. *"aṣṭādaśa-koṭi--suvarṇa-vyayena sarasvatī-bhāṇḍāgārāṇām*

*trayāṇām sthānatraye bharaṇam kṛtam."* Jinaprabha: Tīrtha-kalpa, Vastupāla-saṅkīrtana, Jinaharṣa, *Prabandhakośa,* p.129. The three places were : Anahilvad, Stambha-tīrtha (Cambay) and Bhṛgukaccha (Bharooch). See also Sandesara (1953), p. 38.

7. Diringer (1958), p. 146.
8. Law (1933) 2, p. 670.
9. Gough, pp.1ff; quoted passage is on p. 7.
10. Pandurangi (1978) gives information about the manuscript libraries. See also Janert (1965).
11. See Appendix for a full list.
12. Pandurangi (1978), pp. M & O.
13. Sitaramiah (1983), p. 7.
14. Grateful acknowledgements are due to Dr. K.V. Sarma who brought this to my notice.
15. Bordin & Wuner (1966).

## CHAPTER IV

# PRESERVATION AND CATALOGUING

## I. Preservation

### *A. The Need*

The manuscripts are the carriers of culture. They are the link between the present and the past. Sanskrit in particular was, for a very long period of time (more than 2000 years), the medium of higher education, scientific pursuit and literature. Thus, Sanskrit works are a repository of the multi-farious facets of knowledge. And those works are available today in manuscripts. Hence, it is necessary that we should preserve the manuscripts. Even if the text in manuscripts is printed, it is our duty to look after the manuscripts as a token of gratitude and to give an idea to the posterity about the amount of strain our forefathers took to pass on the light of knowledge. Manuscripts are also useful in tracing the history of scripts. Hence, there is an obligation to preserve these manuscripts in tact for posterity. Prof. M.V. Sitaramaiah touchingly drives home the need for preserving a manuscript along with its microfilm copy. He very aptly asks : "Is it not like ignoring an ailing father after taking his photograph, if a manuscript is neglected just because it has been microfilmed ?"[1]

Paper and palm leaf -- the chief materials for writing books -- get destroyed in course of time. The durability depends on the quality of the material and care one takes about them. Thus, the care of manuscripts pre-supposes a knowledge of the conditions for their destruction. They are generally speaking : time, fire, water, heat, dust, humidity, atmosphere, gases, fungi, ants, rats and last but not the least, human beings.

### *B. Causes of Destruction of Manuscripts*

The causes of destruction of modern printed books apply to manuscripts as well. The manuscripts, however, require more attention than printed books because of the nature of the material, also each manuscript is unique and can never be replaced. Hence each manuscript has to be given individual attention. The manuscripts are to be protected from the adverse effects of environment, climatic conditions, pests and the human being.

Water, fire and wicked men are the primary enemies of books, observes the 10th century critic, Rājaśekhara. The couplet usually written at the end of manuscripts says that the manuscript exhorts one to protect it from oil, water and loose binding and from falling into wicked hands. A wicked person, a mūrkha, has no respect for the books and even is envious of them. Hence, the books may not be safe in such hands.[2] The book, in our tradition, is regarded as an object of worship. That eloquently speaks for having care in handling manuscripts. It is too well known to repeat here that books are susceptible to fire. Water, if it wets, is dangerous as also oil which causes the growth of fungus. If the binding is loose, the leaves are liable for damage. The palm leaf bundles are also to be bound tightly; otherwise the edges of the leaves get damaged.

As with reference to any object in nature, human being is both the preserver and the destroyer. Frequent use guards the manuscripts from the attack of mould or pests. But that only tolls the death-knell of the codex if the person handling it is not careful enough.

#### *Climatic conditions*

The manuscripts are affected by the variation in the level of humidity. If it is low, the leaves become brittle; high humidity helps the growth of mould. Relative humidity is calculated as a percentage of moisture held in the air relative to the total amount of which air could hold at that temperature. 50 to 55% is tolerable for modern paper and for others the limit is 60 to 65%. Low humidity with heat is the greatest enemy of palm leaf manuscripts.[3]

Palm leaf is found to be four times as strong as wood or hand-made paper. It loses its strength due to age but slightly. From the point of view of permanence, palm leaf is an excellent material for records, but for the fact that its resistance to wear and tear is very poor. Old palm leaf has a pH value of 4 and new leaf has pH 5.5 while paper has a dangerously low pH value.

*Environment*

Air is hazardous as carrier of dust and chemical gases (if a factory or a laboratory is close by). Chemical gases are not easy to detect and have an adverse effect on ink and modern paper. Dust, though minute, poses a threat to books by providing breeding resorts to worms and insects.

Coming to the world of other living beings, fungus, insects and rats are the potential sources of danger.

1. **Fungus** : Fungus or mildew or mold (or mould) are particles found in air. While they settle on damp wood, paper, etc., they grow horizontally on the surface of the material and disfigure it. Mold grows when there is high humidity (more than 65%) and when the room temperature is 65° to 95°F. If fungus should occur between leaves, they stick together and they cannot be separated ordinarily without damaging the leaves.

2. **Insects** : There are more than a million varieties of insects noticed by biologists. Only a few of them are harmful to books. *Prabhāvakacarita* refers to palm leaf mutilated by beetles.[4]

(a) ***Silver-Fish*** : The insect is so called because its form resembles that of a fish, tapering backwards and is silver-grey in colour. It is about 13 mm. long. Some name this book-worm and some others differently (silver-moth, etc.). It has long feelers on both ends. It bores holes in the books and is fond of starch (used to smoothen the writing surface), gum and gelatin. Silver-fish shuns light and its activity increases in darkness.

(b) *Cockroach* : Though this name applies to a group of insects - Blattidae - it usually refers to one species, the black beetle. This has more than one thousand sub-species. Some three varieties are found in libraries throughout the world especially those in hot climate. It is a wonderful creature in that it can squeeze itself in a very small crevice. While it can eat anything, it can live without food for days together. The reproductive period is April-October and it multiplies very quickly. The eggs are laid in the edges of books. It also disfigures books by its black excreta. Cockroaches are active in darkness.

(c) *Book-worm* : Though any worm in the book may be called 'book-worm', it is more usually applied to the larvae of the beetle of many varieties. The beetle lays eggs on the edges of books. There are some species like Sitodupa Paniccum that can lay 8,000 eggs in a year. In five to ten days, the eggs hatch and the larvae come out. Immediately, they begin their operation. The larva moves into the book or palm leaf bundle boring horizontally and vertically. It goes on eating whatever is in its path. There is practically nothing that this worm cannot eat. Its excreta too destroys books. Living on and through the books for 15 days, it becomes adult and the life-cycle is repeated. The worms seem to relish the oily part of the ink spread on a palm leaf. That is why we often find only the area of characters eaten while the space around remains intact. Lyctus brunneus is another species which destroys books, it is called ghoon (ghuṇa) in India.

(d) *Termites* : Entomologists distinguish nearly 1500 varieties of termites. These insects which are said to be older than man by least a million years, are the largest group of all insect pests. They inhabit all the world over except the snow-covered continents, Arctic and Antarctica.

Termites are usually called white ants. But these insects are neither white nor do they resemble ants except for the fact that they are also small social poly-morphic insects like ants. The colour of termites is pale yellow or dark brown. It is said that some species in Srilanka are black. Their body is made up of only two parts, the head and the abdomen.

Specialists bring them under the family of isoptera to which are related cockroaches.

The adult male and female insects are winged and they emerge from earth to found new colonies, usually after first rains when the weather is hot and humid. Nature has its own balance, not all pairs survive to prepetuate the family. The wings are dropped during flight and most of them fall a prey to birds, lizards, dogs etc. A whole family is the offspring of a single primary royal pair. We are told that the queen can lay 30,000 to 80,000 eggs in a day, and lives upto ten years.

There are two varieties of termites in the main. One variety is the wood-dweller. This is confined to wood, dry or damp and does not have contact with earth. The other variety is ground-dweller which falls into three types : (1) One group is sub-terranian. Nests are burrowed about a foot below the ground and channels are bored below the ground and buildings to reach food. In other words, the nests of this type will not be in the spot in which the insects are detected but lie somewhere else. (2) The other type builds ant-hills growing upto about six and a half metres with a base diameter of about four metres. (3) The third type builds cellular nests on the ground, on wood, or even on branches of trees. There are some primitive species which have diffused nests. Of all these, the first type poses potential danger than others so far as books are concerned. They are "dwellers of darkness" and shun exposure to light.

Termites are small in size and their body is soft. Still, they are verocious eaters of cellulose. However, they are selective feeders. Thus the damage inflicted by these insects need not be due to their eating. It may be due to the holes bored through by them or due to corrosion because of moisture or bodily secretions.[5]

(e) ***Wasps*** : Wasps do not feed on books. One variety bores holes in wood to build its nest. The other variety called *mud-wasp*, builds mud-nests which stick hard to a surface. The books are liable for damage or disfigurement, if these nests are built in their edges.

(f) *Book-lice* : These are minute insects of the order Corrodentia that attack books. They are also called Psocids. There are also wood-boring beetles.

3. **Rats** : It is well-known that rats attack manuscripts and books and reduce them to pieces. They can easily bore holes in brick walls and wooden cabinets.

## *C. Remedies*

Once the causes of destruction of manuscripts are known, it is easy to look after them.

Darkness is to be avoided where manuscripts are stored. The place must have sufficient light, but direct sun-light should not fall on the manuscripts. When artificial light is necessary, it must not produce heat. Shelves are to be arranged in such a way that there is free movement of air.

Precautionary measures against fire like installation of fire-fighting gadgets - extinguishers, smoke alarm etc., need to be undertaken. Mention may be made here that tests have shown that Indian paint is fire resistent.[6]

Dust must be controlled scrupulously. The manuscripts as well as shelves are to be cleaned regularly and frequently by the use of duster-cloth. The dust is to be wiped and not made to spread. The red-cloth of manuscript bundles[7] are to be cleaned regularly. The floor of the stock-room is also to be wiped frequently with a wet cloth. With regard to palm-leaf manuscripts, arrangements must be made to see that every bundle is cleaned, leaf by leaf at least once in six months. Each leaf is to be wiped on both sides with a cloth. While wiping the leaf, it must be remembered, the hand should not return on the leaf, for that may break it; the hand should move from centre outwards. The manuscripts, paper or palm leaf, may be cleaned mechanically by using vacuum cleaners. The insects, if any, will have to reveal itself through this process.

Maintenance of cleanliness goes a long way in checking the menace of insects and fungi. The person in-charge should be ever watchful. To control insects like silver fish, bookworm and cockroaches, chemical insecticides could be used.

Naphthalene balls or camphor may be kept with paper manuscripts, as it works against silver fish. In Tanjore S.M. Library, for example, some efflorescent chemicals like camphor tied in a piece of cloth are placed between manuscript bundles at regular intervals. Powder of Ghodavaca, a herbal preservative, in small packets or made into pills, may be used - 2 or 3 pouches in a box or shelf. For wrapping manuscripts, yellow cloth is better, for, it is insect repellant. According to Bhattacharya, silk free from book-worm is a more desirable material.[8] In some libraries DDT powder is spread between leaves of hand-made paper manuscripts. Though this method might be helpful as a pest-controlling device, it cannot be recommended because the manuscripts become unworthy of handling, i.e. unless one is prepared to inhale a good part of the powder, one cannot handle it. Also the powder will make the manuscript crumble. It can be sprayed at the foot of the shelves.

Use of Mercuric chloride ($HgCl_2$) is an old method. The chemical is not only very poisonous but also persistent. 5% solution of this is effective against American cockroach.

A less poisonous insecticide is Ammonium thiocyanate ($NH_4SCN$) or Pottasium thiocyanate (KSCN). But one should take care to avoid iron. In Australia, 1% to 2% solution of tri-cresylophosphate in refined kerosene is brushed or sprayed to ward of silver fish and water solution of Pottasium antimonel tartrete or tartar emetic ($K(SbO)C_4H_4O_6\ 12H_2$) is employed. Experiments with Aldrin ($C_{12}H_{12}Cl_6$), Pentachloro Phenol ($C_6CI_5OH$), Pyrethrum or pipernol and Butoxide are being conducted.

Against mold in manuscripts, inter-leaves of tissue paper impregnated with thymol $(CH_3)_2\ CHC_6H_3(CH_3)\ OH$ and an insecticide are recommended. However according to Hughes, it is not yet proved that thymol works against mould.[9] Also thymol vapours are said to have adverse effect. See further.

*Fumigation :*

The manuscripts infested by mildew and insects may be subjected to fumigation in a specially prepared chamber. A fumigation-chamber is an air-tight almirah with shelves made of wire mesh and with glass doors. If the total height is about 180 cms., 4 to 5 shelves may be arranged at about 30 cms. intervals, leaving more space below. In the middle of the lower cover plank, a round (7.5 cms. diameter) hole may be cut and a stainless-steel plate fixed there. The infested manuscripts are to be spread on the shelves A glass plate containing the chemical, Thymol (100-150 gms. per one cubic metre) is kept on the steel plate. Under the steel plate, a vacuum electric bulb of 60 watts is made to burn for about 4 to 5 hours. The heat sublimates the chemical. The vapours pass through the manuscripts above and the insects are destroyed. The manuscripts are to be left in the chamber for two days, then cleaned and restored.

Ethylene Oxide ($C_2H_4O$) fumigation destroys insects and micro-organisms. But this is toxic and explosive. It is also inflammable when mixed with air. Therefore, it is usually mixed with Carbondioxide ($CO_2$). A safer chemical is para-dichloro benzene ($C_6H_4Cl_2$ ). 1.5 kg. of this chemical for one cubic meter is kept in the lower shelf of the chamber. National Archives have tried fumigation with a mixture (1:1) of Carbon tetrachloride ($CCl_4$) and Ethylene dichloride. The mixture is called Killoptera. These chemicals are placed on the top shelf because the vapours are heavier than air. Requirement : 225 gms. per one cubic metre.

Thymol requires a duration of seven days but is found to reduce the tensile strength of the manuscripts.[10] Para-dichloro-benzene is mild but best effective at 65% humidity. Therefore, conditioned silica gel may be used with it. Humidity can also be maintained by a trough of saturated solution of Sodium dichromate ($Na_2Cr_2O_7.2H_2O$) or Magnesium arsenate ($Mg_3(AsO_4)_2.nH_2O$) or Potassium dichromate ($K_2Cr_2O_7$) in the chamber along with the fumigator.

Use of chemicals may smudge carbon inks. Proper precautions are necessary before subjecting the manuscripts to fumigation.

Naphthalene ($C_{10}H_3$), as noted earlier, can be used as a fumigant. It is a cheap and a readily available insect repellent. It is effective even in $30^0$ to 35°C. National Archives have found out that it is more effective than Carbon disulphide ($CS_2$), Carbon tetrachloride or dichloro benzene. About 7 oz (apt.1/2lb) of naphthelene per 10 cft, paralyses cockroach and such common insects in about 1.5 hours.[11]

In the Oriental Research Institute, Mysore, a special kind of oil, an Ayurvedic preparation, is being employed since about 40 years to keep the palmleaf in good condition. The sesamum (til) oil is treated with herbal juice and other insecticide ingredients, which are all a traditional secret. It is prepared locally by two to three persons. The oil when smeared thinly and evenly on the palm leaf (both sides) with a brush, not only cleans the dirt off the palm leaf making the letters legible but also keeps the insects away and the leaf is made pliable. It must, however, be snsured that the oil has dried, before tying up the Ms. Otherwise, fungus may grow and destroy the manuscripts . Before this oil came to be used, the Institute had got a Manuscript-oil from Ceylon, and this author was told that the application of that oil made the leaves stick to each other; hence, the use of that oil was abandoned. Tanjore Library is using Lemon grass oil for the manuscripts in palm leaf.

If the floor and walls are neatly cement-plastered, there is no fear from termites. If the library is housed in an old building, one has to be constantly vigilant to check every nook and corner, periodically.

To fight termites : The almirahs may be kept at least 15 cms. away from ground, wall and roof. Not only is this measure precautionary against termites, but also adds to general cleanliness of the library and allows free air circulation. Appearance of termites at any corner can easily be detected. Legs of wooden almirahs may be placed in stone bowls or enamelled trays containing coal tar creosote in kerosene (1:2). While using this, one should exercise care as this is inflammable. Instead, a strong solution of phenyle in water is also useful. Varnishes and paints check the attack of termites. Varnish prepared from Ortho-chloro-phenol, napthol and petroleum (1:1:40) should be freely applied twice to the wooden structures. 20% solution of Zinc chloride ($ZnCl_2$) in water can also be used. Hot creosote coated twice is most effective and cheap, but the colour would be black and it would be somewhat sticky. R.C. Gupta gives details as to how the termite menace can be effectively kept under control.[12]

Harisagar mentions that panadigrass (used in perfumes) is placed among books to save them from termites.[13]

Of course, if a Manuscripts Library could afford air-conditioning the stock-room, then there is no need to worry so much about periodical cleaning, fumigation, etc. It may be mentioned here that fungus attacks in spite of air-conditioning, if there is humidity.

In case of ink eating away the paper, the manuscripts might be immersed in slightly alkaline solution to reduce the acid contents of the dried ink.

### *D. Repair of Manuscripts*

The manuscripts tend to be damaged, howsoever one may be very careful, due to frequent handling for study and research. Therefore, periodical repair of manuscripts must be one of the items of preservation. The torn pieces are to be carefully glued. Paper manuscripts in book-form are to be checked towards mending injured bindings.

Physical care of manuscripts is to be taken over on priority. Each manuscript has to be given individual attention. Torn pieces are glued together by using tissue paper. The pieces are cleaned - rubbed with rubber-powder for dry cleaning - and placed close together so that the torn line is in close alignment. Tissue paper, about 1 cm. in breadth and of required length, is torn with hand (not cut with scissors, etc.) and placed over and along the joint. It is then hot-pressed. Similarly, the other side is to be given the tissue paper support. A similar treatment may be given to those sheets which are worm-eaten, so that whatever remains may be handled confidently and edges of the sheets of the book are uniform. The palm-leaf pieces may also be restored with tissue paper. Corboxy-Methyl-cellulose paste is useful for paper and Texicryl paste is useful for palm leaves.[14] Cello-tape may also be used.

Worm eaten sheets or leaves may also be given tissue paper support. Broken leaves or torn sheets or gaps may be filled with blank leaves or hand-made paper sheets cut to the required size. This ensure uniformity of size of sheets arrests any further mutilation.

Manuscripts drenched in water should be dried under a fan. The leaves are to be carefully separated and spread for drying. They should not be exposed to sun or dried in an electric heater.

*Lamination*

Lamination is the process of enclosing each leaf or sheet in cellulose acetate or polythene foil. Some use chiffon also for the purpose. There are now automatic machines that do the work.

Paintings and unique manuscripts are to be laminated so that they do not deteriorate due to pests or climatic aberrations. However, the experts say that lamination has its own limitations.

One or two methods of lamination may be noted here. (1) Damaged leaves are placed between thin sheet of polymethyl methacrylate or peropex softened with acetone and pressed at 80°F for two minutes. (2) There is cold lamination process using acrylic emulsion (spineflux) and tissue specially coated with adhesive acrylic rubber. (3) Kathpalia recommends the use of silk (chiffon), flour paste and silk covered with cellulose acetate foil softened with acetone. (4) National Archives recommends a simpler method. The leaf/sheet should be spread on a glass sheet. Cellulose acetone foil piece, a little larger than the manuscript, is spread on it. Over this is placed a piece of tissue paper of the same size as the foil. Cotton swab dipped in acetone is rubbed over the tissue paper and this binds the paper with the original. After it is dry the operation is repeated for the other side.[15]

For all these operations, the leaf/sheet should be dusted and cleaned. It may be cleaned with isopropyl alcohol and then with Toluene. Incised leaves may be rubbed clean with distilled water. Glycerine and water may also be used; the flexibility is restored with camphor oil or citunella or walnut oil. One must ensure oneself whether the ink on the manuscripts is soluble in water. Acidity of paper or ink can be reduced by immersing the material in an alkaline solution like calcium hydroxide or by treating it with ammonia gas.

If incised palm leaves need reinking : (1) It is cleaned and powdered lamp black or carbon black is rubbed with a pad and excess wiped off with a cloth. Then treated with 1% PVA in Toluene. (2) Lamp black is used with 5% oil of camphor in alcohol.

Judith Segal after discussing the merits of several methods, quotes Kate Losty whose method is simpler and appears to have no after-effects : The incised leaves are wiped with a damp cloth adding 1% or 2% glycol for embrittled leaves, and dried between blotting paper under a board. For reinking when necessary, lamp-black and oil of camphor is used. Worm holes are repaired with paper fibres and paste and missing areas with palm leaf pared to fit, using acrylic emulsion, heat set adhesive (texicryl). Written leaves are repaired with fibred Jap paper and starch paste. Mrs. Segal reports the experiments of V. Daniel in British Museum Library. He found best results from soaking a leaf overnight in a 5% solution of Poly ethylene glycol (PEG) in water. Some of the observations in this regard are : the application of PEG 200 penetrates fairly fast; improves the flexibility of palm leaf and makes it hygroscopic and therefore a small amount of fungicide needs to be dissolved in the solution.

It may be noted here Japan has a unique system of preserving ancient paintings. It is a traditional art. The method is so laborious that it calls for utmost patience. Here, even the preparation of the glue involves a complex process. The ingredients of the special glue are to be reduced to very fine paste in a stone-mortar, boiled and kept in jars to be used 12 years later.[16]

The above is a very brief description of the restoration work and shows the direction of work. For details see the literature on the subject in the bibliography.

A proper record of the process or repair should be maintained with reference to each manuscript repaired, noting its problems and methods employed.

Mrs. Segal's observation about repair in general is worth quoting : "When a manuscript needs repairing, it is to admit a basic failure of conservation, a failure, in proper storage and handling."[17] This statement is very much true and serves as warning to the librarian. One need not get dejected if there is an occasion to repair in spite of one's utmost care, for, one has to visit one's physician in spite of being careful about one's personal health.

A list of materials and equipment necessary to clean and repair of manuscripts may be given here :[17]

Materials : Blank palm leaves
Toned thin tissue
Toned long fibred paper
Chiffon
Blotting paper
Release paper

Iso-propyl alcohol
Purified/distilled water for
Cotton swap cleaning

Calcium hydroxide
Calcium bicorbonate to reduce
Ammonium hydroxide acidity

Polyethelene glycol (PEG) 200 for embritled leaves

Para dichloro benzene (PDB) for wormy leaves
Fungicides : Sodium salts of Orthophenolphenate
Lamp black: Essential oil of camphor ] for re-inking

Equipment : Sheet of glass
Light box for tracing
Tacking iron (electric soldering iron with a modifed head and power point
Pressing boards
Sharp knife - scalpel
Paint brushes
Ruler
Scissors
Black Pencils (hard and soft)

*E. Mechanical Reproduction*

To preserve the text in those books which wore out due to frequent handling or which deteriorated due to any other reason, they were being copied manually. This was also the case when a scholar wanted a copy of a manuscript. This process was not only laborious and time consuming but also entailed commission of errors. That was some four decades ago. Now, there are mechanical devices that help in preserving the facsimile of the manuscripts.

Foremost of the devices so far as manuscripts are concerned is microfilming. This has been very handy in preserving the reading in the manuscripts in their original hand-writing. The microfilm occupies less space than its original; it is easy to store and to look after; only it is inflammable. Also copies can easily be prepared for scholars who may need them. However the original manuscripts should be looked after, as long as they last just for preserving them as monuments at least. It may so happen that a look at the original manuscript may decide a doubtful reading.

Microfische and xerography are the other two devices. Paper manuscripts have an advantage over the palm leaf mss. They can be reproduced xerographically (xerox). Not only this is economical but also can be made use of directly, whereas microfilms, microfische/microcard needs a microfilm/microfische reader. Microfische is also printed on a card, hence called microcard; this needs an opaque reader. Microfische is not a convenient device for manuscripts in general and palm leaf in particular.

Indira Gandhi National Centre for the Arts, New Delhi, has, in its programme, the establishment of Kalanidhi, which includes a national library of microfilms and microfische of all manuscripts, catering to the needs of scholars and students. The work is going on with a focus on unpublished material at the first instance.

Recently, the Ford Foundation offered a grant including provision for equipment, to microfilm the manuscripts in the Oriental Research Institute, Mysore.

F. This section may be concluded with a stanza quoted by V.Raghavan from some manuscript.[18] It is self explanatory.

*sambhūṣyam sad-apatyavat,*
*parakarā saṁrakṣyam ca sukṣetravat*
*saṁśodhyam vraṇitāṅgavat pratidina*
*vīkṣyam ca sanmitravat ;*
*babhyam badhyavad aślatham dṛḍhaguṇaiḥ*
*smaryam harer nāmavat*
*naivam sīdati pustakam khal*
*kadāpy etad gurūṇām vacaḥ.*

"(The manuscript) should be a dressed as one's good offspring (is dressed), be guarded from (mis)handling of others like a fertile land, be thoroughly cleaned everyday like a wounded limb, be visited (i.e. handled) (everyday) like a dear friend, be bound fast with a strong thread like a prisoner, be remembered always like the name of the Lord; such a book gets never deteriorated. So say the Masters."

## II. Cataloguing

The concept of library and the arrangement of its contents is not new in India. We have seen earlier that there were huge libraries in Ancient India. Surely, they must had some sort of classification. Unfortunately, we do not have any record to the effect. That there were three buildings and one of them housed sacred scripture might suggest a very broad classification. The counting of branches of knowledge as 2, 3, 4, 14, 18 or 64 speaks for the attempt in classifying the field of learning.[19] The Ánukramanis and the Nighaṇṭus throw light on the idea of indexing and classification which the ancient people had. The Kośas[20] (Metrical dictionaries) have a system of classification, though of words. Some of them have a section in which the words are arranged in the alphabetical order of their final phoneme. There are a few palm-leaf manuscripts in the Oriental Research Institute, Mysore, which are Samskrita-Kannada Dictionaries in the modern sense, i.e. the words are arranged in the alphabetical order of the initial phoneme.[21] The anthologies in Sanskrit literature provide the evidence for the idea of subject-wise classification.[22]

Let us go through briefly the process of preparing catalogues in a printed-books library and then discuss how far the process can work in a Manuscripts Library.

"A Catalogue is a list of books in a particular library arranged according to a definite plan."[23] Cataloguing presupposes classification. The modern printed books libraries have their own system of classification. Those generally followed in India are : the Colon Classification of Ranganathan and the Dewey Decimal System. Both have subjectwise classes - 27 and 10 heads respectively. The books in each class are arranged author-wise.

A master-record of every bibliographic item in the library, as and when acquired is maintained. It is called the Accession Register. It provides a serial number called the Accession Number that identifies each and every item added to the Library, and records information in full about date of accession, the author, etc. in the following order : (1) Date, (of accession) (2) Accession Number, (3) Author, (4) Title, (5) Place of Publication, Publisher's name and address, (6) Year of publication, (7) Volume/Part (if any), (8) Size and Binding, (9) Source (of acquisition), (10) Cost, (11) Class, (12) Date of payment, (13) Remarks.

Incorporating the bibliographical details, catalogues are prepared according to the system of classification adopted. The catalogues enable the reader to look up his/her book and locate it in a very short time. The following entries are given in a Catalogue : (1) Call Number, i.e. the Class Number and the Initial letters of the author's name, (2) Accession Number, (3) Author, (4) Title, (5) Publisher, (6) Date, (7) Volume or part, if any. Each book is given this information. In the case of titles which have no author (example: a journal), title itself is taken under the author. Normally, an Author Index and a Subject Index are prepared. The catalogue follows the classification of books in the shelf.

There are three modes of preparing these Catalogues (Author and Subject) for the use of the reader : (1) Card Catalogue, (2) Book-form and (3) Sheaf form.

*(1) Card Catalogue*

In this type of Catalogue, the information to be provided are typed or written on cards of uniform size and thickness. One card is prepared for each volume in the library. Cross references, wherever necessary are provided with separate cards (example: a book by three authors will have three cards in the Author Index.).

The advantages of this type are : (i) it is easy to consult; (ii) It is very flexible and can easily be manipulated without any hindrance to the system. Cards may be rearranged or replaced as and when needed. The system takes in easily any number of additions (or deletions) at any frequency and grows with the library. Thus, it fully satisfies the 4th and 5th laws of Library Science enumerated by S.R.Ranganathan viz., Save the time of the reader; The Library is a growing organisation.

The disadvantages of the Card Catalogue are: As each and every volume has one Card, sometimes two or three, the Catalogue will be a huge one, set in cabinets. Therefore, it cannot be carried from place to place. A separate space will have to be earmarked in the library. Any one who wants to consult the Catalogue, even within the library, must go to it. There is no question of taking the Catalogue home or consulting it at leisure outside the premises. Only those who use the library in person can benefit from this type of Catalogue.

*(2) Bookform*

The required details are typed or printed (or written) one below the other on sheets and bound together in volumes. Cross references are also provided in their order of sequence.

The advantages of this type of Catalogue are : Several copies of the Catalogue may be got at the same time without any appreciable loss of time. Copies could be kept in different sections of the library and, therefore, one need not go to the particular place for consulting the Catalogue. One could carry it wherever one wants. Even an outsider may have an idea of the wealth of books in the library.

The disadvantage is that it ignores the 4th and 5th Laws of Library Science. It cannot take in any addition. Only supplementary volumes are to be prepared at frequent intervals. This creates confusion and delay in consultation for one has to go through 'several' volumes. If supplements are not issued frequently but at intervals to avoid too many of them, then the reader will be at dark about the recent acquisitions. It must be remembered here that the printed books pour into the library every day. It will be too late by the time the reader locates the book in the library.

*(3) Sheaf-form*

This provides the details of the books on slips of paper

of convenient size and filed in volumes, thus combining the features of card form and book form.

Accordingly, it has the advantages of both the forms. It is flexible and portable. But, there are disadvantages. The size of paper cannot be as small as that of a card which is sufficient for the entries. And then, paper is too thin to withstand frequent use. Hence, slips will have to be replaced very often. In both these cases, there is an unnecessary wastage of paper. Paper slips cannot be set in cabinets.

Taking all these factors as well as the fact that Catalogue is meant for the users of the library, into consideration, Card form is preferred to other forms and is being followed in all the libraries, Indian and foreign.

Now, we may examine these catalogues from the point of view of a Manuscript Library. To begin with, we may note the special features of a Manuscripts Library. (1) The Fifth Law of Library Science has no much of relevance in a Manuscripts Library for the rate of growth of the Library is very low; (2) There is no comparison at all between the frequency of readers visiting a Printed Books Library and that of a Manuscripts Library. Only specialised scholars make use of this Library; in other words, the number of users is very limited and also not restricted to any one particular geographical area; (3) The manuscripts cannot be browsed near the shelves. One should sit in a place and consult a manuscript. It is because of the nature of manuscripts and because of the care one has to take in handling them.

However, even in the Manuscripts Library, it is necessary to have a Master Record - Accession Register - of all the manuscript items (it might include charts, paintings with inscription, etc.) as and when acquired. But the bibliographical details vary from those of printed books. Many Sanskrit works are known by their titles, though in some cases, there may be name of the author handed down in tradition. Some works are, however, anonymous. While preparing the Catalogue, one will have to be guided by the information provided in the 'book' (i.e manuscript). So, the title of books which are invariably found in manuscripts should be given preference. Obviously, there is no necessity for the columns of publisher or year. On the other hand, the script, material etc., are to be noted. Thus, the items of an entry in the Accession Register for manuscripts are : (1) Date (2) Accession Number; (3) Title; (4) Author; (5) Material; (6) Script; (7) Size (in centimetres); (8) Number of leaves; (9) Number of lines per page and number of letters per line; (10) Extent (number of *granthas* and whether complete or not); (11) Condition of the manuscript and date if any (12) Evaluation; (13) Cost; (14) Class Number; (15) Source; (16) Purchase/Donation; (17) Remarks.

The materials and scripts of manuscripts as discussed before are varied. The size, number of leaves/pages, etc., give an idea of the manuscripts. To calculate the extent of contents in a manuscript, the unit is a *'grantha'* which is a unit of 32 letters. It is like speaking of a paragraph in English as having so many words. It is the number of syllables in a verse of the Anuṣṭup metre. The average number of letters per line multiplied by the number of lines per page and the number of pages and the product divided by 32 gives the number of *'granthas'* in a book. The condition - whether good, worm-eaten, mutilated, very old - needs mention. Date, if available, is to be recorded. A scheme of evaluation is followed to determine the cost of a manuscript. This may differ from institution to institution. Broadly, the scheme is as follows: The manuscript of an unprinted work has more value than that of a printed work: If the printed book is out of print, then it is as good as not in print. If a title under either of those two categories is new to the library, it has the maximum value fixed for the category. Of course, it is a treasure, if the title is unique in the manuscript world. The value goes on decreasing as the number of copies already available in the Library increases, with this difference : While even a tenth copy of an unprinted work may be valuable, even a 5th copy of a printed work does not acquire any monitory value. For calculating the purchase price of a manuscript, the rate is fixed per 1000 'granthas', under both the categories. But, sometimes, a Library may have to purchase a manuscript by paying the price asked for by the seller.

Coming to the Manuscript Catalogue, the following information are to be given in the case of a Manuscript : Title, author, class number, script, number of folios/pages, complete/incomplete, Remarks : (Example : with commentary or with/without the original text (in the case of commentary) as the case may be).

*Form of a Manuscript Catalogue*

As observed earlier, a scholar visiting a Manuscripts Library cannot browse the manuscripts near the shelf. Hence, there is no need for the classification of the manuscripts in the shelf. Another reason, more important than this, is that it is not practicable. The manuscripts will have to be classified in the shelf according to the material and not on the basis of subject. Paper manuscripts cannot be shelved with palm leaf manuscripts. Even under paper, the manuscripts will have to be classified according to their size. This aspect must get preferential attention from the point of view of preservation. Often, a Manuscript codex, particularly in palm leaf, would contain more than one title. So, the manuscripts cannot be arranged in the shelf according to the title or subject. So, the Catalogue order need not conform to the order of books in the shelf, or vice versa. One way of arrangement could be to give the manuscripts classifications according to material and size. This Number which is a serial number under the category locates the manuscripts in the shelf easily. The category here is the material. Thus, the palm leaf manuscript bears a serial number preceded by say, PL, palm leaf. Paper is usually in three sizes - half foolscap (bound), foolscap quarter (bound) and loose sheets. Each of these will have a separate serial number preceded by, say PA, PB and PC respectively. A title Index and a Title Index arranged subject-wise are to be prepared.

The Manuscripts Catalogue needs to be not only in the form of cards or Library Register but also to be printed. The copy of a Printed Book available in one library is exactly the same as the copy of the book in another Library. But, it is not true in the case of a manuscript. Let alone copies in other libraries, the copies of a text found in one and the same Library may not be identical; each is "different" from the other. Hence, it is imperative that the Catalogues of all Manuscript Libraries must be available in all Manuscript libraries and also to scholars and researchers in general. That is, every Manuscripts Library must issue its Catalogue in print. As the rate of acquisition is very low, supplements may be issued from time to time and a consolidated one, once after a few years. The perusal of several volumes does not create any confusion because working with manuscripts requires a great amount of patience and care. But, this does not preclude a Librarian of a Manuscripts Library from preparing a Card Catalogue for the use of scholars visiting that Library.

*Descriptive Catalogue*

It is not just enough if a Manuscripts Library prints and makes available its Catalogue - titlewise and subject-wise to sister institutions in the world. Manuscripts Catalogue work is not at all complete without the preparation of a Descriptive Catalogue.

A Descriptive Catalogue, as its very name suggests, is a Catalogue which gives a description of the manuscripts so that a scholar referring to it may visualise it. The ordinary catalogue informs the existence of a copy. A Descriptive Catalogue furnishes details. The Government of India, Department of Education, Sanskrit section, Ministry of Human Resource Development, New Delhi, which provides financial assistance to institutions to prepare and publish the Descriptive Catalogues of manuscripts with them, has prescribed the format as follows :

> A Descriptive Catalogue consists of two parts: Part One gives the physical details of a Manuscript, titles being arranged alphabetically under different subject heads. The order of the columns spread on two adjoining pages are: Call Number, Title, Author, Material, Size (in centimetres), Number of

folios/pages; Number of lines per page; Number of letters per line, Extant (C/Inc.); Condition of the manuscript; Remarks (Whether printed, etc.). *Part two* shall contain extracts of the Manuscript : (a) A few lines in the beginning; (b) a few lines at the end just enough to compare two copies of the same work and identify them; and (c) the Colophon. If the Colophon at the end is not available, a Colophon available elsewhere in the copy is given. If there are more than one copy of a work in the Library, then the extracts may be given from any of them and only difference, if any, in other copies noted. Letter 'E' is prefixed to the Call Number in Part 'one' to indicate that extracts from that copy is given in *Part 'two'*. These extracts are necessary because they are useful in differentiating a manuscript from its namesake and deciding that one and same work is known under different titles.

The Colophon, generally, gives the title of the work, its nature, the name of the author with, sometimes, his titles, his parentage, his patron's name, etc.

### *Catalogus Catalogorum (CC)*

To facilitate reference to manuscript Catalogues of various institutions in the world, Theodor Aufrecht conceived and compiled in Germany, A *Catalogus Catalogorum*, a Catalogue of Catalogues in three parts, (Heidelberg, 1891, Bonn 1896 and 1903 reprint 1962 (Franz Steiner verlag SMBH, Wiesbaden). This was compiled from and gives reference to manuscripts noticed in the Catalogues and Lists of Manuscripts available during his time. The *Catalogus Catalogorum* is an alphabetical register of names of authors and titles of works. Under an author, all works known under the name in the source material are listed. Under the title of a work, the author, if any, and the reference to the Catalogues (Volume Number and page) wherein the work is noticed are provided. This minimises the effort of scholars in locating whether any manuscript of a work is available and if so, in which institution/s.

Reference to the commentaries and super-commentaries are also provided under the title-entry.

Aufrecht's *Catalogus Catalogorum* has many faulty entries but the defect lies not in Aufrecht's magnificent labour but in the source material on which he relied upon. This was noticed as far back as 1935 when more authentic catalogues and descriptive catalogues were available. So, a revision of *Catalogus Catalogorum* was deeply felt by the scholars.

*New Catalogus Catalogorum (NCC)*

In 1935, Dr. A.C. Woolner, Vice-Chancellor, Punjab University, Lahore, wrote a letter to the University of Madras, to revise the *Catalogus Catalogorum*. The University considered and accepted the proposal. A Committee, with MM. S. Kuppuswami Sastri as editor-in-chief and Sri.P.P.S. Sastry and Dr. S. Kunhan Raja as members was formed. The work was started in November, 1935. The first Volume was published in 1949 after which there was a lull for about 15 years. In 1966, Volume II appeared under the editorship of Dr.V. Raghavan, The first Volume was also revised and issued in 1968. Dr. C. Kunjunni Raja took over, after Dr.V. Raghavan retired. Now, Dr. N. Veezhinathan shoulders the responsibility. So far, the 12 volumes covering upto the end of letter 'Pa' are published (1966, 67, 68, 71, 73, 77, 1978, 1992. Volume I Rev.1968).

The method followed is basically that of *Catalogus Catalogorum*. But, Buddhist, Jaina and Prakrit works and authors are also included in the *New Catalogus Catalogorum*. The additional information given about the date and life of authors and the bibliographical details in case the manuscript-text is available in print have enhanced the value of the NCC. However, efforts should be made to see that the pending volumes are published early.

The effort of scholars in pooling together the wealth of manuscripts for their preservation and use of scholars can be understood by the number of catalogues or lists published. Aufrecht based his CC on 98 catalogues/lists. Gidwani and Nawalani mention 500. Katre, 187 enteries of catalogue. Raghavan lists 465, Pingue, 325. Pandurangi, 200 entries. Janert who speaks of 339+36 catalogues, is the most exhaustive regarding catalogues published. Prajapati has physically checked 337 catalogues. He lists 632 catalogues in 25 libraries in Delhi, comprising 1355 volumes covering 6,00,000 Sanskrit, Pali and Prakrit manuscripts and 1,70,000 mss in other Indian languages. Out of 632 catalogues, 361 are those published in India; the other (271) have been published outside India.[24]

## Notes and References

1. *"rogiṣṭhanāda tandĕya photo tĕgĕdiṭṭukŏṇḍu auṣa-dhopacāravannu māḍadĕ, ātanannu sāyu-gŏṭṭantāgu-vudillave ?"* Sitaramiah (1983), p. 5. cf. "We kiss the old shoes... of the saints and we neglect their books which are more holy and valuable relics." Erasmus q. in *Encyclopaedia of Religion and Ethics*, art. Humanists, vol. VI. p. 831 f.
2. *"siddham ca prabandham anekādarśagatam kuryāt. yad ittham kathayanti - nikṣepo vikrayo dānam deśatyāgo 'lpajīvitam; truṭiko vahnir ambhaś ca prabandha-ccheda-hetavaḥ. dāridryam vyasanāvagatir avajñā mandabhāgyatā; duṣṭe dviṣṭe ca viśvāsaḥ pañca kāvya-mahāpadaḥ".* Rājaśekhara : *Kāvyamīmaṁsā*, ch.10, p.53.
   *'tailād rakṣed jalād rakṣed rakṣec chithila-bandhanāt; mūrkha-haste na dātavyam evam vadati pustakam". cf. 'udakānila-caureb-hyo mūṣakebhyo hutāśanāt; kaṣṭena likhitam śāstram yatnena paripālayet.'* q. in Satyendra p.32. *'dyūtam pustaka-śuśruṣā nāṭākāsaktir eva ca; striyas tandrī ca nidrā ca vidyā-vighnakarāṇi ṣaṭ.'* (Gambling, care of books, indulging in drama and sex, indolence and slumber - these six are obstacles for learning.).
3. Segal (1979)
4. *'tadā paṭṭa-truṭir jajñe śalabhebhyo davena vā.' Prabhāvakacarita, śl.* 207, p.338. Rājaśekhara speaks of *truṭika* (termite). See note 2.
5. Gupta (1954).
6. See *Indian Archives*, 5, 1951, pp.172f.
7. In the North Indian Libraries, each manuscript bundle is wrapped separately in a red cloth. But in the South, they are mostly kept as such in racks with or without shutters.
8. B. Bhattacharya (1946) is not aware of dressing palm leaf with oil. He reports that some libraries made use of crude

kerosene. Terpentine oil may be liberally used on the covers with some preservative value.

9. Hughes (1953).
10. See Segal (1979).
11. Kishore (1961); Chakravarti (1946); Kishore & Mehra (1954).
12. See note 5 & 9 above.
13. Harisagar (1946).
14. Chakravarti (1946) b. Goel (1953).
15. Segal (1979); Sannaiah (1971) See also note 11 above.
16. Murray (1980), p.44.
17. Segal (1979).
18. Raghavan (1963), p.12.
19. Vidyā, knowledge, divided into four branches: *'ānvīkṣaki, trayī, vārtā, daṇḍanītiś ceti vidyāḥ'*. Kauṭilya: *Arthaśāstra*, 1.2. Manu adds a fifth *ātmavidyā* (7.43). 14 *vidyās* are sually mentioned: *'aṅgāni* (6) *vedās catvāro* (4) *mīmāṁsā* (1) *nyāya-vistaraḥ* (1); *purāṇam* (1) *dharmaśātram ca vidyā hy etāś caturdaśa*. Four more, *āyurveda, dhanurveda, gāndharvaveda* and *arthaśāstra* are counted to make 18 *vidyās*. 64 *kalās* or 64 *vidyās* are also enumerated; there are variations about the details. See Venkatasubbiah (1911).
20. Eg. Subjectwise: *bhūvarga, manuṣyavarga, vanauṣadhi-varga* and arrangement according to the alphabetical order of the final phoneme like *kāntavarga, cānta, mānta* etc. Hemacandra (1088-1172) has a more complex system in the *Deśīnāmamālā* which has eight *vargas* one each for words beginning with vowels, phonemes in *ka-ca-ṭa-ta-pa-vargas, ya* and *sa*. Each of the *vargas* is divided into two groups: *ekārtha* and *anekārtha*. Under each of these the words are arranged according to the number syllables in the words in order i.e. those having 2, 3, 4, 5 syllables and so on (*dvyakṣara, tryakṣara* etc.).
21. Eg. No. P3831, Oriental Research Institute, Mysore.
22. See for example, *Sadukti-Karṇāmṛta* which divides the collection into five 'pravāhas' which are further subdivided into 'vīcis': Amara-pravāha, Śṛṅgāra-pravāha etc.
23. Sengupta (19S64).
24. Janert (1965); Prajapati (1968).

## CHAPTER V

# WRITING IN MANUSCRIPTS

### A. Manuscripts : Their Form and Size

**Form**: The leaves of a manuscript might be either stitched together or unstitched.

So far as palm leaf and birch bark are concerned, there is no question of stitching them all. To keep the leaves from slipping away or from being shuffled, a cord is passed through them. Birch bark sometimes do not have the cord.

Hand-made paper sheets are not stitched, but kept as loose sheets. No cord is used to keep the order in tact. But, this is not difficult in view of the fact that paper can be easily handled. Machine-made paper manuscripts are available both in stitched and unstitched form.

Satyendra refers to *Daśavaikālika-sūtra* which gives some names of manuscript types.[1] They are: Gaṇḍī, Kacchapī, Muṣṭi, Sampuṭa-phalaka, and Chedpaṭi or Chivaḍi or Sṛpāṭikā.

Gaṇḍī is a manuscript thickness of which corresponds to its length and appears like slab. The book that is wider in the middle than at the ends, is Kacchapī (tortoise-like). Muṣṭi ('fist') is as small as can be held in one's fist. A manuscript with wooden side-boards is Sampuṭa-phalaka. Chedpaṭi is a thin book with only a few leaves.

Satyendra further discusses the names of types of stitched paper manuscripts, as current in North India:[2] Pothī, Potho, Guṭka and Pānāvalī.

Pothī and Potho are centre-stitched books. The size of the paper and thickness of the pothī is smaller than that of potho. Guṭka is a book of the size 15 x 10 cms. It is either centre-stitched or side-stitched. Pānāvalī, also sometimes called pothī', is oblong and stitched at the shorter side.

**Size** : The manuscripts available today are of varied sizes. But all the leaves of one manuscripts will be of uniform size as of any modern book. Selection of particular size, however, depends on the extent of the work to be copied and the purpose, much as in the same way as the size of a book is decided today. Personal liking too plays an important factor. A very small size like 3.5 x 2.5 cms. is chosen, for example, to copy certain religious tracts for personal use. But the purpose of the other sizes cannot be determined easily.[3]

In case of paper, one has a wide range of sizes to choose. As regards palm-leaf, choice is only in regard to its length as the width of palm-leaves is almost uniform. Incidentally, it may be noted that the size of loose sheet (unstitched) paper manuscripts is always oblong.

Bāṇa describes how a manuscript is read. And this indirectly throws light on the nature of a manuscript and how it was handled. The 'book' (*pustakam*) is kept wound by a thread which is unwound just before reading is begun. The 'opened' book is kept on a low stool probably made of cane or reed (Śaraśalākā-yantra). A leaf, evidently of a lesser length than that of the 'book', is kept in it as the book-mark (antaram patram). A few leaves are taken and held together in hand and read out.[4]

**B. Technique**

All the manuscripts, whether palm-leaf or paper and written in any part of the land, adopt a definite and almost a uniform system of writing. It is possible to formulate the principles of writing a manuscript.

As observed earlier, paper and birch-bark are written with a pen while palm-leaves are mostly incised; there are also a few instances of palm-leaf being written with pen and ink. The writing is always horizontal lengthwise and in perfect straight lines whatever may be the script and howsoever long the leaf may be.[5] Writing on birch-bark sheet is parallel to the lenticels. Paper has not any such norm. If the paper is oblong like palm-leaf, writing is horizontal lengthwise. Sufficient margin is left on either ends of the leaf/sheet and writing is full from top to bottom. Even if a text is begun on the same page, it is only 'continuous'. Sometimes, a beginning is made in a fresh line. Even in this case, the previous line is filled by repeating a word like 'śrī', upto the end of the right margin. Perfect alignment is maintained at both ends of the lines. A rectangular space is left blank around the string holes; otherwise, writing is continuous from the left hand top margin corner to right hand margin corner below. While a palm-leaf is invariably written on both sides, paper and birch-bark are sometimes written on one side only.

The kaṇṭha - stylus was used to incise palm-leaf. A few leaves supported by a wooden plank are held in the left hand and written with stylus held in the right hand fist.[6] The scribe wrote either by himself or at the dictation of another. The paper/birch sheets on the other hand were placed on one's lap or on a low stool in front and written.

Almost all manuscripts begin with salutation to Gaṇeśa and/or the favourite deity or Guru of the scribe - (Śrī-Gaṇeśāya namaḥ; Sāmba-śivāya namaḥ; Varadārya-gurave namaḥ, etc.) - followed by the title of the work and the text. Sometimes, the title of the work is written on the left margin. Sectional headings if any, are also mentioned on the left margin. In a text like *Rāmāyaṇa* which has several cantos, a design is written on the left margin against the line in which a *sarga* (Canto) ends and another begins - to draw the attention of the reader. The same design is used usually to indicate the end and beginning of a section/chapter. In the Bakshali manuscript, the design is written at the end of each stanza.[7]

The letters (7 to 8 per 25 mm.) are of equal size, on the same base line and of the same height and same style. The lines are firm but not deep. (*samāni samapadāni samānasani samā śirāḥ; akṣarāṇi pratiṣṭhavyāḥ mṛdūni lalitāni ca.*)[8]

When a text and its commentary are to be copied, there are three modes of doing it : (1) The text is first written continuously and followed by the bare commentary; (2) One verse or a few lines of the text are first written followed by the relevant part of the commentary and that by the next verse or next few lines and the commentary thereon; (3) The text part is written in the middle portion of the page normally with indents on either side and above and below this the commentary relating to the text is written. This is called tripāṭhī or trivallī form and calls for some skill of adjustment when written for the first time and this mode is frequent in paper manuscripts.[9] There is also the Pañcapāṭhī manuscripts where the text occupies in the middle portion and the commentary is written in the space above, below and either side of the text.

One bundle of manuscript often contains several texts. This feature is very common in palm-leaf manuscripts. The title of the texts included are sometimes provided on the opening leaf. Several texts are copied one after another. However, the grouping is not heterogenous. That is, a bundle may contain Vratas, Smṛtis, Upaniṣads, Kāvyas, Nāṭakas, Stotras, etc.

***Pagination*** : The folios are numbered and not pages. The figure appears on the left margin, mostly in the middle part of it, on the reverse side in paper manuscript and on obverse of palm-leaf.

***Punctuation*** : The only punctuation mark that we can come across in the manuscript is the vertical stroke called daṇḍa, single (I) or double (II). In prose passages, a single daṇḍa signifies the end of a sentence and a double daṇḍa the end of a section/work. In versified passages, single daṇḍa is at the end of the first half of a stanza and the other at the end of the same. Sometimes, a double daṇḍa, dash and double daṇḍa, cipher, double daṇḍa (II-II) or (II O II) is employed to denote the end of section. Some scribes make use of the design here. Serial number for stanzas, chapters or sections are put between two double daṇḍa; the first of these double daṇḍa being the end mark of a stanza/section (II 5 II 2 II). In the example given, the first figure refers to the stanza and the other number to section.[10]

Mostly no space is left between words. They are continuously written. In normal writing of any script, each letter is written independently. Joint letters or running hand is not usually found in manuscripts. It may be mentioned here, by way of comparison, that we do find running hand in 'sannads' or official letters preserved in palaces but not on Copper plates.

**Abbreviations** : Abbreviations are also found used for frequently occuring common words. For example : In Āpastamba-Dharma-sūtra, Mss., 'go' is used for 'gotra'. 'o' (bindu) when placed before a consonant indicates that, that consonant is to be doubled; this is common in Prakrit, Kannada and Malayalam manuscripts. Example : saoga is to be read as *sagga*. The figure '2' placed after a word indicates that, that word is to be repeated. Eg: 'punaḥ2' means 'punaḥ punah[11]

**Colophon** : At the end of a work is given the Colophon. There are also instances where certain copies do not have any colophon. A Colophon may be as simple as to mention only the title of the work or may provide information about the poet/author, his titles, parentage, etc. At the end of the sections/cantos of a work too colophons are given. But invariably, these intermediary colophons are simple, mentioning only the title, the number and the name of the section concerned, except for the colophon to the first chapter/canto which is often full.

A colophon at the end of a work may contain one or two or several or all of the following items : (1) title of the work; (2) name of the author; (3) name of parent/s (4) Teacher's name; (5) place of the author; (6) Name of the patron, with/without titles and parent's name; (7) Date of completion of the work. Sometimes, the *grantha-saṅkhyā*, the member of verses (extent) contained in the work is mentioned. This is usually followed by salutation.

**Illustrations** : Diringer writes that "book illumination is the art of embellishing a manuscript book by painting pictures in gold colours". He has not come across instances of book-illumination before the Mughal period. Akbar got the *Rāmayāṇa* and the *Mahābhārata* translated into Persian and the copies were richly illuminated. A copy of the *Mahābhārata* with 169 miniatures - 'one of the finest' - is extant in Jaipur.[12] Works on Mathematics and Astronomy contain some diagrams. In certain cases, they are painted. They are found mostly in paper manuscripts. *Bhāgavatapurāṇa* *Mahimna-stotra* (Puṣpadanta), *Caurapañcaśikā*, *Gīta-Govinda*, *Mahābhārata*, *Rāmāyaṇa*, Jain Kalpasūtras are some of the texts, the manuscripts of which have miniature paintings. The *Śrītattvanidhi* is a treasure of paintings in water colour. A copy of *Prahlāda-caritra* contains drawings on every page. One of the earliest painting on palmleaf is found in the manuscript of *Niśītha-Cūrṇi* of 1100 A.D., deposited in Jain Bhandar, Patna.[13]

**Decoration** : Usually, palmleaf manuscripts do not show any instance of decoration. A striking example is of the *Dhavala* manuscripts of Mudabidri, South Kanara District(Karnataka). Each margin of all the pages of manuscripts is decorated with patterns none of which is repeated twice. Kannada grammar in Sanskrit language written in Malayalam script is very peculiar in terms of calligraphy too. Each page of the manuscript is written in a particular mode - waves; waves with sharp angles; thus giving the appearance of crosses, boxes and so on. The borders of paper manuscripts are often decorated with colour designs. A hand-made paper ms. of *Ṛgveda* (6 aṣṭakas) of about 1640 AD, written in Devanāgarī on both sides, has borders of each page decorated with colours. A copy of *Basavapurāṇa* has each of its 220 folios pages are designed differently.[14] R.B.Pandey writes: "the Buddhist manuscripts of Nepal, the Jain manuscripts of Gujarat and the Brahmanical manuscripts of Rajasthan, Kashmir, Kangra are highly ornamental and profusely illustrated. They contain religious symbols and floral and other decorative designs."[15]

The marginal lines are drawn in paper manuscripts and often they are in a different colour. The accent marks in case of Vedic texts, the daṇḍas are also written in colour ink, mostly red. Some scribes write the Colophon in red ink.

**Corrections** : Errors are bound to occur while copying manuscripts. The scholars using the manuscripts and the scribes of manuscripts knew this.[16] We find corrections made in the manuscripts. But, we are not sure if the correction was done as a part of copying work. It is possible that it could have been due to later revision. In the case of correction too, certain methods are followed.

(1) In a context, letter/s or word/s may have to be omitted. Such of them are marked with dots or small horizontal strokes placed above or below them; or they are enclosed within curved brackets; or the part to be omitted is scored off; sometimes, yellow pigment or turmeric is smeared over such portion.

(2) Replacement or substitution done later is written above the portion to be corrected or in the nearest margin against the line. Sometimes the line number is also given with the marginal correction, particularly, along with those written in the top margin or the bottom margin.

(3) Sometimes letter/s, or word/s may have to be added in a line. Such additions are written above the concerned line or indicated in the margin as in (2) above. The place of insertion is shown by putting a *haṁsapāda* or *kākapāda* (upright or inclined cross, + or x = caret) below the line or above the line. If it is a simple letter to be added, it is inserted in the space between the letters wherein it should have been or it is written just above the line in its place therein. (interlinear writing)

(4) Sometimes the intermediary portions of a very widely known passage are omitted to save space. Such intentional omissions are marked with one or more *'haṁsapādas'* written on the line. Some manuscripts show this with dots or small horizontal strokes.[17]

(5) *Accidental Blanks* : It is possible that a scribe might forget to write on the reverse side of a palmleaf. When it is discovered, to allay the doubts of the reader, it is often

written that 'there is no omission here' (*nātra grantha-pātaḥ*) on the blank page. Blanks in the courses of line should only conversely mean that the portion in question is either lost in the original or too obliterated to decipher. Certain scribes encircle the portion which was difficult to decipher in the original.[18]

(6) *Marginalia* : The writing in the margins of manuscripts is called marginalia. As noted earlier, page/folio number, the titles of sections/chapters/cantos; additions, substitutions or corrections are written in the margins. Various readings as well as meanings/explanations are also other matters found in the margins. Whereas page/folio numbers, titles of works, section etc. are invariably written on the left margin, the other items are written in the margin nearest to the related part of the text.

### (c) Scribe

The scribe is a professional copyist who copies a manuscript or document for others. Lipikara, lipikāra, lekhaka are the Sanskrit terms. The professional document-writers today have kept up the age-old profession against much odds due to advent of typewriters. The government offices in the past had official scribes (as there are typists today). They were called Karaṇika, Kāyastha, Rāja-lekhaka, Rāja-lipikāra. There was Akṣapaṭalika or Divirapati, the keeper of records.[19] Kauṭilya lays down the qualifications of such scribes.[20]

It is indeed a pity that we do not always have the names of scribes who have helped in keeping the torch of learning burning bright down to this day.

Most scribes have declared themselves at the end, by giving their names, date on which the copying was completed, patron or the person for whom the copy was made, the source of the example and so on. Mostly, only a few of these details are furnished.[21] Often the scribe's name is mentioned at the end of Copper plates.

Copying is indeed a very strenuous job. Usually at the end, the scribe craves for the indulgence of the readers to bear with any possible scribal errors and to take utmost care of the copy as it has been the result of strenuous labour on his part.[22]

A scribe's job is, it must be remembered, mostly mechanical. He need not compose a work; he is expected to copy a text fairly and correctly. He may be compared to a modern typist or a type-setter in a printing press. A compositor or a typist composes or types from the author's copy. A proof-reader checks the matter set in types. If there are errors, i.e. if the composed matter is not true to the original in any part, corrections are introduced; a typed copy may be revised; thus the copy is set right. A scribe too may have before him the author's copy or a copy of it made by a person like himself. But this work may or may not be subject to a revision with reference to its exemplar. Thus, it is possible that his errors may remain in the new copy without being corrected. A copy made out of such a copy in similar circumstances, contains not only the possible errors freshly committed but also the errors of the earlier one.

A scribe is prone to visual and psychological errors while copying and each scribe has his own idiosyncracies. That handwriting is highly individualistic is very well-known. In fact, handwriting has been the subject of serious study and it is said that it is an index to one's traits. Even as the mode of writing is different from person to person, particular type of errors can be associated with each scribe. Therefore, what is required of a scribe is faithfulness and carefulness. A scribe must cultivate honesty more than scholarship. Katre uses the word 'fidelity' in this context.[23] Howsoever utmost care one might take, there are chances of failure as it is a manual effort going on for a good length of time and calls for physical strength like vigilant eyes, ability to sit tight continuously etc., as well as mental calmness. Thus, manual reproduction of a book will have its defects and we can have gradations in the trustworthiness of a copy depending upon the fidelity of the scribe manifested therein. However, scribal errors also occur on account of the imperfect knowledge of the script of the exemplar. Katre's remark about the basic qualification of a scribe[24] is worth quoting :

> "A mechanically copying stupid but faithful scribe is better than an intelligent and more qualified but unfaithful scribe."

No hard and fast rule can be prescribed to identify a trustworthy scribe. One has to make a thorough study of the manuscripts for the purpose. As an example, one or two points can be made here: The scribe who makes kuṇḍalas (circles) around letter/s and thus indicates his doubt or inability to decipher the same in his original may be taken as more trustworthy. Similarly, a scribe whose copy contains blank spaces for one or more letters in a line may be considered honest in leaving out the lacunae or those letters that are not decipherable in his original, thus avoiding the temptation of himself making up the lacunae. Similarly, careful and systematic writing may be distinguished from the haphazard writing.[25]

Kṣemendra makes fun of the official scribe : He omits the vowel signs over the letters, causes holes (lacunae), swallows words and letters, he is Kāla himself with ink-smeared face![26]

**(D) Kinds Of Texts**

Generally, an author writes out his own composition. A copy of a text written by the author himself is called *Autograph* copy. Composing a work is different from writing it or copying it. That is, for composing (a poem for example), one need not actually write down; even if it is written at this stage, it is not called 'writing' until a fair copy is prepared. An *Autograph* copy is a copy written by one's – here it is author - own hand. It is possible that the author may dictate his composition or somebody may make copy or copies of the fair copy of the author under the author's supervision. Such copies are also called here 'autograph copies' because they are as authentic as the author's own copy. Thus, today, if an author gets his writing typed and goes through it, the typed script too could be called 'autograph copy'. Before going further, it must be admitted that autograph copy too may not entirely be free from 'errors'. Mistakes might have crept in which we call 'slips of the pen' or scribal errors. This applies to a manuscript as well as to a typed script and a printed copy.[27] Perfection can be assumed if the same copy has been read again and again and corrections introduced wherever necessary.

The copy of a text made from the autograph copy but not under the supervision of the author is called the *immediate copy* : such a copy will have greater authenticity than the later copies.

The text that has passed through several stages of copying is called the *transmitted text* and there cannot be any definiteness as to the number of stages.

In Tibet, copies of a text were made from wooden blocks. The text was engraved on wooden blocks, and copies were printed (xylography) from them and whenever required. This mode of taking out copies, it is obvious, arrests the commission of errors.

As found in the last section, copying was a regular process because of two reasons: (1) That was the only mode of having a copy of a text; and (2) That was the only mode of preserving the text when the available copy was deteriorating. As far as the manuscripts are concerned, there is little possibility of finding the autograph copy of a text older than about 500 years. In fact, the chance of coming across such a copy in respect of recent author too is blank. For, there is absolutely no clue available in the manuscript to reckon a copy as the autograph copy or as the immediate copy or as the copy of a copy. We can only have a plausible guess in certain cases. For instance, if there is a single copy available of the work of an author who wrote not beyond 200 years ago, we may surmise that it is the autograph copy. Thus, the palmleaf manuscripts, of the works of Veṅkappayya Bhūpati (18th century) may be considered autograph copies. Therefore, unless there is a clear indication to the effect that the copy on hand is author's own copy or an immediate copy, it is better not to classify the manuscripts on that basis.

As a contrast, the attention of the reader may be drawn to the documents which are also hand-written, but not directly concerned here. They are the copper plate grants and stone inscriptions. Since the writing on them is indelible and the material not perishable, they can all be taken as autograph copy or immediate copy. In such cases, i.e. when only one copy is extent, the manuscripts are described as 'single manuscripts', or '*Codicum unicus*'.

The immediate copy as the prototype or the source of several arrays of extant manuscripts, arrived at inductively, is called the arche-type and the one which is the source of a smaller array within a larger array is called the sub-archetype.

We may discuss another type of distinguishing the texts (1) Those whose autograph copies are possibly extant; (2) Those whose autograph cannot be expected to be extent; (3) Those which had no autograph copy at any time.

We had referred to the first two categories: Under the first group come those texts whose authors are roughly not more than two hundred years old, and all others under the second. Under the third group only certain works or certain class of works are considered.

The third group may, in other words, be understood as those which have come down in an oral transmission and have no one identifiable author. The *Mahābhārata*, the purāṇas, the Māhātmyas, the *Pañcatantra* and such texts belong to this group. The Vedas have been handed down in an oral transmission for a long time. They were committed to writing late in history. As far back as 8th century B.C. (or even earlier), it was known that oral transmission alters the original and that difference arises in different lines of transmission. And so, to arrest the change that had already occured and give a master pattern, the Prātiśākhyas came on the scene. But no such guard was, however, envisaged in regard to oral transmission of secular texts. With the *Mahābhārata* and the Purāṇas, no doubt, the name of 'Vyāsa' is associated. But 'Vyāsa' or more correctly 'Veda-Vyāsa' was not the name of a person but of an office.[28] Veda-Vyāsa is 'the arranger', 'the systematiser' or simply 'compiler' of Vedas. The same person might have compiled and put together the ballads and anecdotes. These were meant to be expounded orally by professional bards right from the beginning. The bards were trained in schools. Obviously, there were many schools and each school had its own view points and bias with a certain common framework. The bards in their exposition were free to develop in their own way within the ideology of their school. In course of time, the nucleus of the heritage of the bards became enlarged. We have a clue in the *Mahābhārata* as to the stages in which its bulk grew : 'Vyāsa' first related to Janamejaya, the story of the latter's ancestors. 'Vyāsa's' son, Śuka, retold the same to Parīkṣit, the son of Janamejaya. Sūta repeated the narration of Śuka, to Śaunaka and other sages at Naimiśa forest. Surely, Parīkṣit had to be given certain details which Janamejaya could understand. Similarly, Sūta had to add further details for the benefit of Śaunaka and others. Thus, the oral transmission of the story of *Mahābhārata* begun by Vyāsa and continued by Śuka and Sūta, so far as the textual evidence shows, was committed to writing at a later time. Between Sūta and the first writing of the *Mahābhārata* (we do not know when), there could have been any number of exponents. Even later, additions at oral expositions slowly percolated into the written text.

It was observed earlier that an autograph copy too may not be free from errors. In the immediate copy, the errors of the original as well as those that the copyist might commit are found. In the third degree copy, the errors in the examplar (i.e. source of copy or the original with reference to a copy) are there and the copyist might have committed some new errors. In the words of S.M. Katre, "A copy can never be reproduced exactly as the exemplar and the deterioration increases with the number of successive copyings."[29] The correctness of successive copies may be shown statistically as follows (from Katre) : Supposing the autograph copy is 100% correct and supposing the scribal error will be at the rate of 3%, the correctness of the immediate copy is 97%, of its copy 94.09%, next 91.17% and so on.[30] However, the transcription fortunately, does not proceed mathematically. And there are various "arresters" of the scribal errors. Otherwise, the correctness could reduce to a 'zero' not before long. This gives an idea of the transmitted text of a work produced by one author. Those redacted at schools have their own history.

The transmitted texts of epics, etc., with bards of one school were similar because they were like-minded. Consequently, this would be at divergence with those of another school. A geographical area almost fits into a school. A geographical area is marked by the usage of a particular script. Normally, the scribes knew one or two scripts, i.e. of the adjoining areas, besides their own. Those who lived in the borders naturally had the occasion to go through the copies in another script, in other words, of another school. If something new was found, it was incorporated into their copy. That is, the part of transmitted text of one line of transmission was added on to the transmitted text in another line. In times of festivals, melas, rathayātras or in the course of pilgrimages, etc., scholars or bards would come together in different places. During such meeting too, the addition of new material was effected. A copy made from such an exemplar would make the additional material clearly part of the text. This copy will, it need not be repeated, would be at divergence with other copies from the same school. Such a copy or manuscript in which two strands of transmission are found mixed up are called *misch-codex* or conflated manuscript.

Thus, the extant copies found today are the transmitted texts come down in various lines of transmission and many manuscripts the text of which have also the oral exposition besides, are conflated ones.

***Recension*** : Certain texts in popular style and those which have unrestrained oral exposition, allow interpolations in them easily. The *Pañcatantra* and the *Mahābhārata* are such texts. Items can easily be introduced or removed or altered without the least doubt of being detected. If a text in a line of transmission gets so much distorted that when a copy of this line is compared with a copy of the same text from a place afar, then they show more of divergence. They are then said to belong to different recensions. If among the set of manuscripts of a work, the manuscripts array themselves in two or three distinctly different groups, then each of those groups is a recension; example : The *Vālmīki Rāmāyaṇa* has three recensions - The North-Western, The Bengal and the Southern.

## Notes and References

1. Satyendra, p. 156 ff.
2. Ibid, p. 82; Menariya (1979), p. 85.
3. Satyendra, p. 82.
4. "*...tat-kālāpanīta-sūtra-veṣṭanam api nakhakiraṇa-mṛdu-mṛṇāla-sūtrair ivāveṣṭitam pustakam puro-ni-hita-śara-śalākā-yantrake nidhāya ... prābhātika- prapāṭhaka- ccheda - cinhitam antaram patram utkṣipya, gṛhitvā ca katipaya-patra-laghvīm kapāṭikām, kṣāla-yann iva masi-malināny akṣarāṇi danta-kāntibhiḥ, arcayann iva sita-kusuma-muktibhir grantham purāṇam papāṭha.*" ('Keeping on the 'desk' the book that appeared wound by tender lotus fibres in the form of rays of the nails though the binding thread was unwound just then; removing the 'book-mark' indicating where it was stopped in the morning reading session; taking hold of a bunch of a few leaves; read out the purāṇa as if cleansing with the lustre of teeth, the letters blackened by soot and as if worshipping the book offering white flowers.') Bāṇa, *Harṣacarita*, p. 85f.
5. It is interesting to note that Sant Ramadas has given clear instructions about writing in Lekhana-kriyā-nirūpaṇa section of his *Dāsabodha* (Daśaka 19, samāsa 1; pp. 623ff 6th edn. 1847). See Gode (1944)a.
   Schuyler (1908) writes how the palm leaves were marked with lines to maintain alignment of writing: "Before doing any writing, the scribe marks lines, usually five in number, on each leaf by means of strings which are placed in a frame with the ends tied and the rest loose. These strings are then blackened with soot from the bottom of a rice-pot and the strings are placed in position over the palm-leaf and then snapped."
6. cf. Schuyler (1908): "The copyiest then holds the blank leaf in his hand and with the needle point scratches the letters of the text on the prepared surface of the leaf. It is remarkable how the writer holds the leaf in his hand and does not rest upon any surface for steadiness."

7. Kaye (1927).
8. De Silva (1938), p. xv.
9. Mitra, R.L. q. Gough, p 20. Muni Punyavijayaji q. Satyendra, p. 157ff. Śuṇḍa is another mode of writing, writing like the probosis of elephant i.e. tapering. Satyendra feels that Kālidāsa's expression 'kuñjara - bindu-śoṇa' (see note 34 ch.2) points to this. Menariya (1979), p. 79 & 85.
10 See also Satyendra, pp. 34. ff.
11. Buhler, p. 7. Some inscriptions make use of contractions (see Pandey p. 112 and Upadhyaya (1961), p. 260) like *he* for *hemanta*, *di* for *divasa* etc. *Rājaśekhara-carita* (p. 1824), p. 4607, ORI, Mysore) uses *su* and *ra* for *subuddhi* and *rasika-śekhara*, the two characters in the work. See also De Silva (1938), p. xvii.
12. Pandurangi (1978) pp. M & O; Satyendra, p. 160f. The 18th century roll Ms. of *Bhāgavatapurāṇa*, in the British Museum, is lavishly illustrated. It measures 5" x 65" and is written in minute Devanāgarī on thin paper. See Francis (1975) p. 299.
*Śrītattva-nidhi*: fl.size paper, Kannada script, Sanskrit language, Description (dhyāna-śloka) of deities, with their colour pictures. Ms. in Oriental Research Institute, Mysore. Produced in the Court of Mummadi Krishnaraja Odeyar (19th century). Mysore Citrakāra School. 9 Sections Called *Nidhis:*

| | *No. of pages* | *No. of pages with ill.* | *No.of colour pics.* | *Drawings* | |
|---|---|---|---|---|---|
| 1. Śakti-nidhi | 132 | 93 | 246 | - | |
| 2. Viṣṇu | 44 | 38 | 109 | - | |
| 3. Śiva | 62 | 55 | 150 | - | |
| 4. Brahma | 120 | 83 | 257 | - | |
| 5. Graha | 263 | 159 | 398 | 40 | |
| 6. Vaiṣṇava | 66 | 10 | - | 20+ | 4 |
| 7. Śiva | 74 | 35 | - | 94 | |
| 8. Āgama | 113 | 8 | - | 14 | |
| 9. Kautuka | 170 | 16 | - | - | 17 |
| Total | 1044 | 497 | 1160 | 171 | 21 |

13. Diringer (1958), p. 145f. The earliest painting on palm leaf found is the Ms. of *Niṣītha-cūrṇī* of 1100 A.D. in Jaina Bhandar, Patna. Satyendra, p. 61.

14. *Basavapurāna:* No.A 312, f. 220; *Karṇaṭaka Bhaṣābhūṣaṇa:* No. p. 41, f. 262-274. Institute of Kannada Studies, Mysore. Ṛgveda codex of 1640 is in Tanjore.
15. Pandey, p. 118. An 18th century Singhalese palm leaf manuscripts illustrated and a manuscript from Kandy has floral designs on its cover too. Francis (1975), p. 305.
16. *'lipikarāparadhena'*. Girnar Ins. Upadhyaya (1961), *'nyūnādhikam tu saṁśodhya paścāt patre niveśayet.' Vyāsasmṛti.*
17. cf. editor's note : *'iha ekaviṁśater akṣarāṇām avapāto rekhaviśeṣaiḥ anumātum śakyate.' Āryamañju-Śrīmūla-kalpa,* p. 1 note.
*'daivānadhīta-nava-divya-śubhākṣarālī nyāsecchayā nihitakākapadena cakre.' '...kākapadam kākacaraṇā-kāraḥ patitākṣaravijñāna-viśeśaḥ.' Śrīkaṇṭha-carita* with Jonarāja's, commentary 52.10.
18. *Vaṭadruparṇa-sthita-varṇa-melanād athaiṣa bhāṣyam nikhilam patañjaleḥ; lilekha vatsakṣataḍurgrahākṣara - sthale kvacit kuṇḍalanām akalpayat.' ... 'Vatsakṣatam sa pitṛkuṇḍalitam yathāvad buddhyākalayya...'* Rāmabhdra-dīkṣita : *Patañjalicarita,* 6.26; 8.12. Buhler : Kashmir Report, p. 7; Keilhorn (ed.) *Mahābhāṣya,* 2.10 note.
19. Sivaramamurti (1952), p. 20. Akṣara-cuñçu and akṣrajīvana are other words; *Vaijayanti,* p. 137. Kāyastha, Karaṇika are official designations (See *Artha-śāstra, Mṛcchakaṭika*).
20. Kauṭilya : *"amātya-sampadopetaḥ, sarvasamayavid, āśugranthaḥ, cārvakṣaraḥ, lekhana-vācana-samarthaḥ, lekhakaḥ syāt." "lehakaś ced uktam na likhati, anuktam likhati, duruktam upalikhati, sūktam ullikhati; arthotpattim vā vikalpayati iti... daṇḍam kuryāt..." Artha-śāstra,* 2-9. 28; 49. Rājaśekhara desires the poet be proficient in several scripts and be of good handwriting : *"cārvakṣaraḥ nāna-lipijñaḥ". Kāvyamīmāṁsā,* p. 50. Bāṇa's company included Sudṛṣṭi, a *pustaka-vācaka* and Govindaka, a *lekhaka. Harṣa-carita,* p. 42.
21. For example : *'idam grantham mahīśūrapure srī-lakṣmī-nṛsiṁha-svāmi-sannidhau śālivāhana-śaka 1961 vartamāna-vikāri-nāma-saḍvatsara uttarāyaṇe grīṣm-rtau nija-jyeṣṭhamāse śukla-pakṣa-sthiravāsare svāti-nakṣatre sāyāhne asmin śubhadine vasiṣṭhagotrotpanna-nārāyaṇātmja-śrīnivāsarāyeṇa likhitam grantham sampūrṇam."* colophon of *Uttaragītā* Ms. No.C.480/3, ORI, Mysore. See also *Nāranārāyaṇānanda* Baroda, Intd.

22. *'bhagna (v.l. baddha) -pṛṣṭhakaṭigrīvah baddha-(v.l. stadbha) -dṛṣṭir adhomukaḥ; kaṣṭena likhitam grantham (v.l. śāstram) yatnena pari-pālayet (v.l. -pālaya)'. 'yādṛśaṃ pustakam dṛṣṭvā tādṛśam likhitam mayā; abaddho vā subaddho vā mama doṣo na vidyate.' 'bindu-durlipi-visarga-vīthikā-śṛṅgapatti-padabhedadūṣaṇam;- hastavegajam abuddhi-pūrvakam kṣantum arhati samīkṣya sajjanaḥ.'* "Error due to hasty writing, and inadvertance, error with reference to a dot, wrong letter, *visarga*, line, serif, word (substitution)'. This last verse is also found in some copper plates. See for example, Sagare plate of 1379-80 (Nagari) Hg.149, *Ep.Car.*, 3, p. 529.
23. Katre, p. 92.
24. Ibid.
25. The scribe should also keep his materials clean. A bad scribe who sullies the stationery is called 'kulakhaṇī'. See Javaliya (1979), p. 72.
26. *'akāraśirṣa-hārī navadarakārī padārtha-saṁhārī; akṣara-bhakṣaka-melā-lipta-mukho lekhakaḥ kālaḥ'*. Kṣemendra: *Deśopadeśaḥ*, 8.45 (Ed. Madhusudana Kaul, Srinagar, 1923).
27. In the case of the printed copy, mistakes may not be entirely due to the author/proof-reader, for, the printer may be negligent.
28. *Vyāsavidyā* refers to reciting and expounding purāṇas and such works and the person who attended to it was called 'Vyāsa'. cf. A Jain prabandha notes that after the death of Vastupāla, Someśvara abandoned the Vyāsa-vidyā to mark his deep sense of bereavement at the loss of his great friend, and refused to recite the Purāṇas, though pressed by the king. And the king appointed another person named Gaṇapati Vyāsa to do the work (*Purāṇa-prabandha-saṅgraha*, p.80) (1272 A.D.). Sandesara (1952) p.52. Attention may be drawn to the term *Vyāspīṭha*, which denotes the 'stand' for keeping 'books' while reciting.
29. Katre, p. 90.
30. Ibid.

# CHAPTER VI

# VARIOUS READINGS

## Their Causes and Types

We have seen earlier that even the most reliable scribe sometimes nods; his copy will be different from the exemplar in so far as a line here or a line there is concerned. This difference grows inversely to the scribe's grade of fidelity. It also depends to an extent, on the distance of the copy from the archetype and the popularity of the work; greater the distance, greater the possibility of divergence. Popularity of a work will naturally occasion the production of a large number of copies, most of which may not be by competent or professional hands.

However, it must be accepted that the scribes may not be responsible for all the variants. It is possible that authors may have revised their work after sometime. Since neither the revision nor the original is dated, there is no way to differentiate when the copy is separated from the author in space or time.

Each individual has one's own idiosyncracies and these are reflected in one's writing pattern too. Hence each copy comes to have its own peculiarities. In other words, each extant copy of a text will be more or less at variance with another. The divergence may be in the form of addition, deletion, substitution or interchange of a letter, word, sentence etc. upto a paragraph. The form or version of a given passage or its part in a particular text is called reading (*pāṭha*). When two copies of a text vary in their reading, one reading is spoken of as the variant of the other. Such divergence are generally called various readings or *varia lectio* (abbreviated : v.l.).

When there is a variant reading, either of them may possibly be the original reading. Hence one reading is a corruption of the other; it is also possible that both of them may be corruptions of a third lost reading. In other words, all various readings may be called corruptions or errors. These terms here have both literal and figurative meanings. Literally, they refer to all those scribal errors, like jumble of letters making no sense or those writings which are grammatically untenable. Figuratively, it includes all deviations from the 'original' reading or the reading of the exemplar. When one of the variants comes to be accepted, the others are termed corruptions. Eg. in *Rājaśekharacarita* (P.1824, P.2874 - ORI, Mysore), we have :

T : kāvyam vā syān no ya-.

N : kāvyam vā na syād ya-.

If T is accepted N is a corruption. It is necessary to repeat that corruption or error has nothing to do with a reading being intrinsically unsound but refers to the sworving from the original. That is, when a scribe transcribes something different from his exemplar, he is deemed to have erred; though his writing may be grammatically 'correct', it is 'corrupted'.

Now, why does this divergence come about ? In other words, why does a scribe err ? It has been indicated earlier that it is, very broadly, the scribe's inadvertence. It has also been noted that a scribe or a copyist is prone to err due to visual and psychological causes. These causes may now be examined in detail.

If we plod through the handwritings in manuscripts as well as the epigraphs, we find two distinct styles : (1) systematic, uniform, legible and neat writing; and (2) haphazard, illegible and bad writing. On this, it is possible to think that there were two distinct circumstances in which copying was done : (1) open or licensed or protected; and (2) covert or unlicensed or unprotected. In the former instance, the copy was made under the supervision of some authority or a professional scribe did the job for a bonafide customer and there was no secret about it. Thus there was no haste or any sort of pressure or apprehension on the part of the scribe. In the other type, the scribe, professional or not, carried out the work clandestinely, covertly. For some reason, certain people guard zealously the manuscript with them allowing no one to copy it. Naturally, a very interested person might try to copy it even stealthily. This makes the scribe do his job in a situation not conducive for the work, such as poor light, haste, apprehension etc.; attention cannot be focussed on orthography. The remarks of H.Lüders[1] regarding orthography of a copper plate chartar that "badness of orthography is a common badge of all forged grants" applies as well to manuscripts. But so far as manuscripts are concerned, the doubt of clandestine activity is limited to certain parts of them where one copy differs from another copy.

Curiously, there are references to prevalence of clandestine copying; it is not mere imagination. Rājaśekarasūri recounts an anecdote about a scholar Harihara in his *Prabandhakośa:* Once Harihara was asked by Vastupāla about a book he had in his hand. Harihara replied that it was a rare copy of Śrīharṣa's *Naiṣadhīya-carita* and he could lend it for a night. Vastupāla who received the book got a copy of it prepared overnight, bound it with an old thread, wrapped it in an old dirty cloth. Next morning while returning the copy to Harihara, Vastupāla said that he remembered that there was a copy of it in his library. At his orders, the copy was brought after some time. Harihara found that it was really a copy of *Naiṣadha*. But he could guess it was the handiwork of Vastupāla himself.[2]

The Jain Bhandar at Mudabidri has the rare manuscript, a 9th century copy of the Prakrit work *Dhavala*. The authorities of the Bhandar guarded the copy carefully not allowing anybody even to handle it. The efforts of Jain scholars to get it printed went in vain. However the scholars were able to persuade the authorities finally to permit a transcription to be made and preserved in the Bhandar itself, because there were only a few scholars who could decipher the script - 9th century Kannada. It was arranged that the copyist made another copy and it was smuggled out. Later, *Dhavala* was published, but the scholars who edited the smuggled copy are not satisfied with their work.[3]

The scribe transcribing in such illicit circumstances cannot ensure correctness because the work cannot be done with a composed mind. There is no possibility of even taking a second look at the copy, let alone comparing it with the exemplar.

There is another circumstance in which various readings are generated almost without the knowledge of the scribe. We have seen how manuscripts get conflated. A rich person going on a pilgrimage may take his literary friends too with him. Bāṇa, for instance, himself a gifted poet, went round places with a circle of friends, among whom was a *pustaka-vācaka* and a *lekhaka* (calligraphist).[4] Surely, they carried with them the material for exhibiting their art whenever they were called upon to do so. In other words, they carried with them their books. When the reader came across a copy of a work in his possession, he naturally went through it. He might note in the margin of his personal copy, the differences appealing to him. When this copy becomes the exemplar, then the marginal notings may become part of the text or the notings may be substituted for a part of the text.

When even an honest scribe writing in a normal situation is subject to commit errors, then there is no need to repeat that errors abound if the scribe is not so very faithful and careful. Corruptions creep in for two reasons as observed before, visual and psychological. Again corruptions may either be involuntarily or voluntarily committed. In other words, the errors may be accidental or deliberate.

Because it is the human mind and effort that is involved in copying, it is not all possible to enumerate exhaustively the causes of the accidental errors or the motives for the deliberate ones. On the basis of the study of Latin manuscripts, scholars like Jebb, Hall and Lindsay have specified certain types of errors.

Our forefathers too knew of the errors that may occur while writing.[5] Some of them are referred to here. See section on scribe (p.110 ff.)

**Types of Errors**

Broadly speaking there can be only four major types of errors, whatever may be their causes: (a) Deletion, (b) Addition, (c) Substitution and (d) Transference. These may be with reference to a letter, a word, a line/sentence or a paragraph.

***a. Deletion or Omission***

This is mostly a mechanical error. Generally, no scribe voluntarily omits any word or passage. There are deliberate omissions, but they are mostly restricted to works like Purāṇas where sectarian views find a place among the contents which are by and large miscellaneous. In copies of such works, it is possible for a scribe having a particular orientation to omit such passages as are not palatable to him.

*(i) Simple omission*

Due to oversight and more due to carelessness or negligence of the scribe, there occurs omission of a letter, a word or even a line.

Examples :

1. *Ye mad viṣa-vāsinaḥ* for *ye mad viṣaya-vāsinaḥ*. (D6, A5. *Rāmāyana*, 1.2.8)
2. *upacārmātram bhakti. t* omitted in between. (Ka, Kha *Dhvanyāloka*, p.28)
3. *kṣoda-kṣamatva* for *-kṣamatattva*. (Ga. *Dhvanyāloka*, p.4)
4. *hiraṇya-pragrah* for *-pratigraha*. (Kha. *Arthaśāstra*, p.41)
5. *nanandado* for *nānandado*. (M. *Kapphiṇābhyudaya*, 18.44d)
6. ahiṁsā satyam anasūyatā .... *śaucam* omitted after *satyam*. (Gha. *Arthaśāstra*, 1.2.1.)

*(ii) Omission of serifs*

The vowel signs that are put above and below the letters are called serifs - those of i/ī, e/o, ai/au; u, ū and ṛ. These are sometimes omitted.

Examples :fc

1. *kinta yā* for *kintu yā*.
   (N. *Kapphiṇābhyudaya*, 6.3a)
2. *subhravaḥ* for *subhruvaḥ* (D 14. *Rāmāyaṇa*).
3. *vātāśanā for vātaśoṇa*. (D 34. *Rāmāyaṇa*).

*(iii) Haplography*

When the same or similar phonemes occur in a series, one or two of them tend to be dropped. This is called haplography. Words between two words having similar phonemes are often dropped along with one of the similar phonemes. Such an error is called tele-haplography. It is possible for the scribe to jump to a line further off instead of going to the very next line, if those lines began or ended with the same phonemes, thus skipping one or several lines.

Examples :

1. *prada -hanumat* for *pradahatu hanumat-*
   (B 192, B 351 ORI. *Mahendra-vijaya-ḍima*. 1.1)
2. *gurvakṣaram tadbhavanāṁśakeṣu*
   *tadbhavanam* omitted in between.
   (P, 404, ORI. *Utpala-parimala*, ch.97)
3. *śaraśaśivakṛta-* for *śara-śaśi-śiva-kṛta-*
   (ibid. ch.101).
4. *dakṣiṇam ca abhimata* ... *ceṣṭam dakṣiṇam cakṣuḥ*.
   Words between *ca* and *cakṣuḥ* omitted.
   (ibid. ch.95).
5. *teṣām svābhāvikī* ... *naisargikī teṣām tāvat*.
   Words between *teṣām* 1 and *tāvat* omitted.
   (Gha. *Dhvanyāloka* Locana, p.164)
6. *arthaśabdadharma eva pratipāditaḥ* ... *śabdadharma eva śabda-dharmatvam*

Words between first *eva* and *śabda-dharmatvam* omitted.(Gha. *Dhvanyāloka*, p. 120)

7. *puropavanaspatīnām* for *puropavana-vanaspatīnām* (Gha. *Arthaśāstra*, 3.19, p.247).
8. *kṣmāpa–padma–* for *kṣmāpa–pāda–padma–* (Dharwad plates of 1247. *Ep. Ind.*, 34.7)

Katre speaks of omission of seemingly unimportant words (See Katre (1941), p. 60).

### *b. Addition*

We find additions in a text from a letter to a whole chapter. Such additions may occur not only accidentally or mechanically but also voluntarily or deliberately. The intentional insertions are termed interpolation. This term usually has a derogatory sense as meddling with the text. Such interpolations will have to be undetectable. So this could be expected of a text the language of which is easy. Works like the Purāṇas and the *Mahābhārata* are the first to be considered in this connection. Not only the language but also the versification does not need any sophistication. The contents are varied making it easy to insert passages and they cannot be detected.

Insertions or interpolations may be found in other works also. But not all insertions deserve to be condemned this way. Addition of letter/s may be with a view to give a readable and understandable text when the exemplar was in a bad state being mutilated, torn, worm-eaten or worn out. Some conscientious scribes have marked their insertion by encircling them. There is only a reference to such practice in literature, but so far no evidence is reported. Rāmabhadra–dīkṣita says so in his *Patañjali-carita*:[6]

*vaṭadru-parṇa-sthita-varṇa-melenād*
*athaiva bhāṣyam nikhilam patañjaleḥ;*
*lilekha vatsakṣata-durgrahākṣare*
*sthale kvacit kuṇḍalanām akalpayat...*
*vatsa-kṣatam sa pitṛkuṇḍalitam yathāvat*
*buddhyākalayya lipi-jālakam antarantaḥ...*

Some have confessed that they have added their own composition. Bhūṣaṇa-Bhaṭṭa, son of Bāṇa, is one such. He writes that he thought of continuing and completing the *Kādambarī* which his father could not complete:[7]

*yāte divam pitari tad-vacasaiva sārdham*
*vicchedam āpa bhuvi yas tu kathā-prabandhaḥ;*
*duḥkham satām tad-asamāpti-kṛtam vilokya*
*prārabdha eṣa ca mayā na kavitva-darpāt.*

One Dāsa-śarmā, son of Mañju, declares that he filled the lacunae caused by over use etc., in *Śānkhyāyana-Śrauta-sūtra-bhāṣya:*[8]

*bhāṣyakāra-giram yatra vinaṣṭam lekhanādinā;*
*akṣaram tad dāsaśarmā mañju-sūnur akalpayat.*

The unintentional or involuntary additions are mostly instances of dittography, repetition of single letter/s etc.

Examples :

1. *agre pradarśayiṣyate* for *agre darśayiṣyate.* (Ga. *Dhvanyāloka*, p.12)
2. *samādhir ity ākhyāyate* for *samādhir ākhyāyate.* (Ka. *Kāvyālaṅkāra-sūtra*, 3.1.18)
3. *bhojayitvāśiṣo vācayitvā daśa pūrvān...* for *bhojayitvā daśa pūrvān...* (P.404. *Utpalaparimala*, ch.102).
4. *saptasu yaticchedaḥ* for *sapta sukhayati-cchedavāān* (P.404 *Utpalaparimala* ch.104)
5. *dīkṣitasyābhiṣecanam* for *dīkṣā tasyābhiṣecanam* (*ka* etc. *Arthaśāstra*, p. 42)

Sometimes marginalia gets inadvertantly incorporated into the text:

Examples :

1. *kāvyalakṣma-vidhāyibhiḥ bhaṭṭodbhaṭaprabhṛtibhiḥ* for *kāvyalakṣma-vidhāyibhiḥ* (MB. *Dhvanyāloka*, 1.4. p.6)
2. *bhaṭṭodbhaṭaprabhṛtibhiḥ tato neha* for *tato neha.* (Ga Ibid.)

3. *jīvantī-śvetā-girikarṇikā-muṣkaka-* for *jīvantī-śvetā-muṣkaka-*
   (Gha. *Arthaśāstra* p.44. *śvetā* and *giri-karṇikā* are synonyms).

Sometimes addition is resorted to with a view to improve the reading for easy understanding :

Examples :

1. *matipravivekān* for *matipravekān*
   (Ka etc. *Arthaśāstra*, p.36)
2. *kūpas tu tṛṣām hanti* for *kūpas tu tṛṣam hanti*
   (Mys. *Dṛṣṭāntaśataka* 13)
3. *tātparyeṇa artha-prakāśanam* for *tātparyeṇa prakāśanam.*
   (Gha. *Dhvanyāloka*, p. 28.)

Devotion and convention may cause an unnecessary addition :

1. *abhīpsitārtha ... tasmai (śrī)gaṇādhipataye namaḥ.*
2. *kāyena ... (śrīman) nārāyaṇāyeti samarpayāmi.*

### c. Substitution

Substitution is mostly an intentional error. The intention may be wanton, i.e., a substitution for which there can be no valid explanation. Or it may be to solve a difficulty of a reading either faulty or having an unusual word or form and therefore mistaken as faulty.

Examples :

1. *vyavahitam* for *vyavasthitam.*
   (Gha. *Dhvanyāloka* 3.33 p.204)
2. *yena brūmaḥ* for *tena brūmaḥ.*
   (Ga. ibid. 1.12)
3. *nadīnadānām* for *nadīnadāni*
   (M. *Kapphiṇābhyudaya*, 18.44 a)
4. *sāmajasyeva samupuyayau* and *-eva samāyayau* for *sāmajasyeva ayam yayau.*
   (*Kādambarī* (Chowkhamba) p.350)
5. *teṣām antevāsino 'pi* for *teṣām antāvasāyino'pi*
   (Ṅa, Jaya. *Arthaśāstra*, p. 33)

6. *apanītāni* for *apācīnāni* (N.S., *Rāmāyaṇa* 5.34. 78d)
7. *yadi vācam pravakṣyāmi* for *yadi vācam pradāsyāmi.* (Rāmāyaṇa, 5.30. 18a).
8. *māheśasya for māheyasya* (P.404 *Utpalaparimala*, ch.104)

The substitution occurs semi-voluntarily also. A synonym is substituted for a frequently occurring word:

Examples :

1. mahārāja, janādhipa, narādhipa ; muni, ṛsi these synonyms are mutually substituted. (*Mahābhārata*).
2. *-madhya-daśanāgra-* for *-madhya-radanāgra-* (P. 404 *Utpalaparimala*, ch.95)
3. *kaiścit paṭhyamānaḥ ślokaḥ nācāryakṛtaḥ* for *kvacid dṛśyamānaś ślokaḥ* etc. (ibid., ch.82)
4. *śvasantam iva pannagam* for *niśśvasantam yathā nāgam.* (Sukthankar (1933), p.xxxvi)
5. *svacchāyā-vijitendavaḥ* for *svacchāyāsitendavaḥ.* (Ga. *Dhvanyāloka*, 1.1)

Substitution may result from false recollection. When one is copying certain phrases which may be similar to the phrases in another part of the same text or in an entirely different text, may be recollected and words following the phrase in that context will be written.

Examples :

1. *praṇamya paramam jyotiḥ vāmanena* is copied as *praṇamya paramātmānam...* (Ka. *Kavyālaṅkārasūtra-Vṛtti*, 1.1.1)
2. *rātrāv atra vivāhamaṇḍaptale* for *rātrāv atra vihāra-maṇḍapatale* (Ka. *Kāvyālaṅkāra-sūtra-vṛtti* 1.2.13,ill.)
3. *na lokāntara-niṣṭhā-* for *na lokāvayavaniṣṭhā-* (*Siddhāntakaumudī*, 6286.3.69)

Substitution is resorted to in avoiding archaisms and such textual difficulties.

Examples :

1. *naiko munir yasya* for *naiko ṛṣir yasya.* (hiatus between *-o* and *-ṛ* is avoided).
2. The hyper-metric line *vinatām viṣaṇṇavadanām* has the v.*l: vinatām dīnavadanām; viṣaṇṇavadanām kadrūḥ; viṣaṇṇarūpām kadrūḥ.* (*Mahābhārata,* 1.20; Sukthankar, (1933). p.xciii)

***d. Orthographic Confusion***

When a copyist conversant with one script and familiar with another, copies from either of them to the other, the scribe is liable to commit certain errors due to confusion of letters. The orthographic similarities cause this semi-voluntary error.

*Ex.* The editor of *Kapphiṇābhyudaya* notes[9] that there are many instances of confusions in Oriya script. *aṅga* comes to be written as *aṁśa* (6.47c), *rāga* as *rāsa* (14.2a), *gaja* as *gada* (3.33c), *bala* as *nala* (5.2a).

Katre notes[10] that there are such similarities between Śāradā and Devanāgarī scripts as for ex: between *m* and *s*, *u* and *t*, *ṣ* and *th* (so *tathā* becomes *uṣā)* etc.

In Nandināgarī there is the possibility of confusion : *para* to *pha* and vice versa; śva, sva and kha, eg.

*-khagati- and -svagati- for -śvagati-*
(Pb, W. *Vṛttaratnākara, 3.36)*

The Devanāgarī of Jains as observed by Katre[11] is peculiar in that there is a frequent interchange between *c*, *v* and *b*, *tth* and *cch*. etc.

***e. Transposition (Anagramatism)***

Phonemes and words get transposed involuntarily. It may be effected voluntarily to guard against possibility of metanalysis.

Examples :

1. jñāne na cānyo becomes *jñāne ca nānyo.* (Mt. Md. *Mahāvīracarita.* 3.37d)

2. *trāyatām vo pra...do madhuripoḥ nakhāḥ* for *trāyatām vo madhuripoḥ pra...do nakhāḥ*. (Ga. *Dhvanyāloka*, 1.1)
3. *alokasāmyam pratibhāviśeṣam parisphurantam samabhivyanakti* for *alokasāmānyam abhivyanakti parisphurantam pratibhāviśeṣam*. (Ka, Kha. *Dhvanyāloka*, 1.6)
4. *upamā rūpakam caiva dīpakam* for *upamā dīpakam caiva rūpakam*. (C. *Nāṭyaśāstra*, 17.43)
5. *vijānātu* for *vinā jātu* (Ag. C. *Nāṭyaśāṣtra* 17.40)
6. *vana-nadī* becomes *nava-nadī* and gets corrected to *naganadī* and *nadanadī* (*Meghadūta*, 26/28)
7. *-malanā-* for *-manala-* (M.*Kapphiṇābhyudaya*, 6.62 b)
8. *bindu-sauvīraś cāja māna-* for *sauvīraś cājabinduḥ māna-* (Kha. *Arthaśāstra*, p.16L)
9. *āsanna-kāṣṭha-caitya-devatā* for *āsanna-caitya-kāṣṭha-devatā*. (Gha, Jaya. *Arthaśāstra*, p.43)
10. *-anutarasya* for *-anuratasya* (P. 404 f.85 *Utpalaparimala*).
11. *svabhāvajātāni ratnāni* for *svabhāvād ratnāni jātāni*. (P. 404 *Utpalaparimala*, ch.77)
12. *idam vacanam abravīt* becomes *vacanam tv idam* (B2. *Rāmāyaṇa*, 1.9.6)

The editor must patiently go through the varieties of readings and consider their relative aptness from the point of view of orthography and context. The principle of interpretation should be adopted: *sthitasya gatiś cintanīyā*. Also the various readings have, surprisingly, a primary role in ascertaining of codices (See ch. VIII).

## Notes and References

1. Lüders, *Ep.Ind.*, 4.49, p. 334.
2. Rājaśekharasūri: *Prabandhakośa*, p.60, *ekadālāpitaḥ hariharaḥ: 'paṇḍita, ko 'yam granthaḥ ?' paṇḍito vadati - 'naiṣadham mahākāvyam.' 'kaḥ kaviḥ'. 'śrīharṣaḥ'. vastupālena gaditam, 'tad ādarśam darśaya tarhi'. paṇḍito brūte - 'nānyatrāyam granthaḥ. caturo yāmān arpayiṣyāmi pustikām'. arpitā pustikā. rātrau sadyo lekhaka-niyogibhiḥ lekhitā navīnā pustikā. jīrṇa-rajjvāvṛtā. vāsanyāsena dhūsarī-kṛtya muktā. prātaḥ paṇḍitāya pustikā dattā. 'gṛhyatām tad idam svam*

*naiṣadham. gṛhītā paṇḍitena pustikā. mantriṇā nyagādi: 'asmākam api kośe kilāstivedam śāstram iti smarāmaḥ. vilokyatām kośaḥ. yāvad vilambenaiva kṛṣṭā navīnā pratiḥ. yāvac codyate, tāvat 'nipīya yasya kṣiti-rakṣiṇaḥ kathā' ity ādi naiṣadham udghāriṣṭa. dṛṣṭvā paṇḍita-hariharena uktam - 'mantrin tavaiva māyeyam...'*

3. In 1895, it was decided to transcribe the Dhavala manuscripts on the paper. The work was completed in 1922. In the meanwhile, one copy was smuggled out to Sahranpur. The copy was also in Kannada script. Hence a Devanāgarī transcription was attempted and completed in 1929. By this time one more copy was smuggled out. Its transcriptions are now found at Amaravati, Karanja, Sagar and Arrah. On the basis of these copies, Hiralal Jain took up the edition of the work in 1938 and completed it after 20 years (1958). Hiralal Jain: *Contribution of Jain Dharma to Indian Culture*, ch.II, section on Śaurasenī-Āgama. Translated into Kannaḍa: Mirji Aṇṇārāya: Bhāratīya Saṁskṛtige Jainadharmada Kŏdugĕ, Sholapur: Jaina Sahitya Samraksaka Sangha, 1971. p. 91. In 1960, the Oriental Research Institute of the University of Mysore acquired a microfilm copy of the entire palm leaf codex. Thanks to the then Director of the Institute, Shri. H. Deveerappa and his team Vidwan K.S.Varadacharya, Pandit and Shri. C.S. Srinivasan, photographer.
4. *...pustaka-vācakaḥ sudṛṣṭiḥ ...lekhako govindakaḥ ... Harṣacarita*, ucchvāsa 1 end, p.42.
5. See Gode (1940); Sarma, K.V. (1982); Shivaganesha Murthy (1984), etc.
6. *Patañjali-carita* of Rāmabhadra-dīkṣita, 6.26 & 8.12. (Kāvya-Mālā 51, NSP 1895).
7. *Kādambarī*, part ii Chowkhamba, Varanasi, 1965, p. 2, Śl.2.
8. *Śāṅkhyāyana-Śrauta-Sūtra-bhāṣya* of Varadasuta Anārtīya, Adh. 9 & 10 end. Ed. A Hillebrandt, Calcutta, 1888, vol. 1, Preface p. ix. One Amṛtānanda of the last century writes that he added three cantos (14-17) to *Buddhacarita* because he could not find a manuscript of the rest of the text. See Keith, A.B. (1920) : *History of Sanskrit Literature*, Oxford, Repr:1956, p. 58.
9. *Kapphiṇābhyudaya*, intd. p.xii
10. Katre, pp. 56f.
11. Ibid.

## CHAPTER VII

# CRITICAL RECENSION

Making copies was a necessity and was in regular practice among the book-lovers of the past. Those who wanted to possess a copy of a book for themselves had to make their own copy or to get it copied for them. When a copy frequently used wore out, a new copy was called for. The process of copying, be it professionally done or not, is a tiresome and time consuming manual labour. And we have seen how copying involves varieties of voluntary and involuntary errors. Thus every copy, even when several copies were made at a time, had its own situation and therefore different from others. When one is confronted with divergences, the question of accepting a reading and rejecting the other arises. It may be done ecletically or certain norms may be followed.The copyist often played a dual role of being a copyist as well as a redactor. The obviously as well as the seemingly erroneous writings were corrected. In other words, a writing may appear grammatically incorrect to a redactor or a redactor may suspect a scribal error where there is none actually. The redactor may adopt a reading in another copy, finding it better or may emend it. Thus the redaction complicates the problem than solving it.

On the other hand, if readings are chosen after careful consideration of why and how of the variants and other factors, then the text so constituted is called a recension. Further if all the data considered are also provided, then it is called a critical recension. The expression critical recension, though tautological, has come into vogue. The term recension is defined in the dictionary as "an editorial revision of a literary work especially on the basis of critical examination of the text and the sources used."

After a painstaking thorough study of the variants as well as the nature of the codices, certain principles are formulated. A text constituted after following these principles is called critical recension.

Critical editing is the process of finding the most plausible reading which the author could have written or the one nearest to it from among or on the basis of the various readings provided by the manuscript copies. Simply printing the text as found in a manuscript copy, when it is known that another copy exists, is not worthwhile in spite of correcting the obvious errors. However, such editions are not totally valueless. They can well be regarded as neat copies the text of which does not get corrupted further. Consultation of another copy minimises, if it does not solve altogether, the problems of the editor.

The epigraphs stand on a slightly different footing. The emphasis, here, is on decipherment because these documents are those which were produced at different periods of history and engraved mostly by persons who might not have been conversant with writing formally. This is particularly true of stone inscriptions.

## METHOD

Scholars who have critically edited Sanskrit or Prakrit texts for the first time have mostly followed the model of the method formulated for Greek and Latin texts. Our ancestors too had the basic ideas of editing. The commentaries exhibit a clear awareness of certain principles which, however, have not been clearly enunciated.

The fundamental aspects of critical editing can be noted here. The actual process of editing differs from work to work because each text has its own problems. The codices of each text have their own history and peculiarities. Hence each text has to be tackled individually, adapting the general principles. For example, the codices of āgama works are replete with grammatical errors; the Devanāgarī manuscripts of Dvaita works have orthographic peculiarities.

The process of critical editing consists of two broad divisions: (1) The text to be presented as nearest as possible to the author's original, on the basis of available material. (2) The consideration of question of authorship, date etc, of the author, the influence of earlier works in the field on the author, in other words, the sources and the influence of the author on later works, the significance of the work and so on.

The former section is called lower criticism and the latter, higher criticism.

**A. Lower Criticism**

Lower Criticism can be distinguished into three stages. They are (i) Heuristics, (ii) Recensio and (iii) Emendatio. Some scholars speak of only two stages including heuristics in recensio but it does not give a comprehensive picture.

(i) *Heuristics*

As observed above, the text is arrived at after a critical evaluation of the available data. Hence the necessity of putting together all the material available in a methodical way. This in turn requires a knowledge of the availability of the material. When one decides to prepare a critical edition of a text, *the New Catalogus Catalogorum* is to be perused[1] and the libraries where copies of the text are deposited are to be noted. The entries under known alternative titles of the work on hand or a possible alternative are also be checked. Suppose one has taken up *Meghadūta* or *Dhvanyāloka*, then the entries *Meghasandeśa* or *Sahṛdayāloka* are also to be checked.

The commentaries that may be available on the work on hand, the works in which references to the one on hand may possibly be found and other such related works are also to be noted.

The details of the beginning and end of copies of works which may bear similar titles are to be compared. For this, the descriptive catalogues are to be consulted.

The originals of all the copies available are to be collected. Only originals or their mechanised copies like microfilm, xerox etc., are to be sought and not manual copies. For, in the latter case, there is the possibility of further commission of errors which cannot easily be verified with reference to the originals which are known to exist. And certain relevant information like erasures, over-writing, etc., may not come to the notice of the editor.

Then each copy of the work is to be studied thoroughly from the point of view of orthographic peculiarities and scribal stylistics. Thus the trustworthiness of the codices can be determined. After the study of individual copies, the evidence provided by all the extant copies are to be considered together for constituting the text. The text-tradition in respect of even single letters is to be observed and studied. This encourages the editor to discover the original or near-original readings for himself. Not only the evidence found in the extant codices but also that in the commentaries, anthologies and allied works is to be taken into consideration. Variants have to be compared for agreement and disagreement. In other words, they are to be collatea. For the purposes of collation, the readings are to be recorded methodically. The manuscript which appears more trustworthy than others is to be taken as the basis and the readings of this copy should be collated with the readings of others.

*Siglum*

To identify the reading as of a particular codex, the several codices consulted are to be given an identification mark. It is called siglum (pl. sigla). A very simple mode would be to name the codices A B C etc. or use Indian alphabets Ka Kha etc. But an intelligent way would be to use a symbol by which the codices are better identified. The codex may be named after its script. Eg. D(evanāgarī), G(rantha), O(riya) etc. Sigla may refer to the source of the codex. Eg. M(adras), Ar(rah), My(sore), B(aroda) etc. If more than one codex are to be identified in the above scheme, then numerical figures inferior or normal could be used. Eg. The three Devanāgarī codices or two Tanjore codices may have the sigla respectively as, D1 D2, D3, or $D_1$, $D_2$, $D_3$

and $T_1$, $T_2$, or T1, T2. Some scholars suggest that the age of the copy should also be included in the siglum. Thus $K^{13}$ means a Kashmirian codex of the 13th century. If the date is doubtful an asterisk may be used along with the numeral. Eg. $C^{14*}$ means Calcutta codex of circa 14th century.

It may be necessary to assume the existence of a non-extant manuscript to explain the relationship of the extent codices. The sigla for such codices may be formed by using lower case Roman alphabet or Greek alphabet with an asterisk. Eg. $a^*$ $b^*$ $\alpha^*$ $\beta^*$ etc.

Sukthankar classifies the *Mahābhārata* codices on the basis of their scripts and an inferior figure is attached to indicate its serial number among the codices in a script group. Thus $D_1$ $D_4$, $G_1$ $G_8$ etc.

An editor can also form the siglum that indicates both the source and script. Eg. Mt Md mean respectively, Madras codex Telugu script and codex in Devanāgarī script from the same source.

*Collation*

We may now discuss how the readings are to be noted for collation. When there are three codices to work on, the following method may be adopted. The text as in one of the codex, selected as the better than either of the two, is copied on sheets of paper. Sufficient margin is left on either sides of the page. Or the lines may have sufficient space in between. This copy is compared with the other two manuscripts, word by word. Whatever divergence discovered is recorded on the nearest margin or in the space above the concerned part. The siglum must be recorded with each such entry without fail. Or the variants of each of the codices may be entered in one coloured ink each. Not only simple variations that are to be recorded, but other related evidence like erasures, interlinear addition, addition in the margin, blank spaces etc., also to be duly noted. Some convenient abbreviations may be formulated. For example:

| | |
|---|---|
| w | for worm-eaten |
| m | for mutilated |
| b | for blank space |
| a | for addition in the text part |
| am | for addition in the margin; this may be accompanied by t(op), r(ight) l(eft) or b(ottom) |
| cr | for corrected to (text part) |
| crm | for corrected to (in the margin) |
| nf | for not found |
| (d) | for deleted using curved brackets |
| ḍ | for deleted with dots below |
| b | for deleted by striking out |
| il | for interlinear writing |
| tr | for transposed |
| h | may be added for a different hand, if clear |
| c | for commentary |

This method holds good where the number of codices to be collated is two or three. If the readings are not too many, this can be adopted to collate more than three manuscripts also.

A different method will have to be adopted if the codices are too many and the readings are also expected to vary. Collation has to be done on a specially prepared sheet called collation sheet. Lines are drawn horizontally and vertically so that small squares are formed. The squares are to be as wide as to write a single letter (i.e. 8 to 10 mm.).

As in the earlier case, a comparatively better or more trustworthy codex of those under consideration is selected and its text is written in the first row of squares, one letter in each square. Length of the text may be conveniently divided. If the text is versified, two pādas of Anuṣṭup metre (16 letters) or one pāda of a bigger metre (upto, say 22 letters) may be taken as a unit, one line in the collation sheet. In case of text in prose, the length of line depends upon one's practical convenience. Of course, the preparation of sheet is to be planned before-hand or adapt the same to the text on hand. In the subsequent rows the readings from other codices are to be recorded. On the left side and against a row, the siglum of the codex is entered. Some space may be left on the right side for recording any relevant information. In recording the evidence from the sources, it is not necessary to fill all the squares, but only those which are different from that in the top line. In other words, a blank square in a row means that that letter in the particular source is identical with the one in the top line.

Collating the evidence of manuscripts in this way makes it possible to arrive at fixing the mutual relationship of the codices consulted. The relationship between two codices can be in two ways: they may either be exemplar and copy or sister copies i.e. copies of one and the same exemplar. This helps in tracing the genealogy of the codices of a work. Such a chart wherein we can show the relation of the codices of a work is called stemma codicum, tree of codices. Chalking out the pedigree of codices aids in determining the possible earlier reading. A stemma codicum of, say, five codices may appear like this:

The sigla of the codices: A B C D E

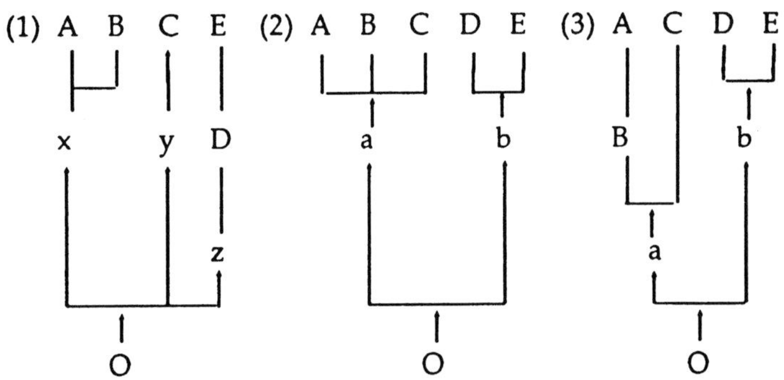


Only three sets of relations are shown here. The manuscripts may array themselves in many more ways.

*Secondary Sources of Evidence*

The evidence of manuscripts are the primary ones for fixing the readings of a text. The manuscripts of a text may also be called the direct evidence. Apart from this source, a commentary on a text or its translation will also provide the basis for a critical appraisal of the text. Such of the works as forming source of evidence are called testimonia (sing. testimonium). It is also referred to as external or indirect evidence. This includes not only all those works which are directly and closely related to the text on hand but also those that may contain quotations from it. Thus there are many sorts of secondary evidence.

*(a) Commentary*

Almost every Sanskrit text has a commentary on it. Some works which are popular or considered standard have scores of commentaries to their credit. *Meghadūta* and *Kāvyaprakāśa,* for example, have nearly fifty commentaries each. Most of the commentators are earlier than the available codices and they provide a clear evidence of the readings current and accepted in their times. Though these commentaries have also come down to us in a line of transmission, the chances of corruption of the readings adopted by them are rather rare. Often the commentators mention and discuss the variants and add to our knowledge of the situation. Devarājayajvan, commentator on the *Nighaṇṭu-Nirukta,* notes the value of a commentary in textual criticism.

All the codices of *Nighaṇṭu-Nirukta* that Devarāja had collected, were in chaos. He writes, it was difficult for him to arrive at correct reading; the lack of an earlier commentary made his attempt more strenuous : *"evam vyākīrṇeṣu kośeṣu...kasyacid vyākhyānasya abhāvāt, naighaṇṭukam kāṇḍam utsanna-prāyam āsīt."*[2]

*(b) Translations*

Even from ancient times, people have been widening frontiers of their knowledge by translating into their own language, a text in another language. Sanskrit texts are no exception to this. Works like *Pañcatantra,* Upaniṣads and some of the Buddhist works have been translated into languages outside India. Even within the country works like the *Mahābhārata* and the *Rāmāyaṇa* have been translated into all regional languages. The translation in any language of a text in Sanskrit, could be consulted as secondary source. The value of a translation as source increases as the date of translation is nearer the author of the original. It is well known that it was the Chinese translation (683 B.C.), that revealed the extent of the *Buddhacarita* of Aśvaghoṣa to be twentyeight cantos while only thirteen cantos were available in Sanskrit original.[3]

An editor can also try to re-present the original on the basis of the translation. *Śaivaparibhāṣā* of Śivāgra-yogi, for instance, is a text in five chapters. When the Oriental Research Institute, Mysore (1950) took it up for editing, neither of the codices it had (one of ORI, Mysore and another of Adyar), did contain the last chapter. Nor any library reported about a complete copy. But there was a Tamil translation of the entire text available to the editor, late Vidwan R.Ramasastri. He retranslated the Tamil version, so that he could present a complete text. When the script was about to be sent to press, a codex complete with text and translation was reported from Devakota. On comparison, it was surprising that the retranslation appeared just like author's copy only. It was even better than the copy procured from Devakota. Sastriar did not yield to the temptation of retaining his attempt, true to his editorial spirit.[4] Unfortunately, he did not even allow it to be printed as an appendix.

*(c) Anthologies (Florilegia)*

It is human tendancy to have with oneself the best part of the writings of master poets. Thus, there are compilations of quotations and sayings or of poems and essays. These are collected and arranged by people at different times in accordance with their own taste and temperment. Such works are generally called anthologies. Anthologies of poems are found in Sanskrit too and are called kośas. Verses which are complete in themselves (muktakas) are selected from various poets and are arranged topicwise. Several verses under a topic, taken from the same work, will be set together and generally in the same sequence as in the source. At the end of each śloka or group of ślokas from an author, the name of the author as known to the compiler is given (eg. *bhāsasya*). If the author is not known, the same is recorded (*kasyāpi*). But the compilers are not always trust-worthy in this aspect for certain ślokas which are of older poets are shown as those of later ones. Of course, the hand of copyists/redactors in this cannot be ruled out. However, if the passage of a text being edited is found in a kośa, the evidence found therein can also be taken into account. Sometimes it may solve or pave the way for solution of a problem.

Vallabhadeva in his *Subhāṣitāvalī*, for example, has extracted a couple of verses from *Dṛṣṭānta-śataka*. The sequence of the extract is as in the extant text but for one stanza. The contents of the Śataka is varied and each stanza is independent of the other. The author does not seem to have any logical order in his work; any stanza can be anywhere. Perhaps Vallabhadeva may have preserved an earlier reading. Because Vallabhadeva is certainly earlier to the available manuscripts of *Dṛṣṭāntaśataka*, the śloka may be retransposed to its place on the basis of *Subhāṣitāvalī* vis-a-vis the manuscript evidence.[5] True, it cannot be lost sight of the fact that *Subhāṣitāvalī*, the text of which may be earlier, too has come down to us through a manuscript tradition. But a critical edition of the anthology (in the present case, there is the excellent edition prepared by P.Peterson), makes it trustworthy. This aspect should be borne in mind while using anthologies as a source.

Conversely, the original sources of the compiler, so far as available to us can be useful in the critical edition of an anthology. The Keladi king Basava-bhūpāla, for instance, has written a work, *Śivatattva-ratnākara*. It is encyclopeadiac in character, having the *Mānasollāsa* or the *Abhilaṣitārtha-cintāmaṇi* as the model. It is a combination of extracts from various branches of knowledge.[6] The editor of first two volume of the work, Vidwan R.Ramasastri has provided in the foot-notes the references to the sources and he told this writer that comparing the manuscript text with the original sources has been immensely useful.

*(d) Quotations*

Śāstra works contain direct quotations from allied works with or without acknowledgement. Such quotations are sometimes most valuable in deciding the readings of respective works. The reading in such quotations may be taken to reflect the views of the elect i.e., the reading in a given context of a work is the one accepted by scholars in a particular time.

Example: 1. Someśvara in his commentary *Saṅketa* on *Kāvyaprakāśa* cites a line from *Vakroktijīvita: santi tatra trayo mārgāḥ*. This solved the problem of the text in De's edition which read: *samprati tatra yo mārgaḥ* (1.24a).[7]

2. *Nandi-sūtra* provided corrections to the corrupt passages of *Arthaśāstra*, as R. Shamasastri, the editor, has discussed: *dīrgham tṛṇam iti cārāyaṇaḥ* among other v.l., becomes: *tṛṇam iti dīrghaś cārāyaṇaḥ*.[8]

3. Krishnamoorthy has drawn immensely from *Kalpalatāviveka* in revising the text of *Dhvanyāloka*.[9]

4. Bhaṭṭoji Dīkṣita, in his *Siddhānta-Kaumudī*, cites lines from poets. To take an instance: under *bhuvaś ca* (3.2. 138/3118), he writes: *chandasi ity eva; bhaviṣṇuḥ katham tarhi 'jagat-prabhor aprabhaviṣṇu-vaiṣṇavam'* (Māgha. 1.54) *iti. niraṅkuśāḥ kavayaḥ*. Under 1.3.76/2742, Dīkṣita writes: ***nṛpaḥ avāluloce***: further he questions, ***katham bhaṭṭiḥ***.

5. Hemacandra, quotes profusely, from *Abhinavabhāratī*, the commentary of Abhinavagupta on the *Nāṭya-Śāstra*.

*(e) Obvious imitations*

Many of the works are written in clear imitations of certain works. Sometimes the model is acknowledged. Most of the gīta-kāvyas, for example, are modelled on the *Gīta-govinda* of Jayadeva.[10]

*(f) Epitomies and adaptations*

Paraphrases of larger works go a long way in aiding textual criticism in respect of the concerned works.

Example : *Bhārata-mañjarī* of Kṣemendra, an abridgement of the *Mahābhārata* has been consulted by Sukthankar while constituting the Kashmirian redaction of the *Mahābhārata*. The three Sanskrit adaptations of the lost *Bṛhatkathā* are well known. Jinasena's *Pārśvābhyudaya* is another good instance in this context. Jinasena adapts *Meghadūta* into his own kāvya. Each of the *pādas* of the verses of *Meghadūta* is made the fourth *pāda* of his stanza in the same order. In other words, by grouping the successive fourth *pādas* of the stanzas of *Pārśvābhyudaya*, the stanzas of *Meghadūta* are formed. This provides evidence for the order and the number of stanzas of the *Meghadūta* as well as the readings as accepted during the times of Jinasena.

*(g) Parallel versions*

Texts like the Purāṇas have mostly come down in oral transmission also. They abound in episodes (*upākhyāna*) and glorification of places, seasons and so on (*māhātmyas*). This causes parallel versions. The episode of Śakuntalā (in the *Mahābhārata*), for example, has a parallel version in the *Padmapurāṇa*.

***(ii) Recensio***

The first stage is thus, the methodical collection and analysis of all the evidence in respect of the readings of the text concerned and their study with a view to form a pedigree of the codices. This paves the way for the next stage.

The second stage, recensio, calls for the critical acumen of the editor. The editor has now before him a table of various readings and other information gathered from the codices as well as the evidence culled from the testimonia. It has also been possible to know the mutual relation of the codices. The problem now is to choose from among the variants a reading which might have been intended by the author or the one nearest to it and formulate a recension. The editor will have to interpret and weigh the evidence presented. He has to be careful and openminded. Just because a codex is late or a codex is full of obvious mistakes, the codex cannot be brushed aside or disregarded. For, that may give a hint to, if not a chance preservation of, the acceptable reading against the doubtful reading of the oldest or best codex. The method may appear ecletic i.e. choosing one here and another there, but it is not so because the choice does not depend on the whim and fancy of the editor. On the other hand, the choice is guided by certain principles. Every reading is decided only after a debate over its aptness. That is why the recension formulated thus is called critical recension. However an element of personal attitude of the editor affecting the interpretation cannot be ruled out. It is because of this that an editor is required to place all his material before the scholars.

### *(iii) Emendation*

The editor may come across a point where none of the readings may satisfy him as having been composed by the author. Or the evidence may not be adequate enough to arrive at a conclusion. This difficulty is not peculiar to codex unicus but may arise even if there may be several copies.

If none of the variants is meaningful in a context or is grammatically incorrect or does not satisfy the metrical and other contextual requirements, the editor may effect an amendation. He may suggest a reading which is more plausible so that the text presented may be understood properly and easily. However, one has to exercise utmost discretion while resorting to emendation. An emendation if it should be conceivable, should satisfy the two probabalities - the external and the internal.

## B. Higher Criticism

This aspect is not directly connected with the selection of readings but concerns itself with a text and its contents as a whole. Because the sources of the author and his influences are probed, and not mere genuineness of a particular text, it is called higher criticism. In fact, higher criticism cannot strictly be spoken of as a stage, for, this aspect of study begins along with the selection of a text for editing. It continues during the course of the editorial work as well. It even forms the basis for the entire editorial process. Its completion follows the finalisation of the recension. From this point of view, it may be conceded as the fourth stage.

Lower criticism involves much of mechanical work: recording, comparing, collation and so on. Higher criticism rises above. It is, in short, an assessment of the author's work. The style, the language, the literary aspects, the sources of the work, the life of the author, his equipment, the circumstances that made an author compose the work, the situation in which the work might have been written, the influence of earlier writers in the field on the author and the author's influence on later writers, the contribution of the author to the field concerned, thereby determining the place and value of the work on hand, leading to its popularity or otherwise– all these as well as other allied issues fall under this category. Obviously, tackling these questions requires critical acumen, a keen sense of appreciation and a thorough grasp of the history of the particular branch of learning in addition to a good understanding of every line of the text. With all these equipment, the lower criticism too will be smooth and will have optimum results.

Higher criticism need not necessarily follow the editing of a work. Any person can independently take up the study on these lines of a work in print. This aspect is considered here because an editor of a critical edition of a work will be in a better position as he will have done close study of the text enabling him to a critical appraisal easily.

**Notes and References**

1. *New Catalogus Catalogorum*, Madras: University of Madras, vols. 1 to 12 of *pa*, 1966-92. *Catalogus Catalogorum* of Aufrecht, Heidelberg 1891 and Bonn 1896 and 1903, 3 parts.
2. *Nirukta* with the *bhāṣya* of Devarājayajvan, p.1.
3. *Buddhacarita* has 13 cantos plus 3 added by one Amṛtānanda. The Chinese (414-42 AD) and the Tibetan

versions contain 28 cantos. Keith (1920), *History of Sanskrit Literature*, p. 58.

4. Vidwan Ramasastri had conveyed this to me personally.
5. *Dṛṣṭānta-śataka* (Ed. Jivananda Vidyasagara, Calcutta, 1883 3rd edn.) verse 12 should be numbered as 2 on the basis of *Subhāṣitāvalī* of Vallabhadeva (Ed. P. Peterson, Bombay, 1886).
6. *Śivatattva-ratnākara*. Ed. S.Narayanasvami Sastri (Vol.1), R.Ramasastri (Vol.2), P.Maribasavaradhya (Vol.3), Mysore: Oriental Research Institute, University of Mysore, 1965, 69, 84.
7. Krishnamoorthy, K. (Ed.) : *Vakroktijīvita*, Dharwar: Karnataka University, 1983, Intd. xxiii and Krishnamoorthy (1983), p. 48.
8. See Shamasastri's Introduction to his 2nd edn. of *Arthaśāstra*. Oriental Research Institute, Mysore, 1991, 5th edn., p. 88. (Intd.)
9. "The pride of place among them (testimonia) goes to the anonymous *Kalpalatāviveka*. .. It contains the bulk of the *Locana* and the *Dhvanyāloka* almost like a transcript. It is also interesting that it has some *kārikas* not found in any other edition." Krishnamoorthy (Ed.): *Dhvanyāloka*, Dharwad, Karnataka University, 1980. Intd., p. xiv.
10. *Śāntāvilāsa* of 'Hariśāba'. Ed. R.S.Shivaganesha Murthy; Malladihalli: Anathasevasrama, 1987, Intd., p.7.

# CHAPTER VIII

# PROCESS OF CRITICAL EDITING

## 1. Genealogy of Manuscripts

A knowledge of the mutual relation of manuscripts is essential as a prelude to the consideration of the principles underlying critical editing. It is necessary to acquaint oneself with the pedigree of codices; how the extant codices could be arranged in a genealogical table. If our ancient copyists had the habit of writing their names, address on the books and if they invariably mentioned whose copy was their exemplar or if they had mentioned the date of copying, this problem would not have been there. It is very very rare that the name of the owner is written on the codex. While as a rule, the source is not mentioned, very rarely do we come across the statement that the copy was made for so and so. Perhaps in one or two instances, the source is also referred to. Though often the date is mentioned, in most of the cases, it is not verifiable as only the name of the year (in the 60-year cycle) and the month etc. are noted. In the absence of such clear indication, the onus of the editor is more in arranging the extant codices in a family tree.

Because the codices have come down to us in a chain of successive transmission of copies, and go back ultimately to one archetype, a relation among the extant codices is obvious. There are two such possible relations: (1) One codex (or more) may be the direct descendant of another extant codex; (2) The extant codices may be descendants of one or more non-extant codices; in other words, the extant codices may have either sister or cousin relation among themselves.

Thus tracing back we may discover several points of convergence and ultimately to one archetype. On the basis of this, a reading common to each branch can be arrived at, thus reducing the number of variants for comparison.

A general principle in this is that identity of reading, accident apart, implies identity of origin. If there are, say, eight copies and five of them array in one group and the other three in another group, having common or nearly common readings. Then it may be concluded that these groups have an ancestor each. The expressions 'identity of reading' and 'common reading' do certainly appear strange when every copyist is expected to copy faithfully the exemplar. But we have already seen that no copy is identical with its exemplar. It is in the corruptions, variants, that identity is established.

Omissions, in particular, provide the surest test of affinity, writes Hall.[1] The 'errors' as indicative of affinity of codices, are of two types: (1) Peculiar errors and (2) Separating errors. A scribe copies as it is in the exemplar and as already observed each scribe has his own idiosyncracies. These are peculiar to individual scribes, and when they are not common with another copy, they are called peculiar errors. Errors which appear syntactically plausible come to be retained. Such errors separate a codex from others; hence called separating errors. The errors found in some copies of a text but not in other copies, are called conjunctive errors. It is on this type of errors that the genetic relation between codices are spoken of. However, it is assumed that no two scribes commit the same kind of mistake in the same place.

When two copies of a text, say, A and B are compared, it may be found that all the errors of A are found in B, but some errors are peculiar to B, then B may be taken as derived from A. On the other hand, if it is found that all errors of B are found in A, along with some which are peculiar to A, A may be apoken of as derived from B.

If A and B were to be found having errors peculiar to each of them but agreeing otherwise, they must have been derived from a common exemplar. If A and B do not agree, then they belong to different transmission lines. This mode of tracing is possible in the case of non-conflated manuscripts. Thus genetic relation is established.

The number of relationships possible varies according to the number of manuscripts utilised.

Supposing three manuscripts A B C are utilised for editing. Then the possible relations of the three manuscripts will be 22. They are shown by the following table:[2]

**Types/No. of possible relations**

| I/6 | II/3 | III/3 | IV/6 | V/1 | VI/3 |
|---|---|---|---|---|---|

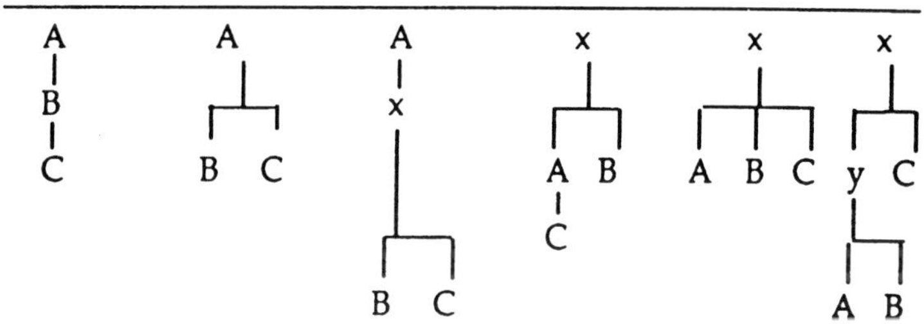

Notes on the table:

**Type I:** Of the three manuscripts, one may be the copy of the other of which third is a copy. Such a relation decides that only one of them is important. In other words, it is as good as having a single manuscript.

**Type II:** In this type two manuscripts may be the copy of the other. Here also it amounts to having only one manuscript.

**Type III:** This does not substantially differ from the type-II. Only it is found that the two manuscripts are not direct descendents of the other.

**Type IV:** This type is similar to type-II Only two manuscripts are useful because the other manuscripts is only a copy of one of the two.

**Type V:** The three manuscripts may be the descendents of a non-extant exemplar. Each of them will have independent importance.

**Type VI:** All the three in this type, have equal importance. Two of them form one branch and the third a separate branch.

Thus if the manuscripts have the relationship of the types V or VI, then all the manuscripts are valuable in editing.

To illustrate: Suppose we have 12 copies of a text. Let us name them: A B C D E F G H I J K L. After due comparision, if it is found that A B C D and E form one group having sister relation, then they point to a common parent, say, y*. F and G, and H, K and L form two groups derived from, say, m* and n* respectively; if these two groups together bear resemblance to J then m* n* and J go back to a common ancestor, x*; I is very clearly a copy of A. m, n, x and y are not extant but they are assumed to explain the relation of the extant codices. x and y are derived in turn from one archetype which also is not extant. This may itself be the original or the immediate copy of a lost original. The whole lthing may be tabulated thus:

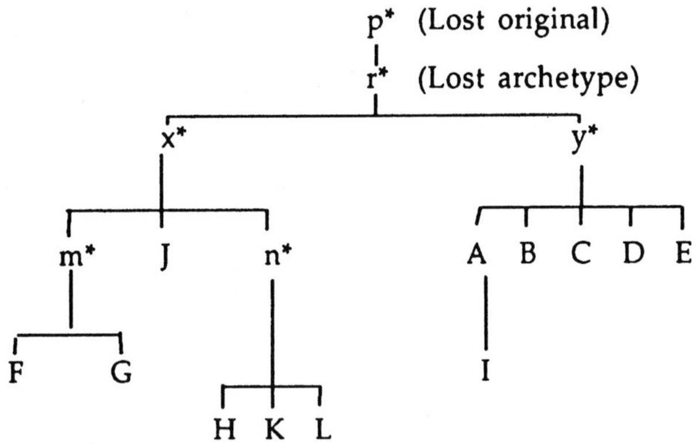


In this stemma codicum, I has no independent value except where A is damaged. The readings of m can be fixed on the basis of F and G. Similarly H K and L help in constituting n. When F and G disgree, the readings may be compared with H K L or J. m becomes doubtful if F or G do not agree with any one of the other four. Similarly, if H K and L disagree, the reading may be compared with F G or J and if there is no agreement with any one them n becomes doubtful. x may be constituted on the basis of m n and J. If these disagree, the readings should be compared with A B C D or E. At least there should be agreement with any one them. Else, x becomes doubtful. y is constituted on the basis of A B C D and E. If there is disagreement among them, the reading is to be compared with m n or J Now the original or near original reading can be arrived at by comparing x and y.

When the codices in a family branch vary and are independent in their reading, then their parent copy becomes doubtful. While all the variants have a claim to be the original, the transitional or documentary probability and intrinsic probability are to be considered.

Sometimes, two readings may come to have equal weightage. Then the divergence might reach the author as well. It is possible that the author might have revised after some time he wrote a text for the first time. By the time of his revision, copies will have got circulated. Later revised copy also gets circulated. Thus giving rise to variants at the very source. An instance in question would be a line from *Abhijñāna-Śākuntalam*[3]:

*mṛduni mṛga-śarīre **puṣpa**-rāśāv ivāgniḥ.*
*mṛduni mṛga-śarīre **tūla**-rāsāv ivāgniḥ.*

Perhaps Kālidāsa first wrote *tūla-* and then revised it to *puṣpa-*.

The copies from which the variation might have begun are called variant bearers and the readings of these are considered for the constitution of a text. In the above case, they are x and y and the immediately preceding common source for the variant bearer is the archetype.

If r in the above stemma had come down in three or more lines of transmission, it may be constitued through agreement between any two of the sub-archetypes. If the branches give divergent readings or when the agreement between any two is accidental and independent of each other, there can be no certainty of the reading of r. Here the testimony of testimonia will be helpful in deciding.

The reading supported by the codices alone is called transmitted reading, while that which is supported by testimonia too is called traditional reading.

The problem is not so simple as above in the case of works like the *Mahābhārata*. The manuscripts of such works will not have come down in pure lines of transmission. They are subject to what is called conflation.

Two lines of transmission will have influenced each other and the codices cannot be arranged into clear branches.

Supposing there are 8 codices: A B C D E F G H which may be arranged in the following table:

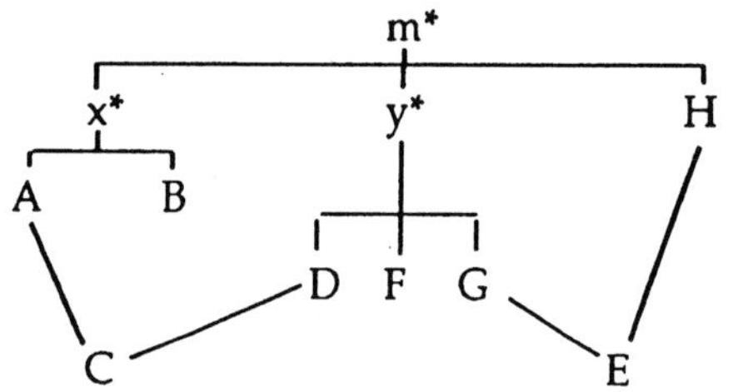


In this, C and E are conflated manuscripts or misch-codices.

A good instance of acknowledged conflation is *Hitopadeśa*. In the introduction, Nārāyaṇapaṇḍita writes that he has written the *Hitopadeśa* taking stories from the *Pañcatantra* and another (not specified) text : *pañcatantrāt tathānyasmād granthād ākṛṣya likhyate.*

In the case of those manuscripts which are known to be conflated: The agreement among the independent version will have to be postulated as original. If they are at variance, then the reading which is documented by the largest number of independent versions will have to be taken as the basis and it has to be supported by intrinsic probablity. The reading of the manuscript which can be relied upon as accurate may be accepted as a stop-gap. In these cases it may also be useful find out how the other readings might have arisen.

Edgerton has discovered four independant streams in the transmission of the *Pañcatantra* text, and there are traces of a fifth one too. The four streams are:

1. Tantrākhyāyikā, Pūrṇabhadra and Simplicior.
2. Southern *Pañcatantra*, Nepalese *Pañcatantra* and the *Hitopadeśa*.
3. The *Bṛhatkathā* versions of Somadeva and Kṣemendra.
4. The Pahlavi versions.

**Pedigree of Mahābhārata Manuscripts**

(V.S. Sukthankar)

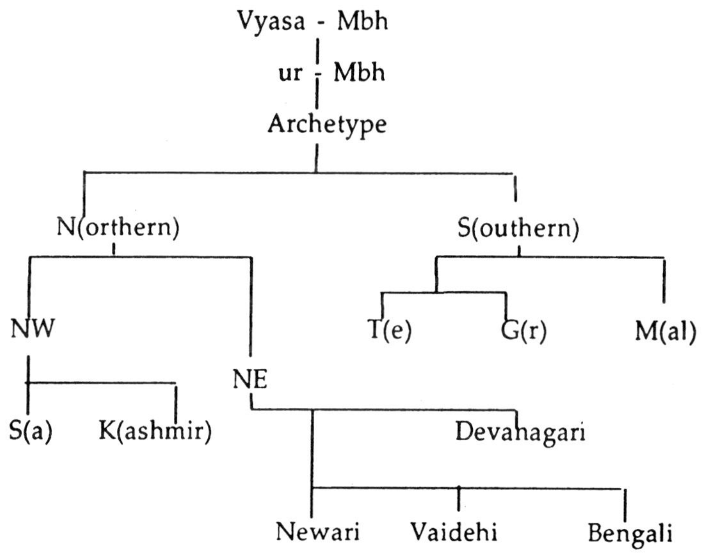


**(2) Emendation**

The purpose of textual criticism is the restoration of a text to its original form as far as possible. The basis is the evidence provided by the manuscripts. The role of the editor comes in when the manuscripts present diverging variants. The editor has to formulate certain tests by which he can judge the suitability of a reading in a context. It is obvious that the parameters for the test in the first place is the diction of the author and secondly the mutual relation of the various readings from the point of view of orthography and linguistics.

The reading with which all codices agree (called transmitted reading) or the reading supported by the codices as well as testimonia (called traditional reading) may make no sense; because of it there may be a glaring contradiction; its form may baffle any grammatical explanation; it may be a mere repetition though a synonym; it may pose a metrical difficulty; or there may be some disjunction in the thought sequence. Or none of the sources may have an identical reading. In the former case (transmitted reading), the reading is very much there, there is the documental support. In the second case, the problem is one of selection.

In such a situation the editor may suggest an emendation, a correction. This suggested alternative should satisfy intrinsically as well as extrinsically. Every reading, as pointed out earlier, will have two probabalities: intrinsic or internal, and extrinsic or external. The suggested reading should fit into the context, be befitting to the diction of the author. That is the emendation should appear an intrinsic part of the text. It must satisfy the metrical requirement if the text is metrical.

Further the proposed reading should have transcriptional or documentary relation with the various readings available. In other words, one must explain orthographically how the reading - considering the proposed as the original - got corrupted into the present readings. This is called external because, it does not refer to the text or the author but to the mode of writing it, to the copyist. The question would be, for example, why the copyist wrote - *saṅkhyā-* when his exemplar had *-śayyā-* (in *prameya-śayyā-paripūraṇāya, Dhvanyāloka-Locana,* p. 79, l.3)

These tests are applied to variants when doubtful. When a new reading is proposed, it is called conjectural emendation. But this does not arise due to doubt or uncertainty but due to the fact that none of the available readings satisfies the context. In spite of this, it must be conceded that the conjectural emendation is a conjecture and it cannot be passed off as the original with absolute certainty.

If it is not possible to find a reading which satisfies both the probabilities simultaneously, then the intrinsic probability should be preferred to extrinsic probability. The reading that fulfils intrinsic probability only, can be accepted as plausible, as a stop-gap. Because it bears no relation to the extant reading - resemblance etc., it can not be accounted how the various readings came into being. The readings that is probable transcriptionally only, has no much value. It may not even fit into the context. It is as good as one of the variants themselves which have not merited acceptance.

Thus emendation is a process which involves wide knowledge of and deep insight into the diction of the author concerned, along with a sound knowledge of the language as well as the field or fields to which the work in question belongs. The text-critic should be familiar with the varieties of scripts, lexicon etc. Emendation must be preceded by good deliberation. It is the most formidable task of a text-critic.

In spite of this onerous nature of emendation, an editor may be tempted to resort to it often. Sukthankar warns that a text-critic should not resort to precipitate emendation. He is of the opinion that interpretation of the evidence should be preferred to emendation. The editor should not ignore the clear and unanimous testimony of the codices.

### *Two Schools*

There are two schools in regard to emendation. One school has the view of 'scientific interpretation.' Followers of this school are conservative and say that the readings that may appear unacceptable are to be interpreted rather than emended. The other school holds the view that faults shall not be allowed to remain. Corrupted passage i.e., those contexts where none of the readings available is useful, are to be emended. If attempts are not made to correct or emend, then the constituted text will not be meaningful and may even cause misinterpretation of the text. Even though a proposed emendation may not have a claim to be the original or near original, it can at least be a stop gap. It can be accepted for the time being, till fresh evidence comes forth. 'Stop-gaps should be preferred to debris.'[4] Further, it is the editor that can make a conjecture for he will have a better insight into the diction of the author and the idiosyncracies of the scribes. If he does not do it, then the constituted text loses its value.[5]

The protogonists of each of these two schools are right in their own way. Also, it is not advisable to follow either of them wholly. So a via media has to be struck. The doubful traditional reading is to be interpreted. It should be tried to see if some relevant meaning can be elicited from the reading in question. But one should not resort to forced or round about interpretation. Instead of forcibly eliciting the required meaning, if it is possible to substitute it with a suitable reading that illuminates the meaning of the context, then there is no reason why it should not be adopted. Hence the individual situations are to be taken separately and given the treatment they deserve.

### 3. Canons of Critical editing

No universal canons can be prescribed. The principles have their own limitations. On the basis of experience, some broad principles can be formulated. The evidence of the codices and testimonia is the basis and the task is to apply the principles intelligently, skilfully and systematically for utilising this evidence to constitute the near original text if not the original itself.

Sanskrit authors, poets in particular, bring in to their work all their learning in the diverse fields of knowledge. Therefore, the editor, must be careful in derecognising an unfamiliar expression, it may be an expression with a technical sense in some science.

(1) When the pedigree of manuscripts is traced, a reading common to a branch can be settled. This reduces the number of variants for final comparison. Generally, the agreement among the independent manuscripts must be taken as the original reading. If the sub-archetypes vary, then the transcriptional and intrinsic probabalities are to be considered. Thus the evidence has to be examined

irrespective of the number of manuscripts. "Codices are to be weighed, not counted."[6]

In other words, 'in a camparison of variants, the larger arrays of manuscripts represent the earlier divergence; the smaller always represent the later.'[7] In the table earlier (p.157) five manuscripts out of twelve form one branch. The other six form the sub-branches of one, two and three respectively The latter being lower down in transmission than the former, and therefore later, the readings of the former are preferable.

(2) In the pedigree, if the reading of any one codex in one of the lines of transmission (say, y*) agrees with the reading of any one codex of another line of transmission (say, x*), then that reading has a claim to be original because that must have come down from the archetype only and cannot be accidental.

(3) If there is agreement between the readings of the two reconstructed sub-archetypes (x* & y*), then that reading has claim to be the original. If they disagree, they are the variants bearers and the decision to accept is to be taken in respect of those which fulfil the internal and external probabalities. Supposing the readings in the two have equal claim, satisfying both the probabalities, then the editor accepts with doubt one of them, which appears more plausible.

(4) If there are only two lines of transmission, then the earlier of them is to be given preference. If there are more than two lines then the reading common to any two branches can be regarded as that of the archetype.

(5) Prefer lectio difficilior. Prefer the harder reading. This is one of the most commonly recommended principle. There is the possibility of a scribe deliberately altering by substitution or otherwise, the reading of the exemplar, if he finds it difficult to understand. He may even consider it a mistake. In order to make the text clearer or 'correct', a simpler form or word is substituted. Archaisms, solecism, peculiar constructions of the original tend to be altered like this.

Eg. *triyambakam* and *trilocanam* are the two readings in *Kumārasambhava* 3. 44d. The former is an archaism to avoid which the latter may be a substitution. In *Mahābhārata*, Araṇya, 228. 12ab has several variants. Of them *ārabhadhvam*, the reading in a single manuscript, has merited preference. When we discover that *ārabhadhvam* is used in an unusual sense, it explains the variants: the copyist altered the reading to make it 'intelligible'. This did not satisfy a later copyist who altered it in his own way.

**text**[8]: *atha yūyam bahutvāt* ***tān ārbhadhvam*** *kathañcana.*

| | |
|---|---|
| $S_1K_1$ *tān ālabheyuḥ.* | $K_2$ *tān ālabheyam.* |
| $K_3$ *tān nārabhedhvam.* | $K_4$ *ca nākṣipadhvam.* |
| $B_1$ *tānakṛtadhvam.* | $B_2$ *tu tāllabhadhvam,* |
| $D_c$ $D_6$ *tān nārabheran.* | $B_3$ $D_4$ *tān ārabheran.* |
| $D_{1\text{-}4}$ *tān nākṣipadhvam.* | $G_{2.3}$ *tān nārabhadhvam.* |
| $G_4$ *tān nārabadhvam.* | $\acute{M}_1$ *tān parādhyān.* |
| $M_2$ *tān ārabhadhvam.* | |

Therefore, a reading which appears unusual, morphologically or semantically, is to be preferred. Again the rule may not be applicable blindly. It may not hold good in each and every case. There may be an error which poses harder than the true one. Such pitfalls are to be avoided carefully.

(6) It may so happen that the transmitted reading may be hopelessly bad; the testimonia too may not be useful. Then the editor could suggest an emendation. The need for utmost restraint on the part of the editor in this exercise has already been discussed.

(7) As said earlier, the principles that may be formulated are very general in nature. The evidence of the manuscript will not always be enough. Testimonia may throw welcome light. But, one should not forget that it is an intellectual endeavour that is under consideration; it does not always conform to any hard and fast and universal pattern. We may recall here what Hall says at one point: "A critic must be more than a palaeographer".[9] So the editor should rise above his individual self. He should develop the

faculty of *sahṛdayatā* with the author; he should become one with the author.

Such an attempt when genuine, should not be branded as subjective. If the editor remains as such but claims originality to his constitution, then only does rise the question of being subjective. But when the editor can completely lose himself in the author, there need be no hesitation in accepting the constituted text as original. It may be an ideal; but it is worth striving to achieve it.

**4. Problem of Prakrit texts**

Though Prakrit literature is wide enough, and many texts have been printed, scholars do not seem to have given sufficient attention to the problems of textual criticism in respect of this literature.

The dimensions of the problems are not simple. First, it is not one or two dialects that come under Prakrit, but several. Śaurasenī, Māhārāṣṭrī, Māgadhī, Ardhamāgadhī, Paiśācī and Cūlikā-paiśāci are the main ones recognised. We have Jain-śaurasenī and Jain-Mahārāṣṭrī varieties. Apabhraṁśa, too is considered under this head; but it is itself a different world. One of the Prākrit grammarian, Mārkaṇḍeya, himself records not less than twentyseven varieties of Apabhraṁśa. Thus the question of Prakrit texts is complex.

Secondly, as regards the linguistic features of these languages, we are confronted with the grammarians on the one hand and the manuscripts on the other. There is no clear indication that a work is in a particular Prakrit dialect. On the basis of geographical, chronological and other consideration, one can surmise that a work could be in one Prakrit dialect. But the manuscripts of the work do not allow us conclude that way. Now comes the critical question - whether the manuscript evidence should be given preference over the regulations of grammar. As a student of manuscriptology, one may be tempted to go with the manuscript evidence. But one has to exercise utmost caution here. Though there are more than ten Prakrit grammars and several commentaries written on each of them, Prakrits have not been studied with the same ferver and care as Sanskrit was studied. The very fact that these grammar texts and their commentaries are written in Sanskrit, points to this. Hence Prakrit as a whole is deemed simply to be a deviation from Sanskrit in spite of the knowledge of varieties. The copyists do not appear to be mindful enough to maintain a particular dialect. It is only a person who knows the dialects that does not mix up forms like *hoü* and *phuradu*, *rīo* and *jayadi*.

Expressions like *kaï* which may be understood as 'poet' (*kavi*) or as 'how many' (*kati*), might prompt a copyist treat it as causing confusion and 'correct' as say, 'kavi' Thus scribes add to the complexity the problem. The edition of *Karpūramañjarī* brought out by ManoMohan Ghosh (1939) raises certain issues which may be spoken of as the basic issues. Sten Konow (1907) who had edited the text earlier, used eleven manuscripts. He proceeded with the assumption that Rājaśekhara wrote the play in two prakrits: Śaurasenī (prose) and Mahārāṣṭrī (verse). And corrected the text according to the grammar completely ignoring the evidence of manuscripts. While Ghosh relied on the manuscript evidence only. Unfortunately, the method of either of the scholars can not be approved because there is no such precept that prose and verse are to be written only in Śaurasenī and Mahārāṣṭrī respectively, and on the other hand, the manuscript evidence strikes at the very features of dialects.

S.R.Banerjee (1988) writes : 'time has come to formulate some rules or norms for Prakrit Textual Criticism'. Before any such attempt can be undertaken, the linguistic features of the different dialects in different periods of history are to be settled. The observations of the grammarians are to be studied comparatively and to be verified with the inscriptional evidence and evidence of manuscripts of Prakrit works. The works that the different grammarians might have had before them may also be determined so that the rules framed by a later grammarian may not be taken into consideration while dealing with the text of an earlier work.

## 5. Other Editorial Tasks

There are certain features that are essentially to be found in a critical edition of a text and certain others which are desirable and useful.

An editor collects all the extant copies of the text in original or their mechanised copies like microfilm, micro-fische, or xerox. The copies are studied individually and their mutual relation and trustworthiness are arrived at. Then the copies are collated; the help of testimonia is exploited and the critical recension of the text is constituted. Of the several readings that the editor comes across in a context, only one is accepted. There may be cases of doubt and conjectural emendation. Now, the editor's task is primarily to arrive at a critical recension. But it is not enough if only the constituted text is placed before the world of scholars; a description of all the above mentioned facts and features are to be presented. This constitutes the essential part of a critical edition because this vouches for the criticism involved in the constitution of the text.

*Manuscript and related material*

Each of the manuscripts on which the edition is based is to be described. The source, the catalogue number (if from a library), material, size, number of folios, number of lines per page, number of letters per line, extent, condition, missing leaves, if any, date and name of the scribe etc. (if mentioned) and any other feature of codex that the editor may feel useful - are to be provided.

Besides, a note on the orthographic peculiarities, style of writing (haphazard or steady etc), blank spaces, marginalia, interlinear writings, erasures and other modes of correction, whether the handwriting is uniform or not, peculiarity of pagination, damage through mutilation or worms, decoration and illustration if any, - in respect of each codex is to be given. In clarification of the extent, if incomplete, the portion collated must be mentioned clearly. If several codices are partially collated, a table showing the particulars is helpful. In other words, all details that may be useful to the reader in forming an idea of the codices are to be furnished. The sigla given to the codices should also be indicated appropriately.

The editor makes use of testimonia as well. Hence the number of commentaries on the text known and available, the number of commentaries utilised, the translations etc., consulted are to be noted with relevant details.

A chart of the pedigree of the manuscripts is to be given depending upon the number of manuscripts involved.

Of course, material under all of the above particulars may not be there in every case. But the mention of the details of the manuscripts collated is a must and an editor cannot be excused for forgetting this. In many of the texts published in the Trivandrum Sanskrit Series only this part is given. Conversely, the editor of *Anubhavasūtra*, for example, does not specify which are *a, ka, ya* and *kṣa* on which the edition is based.[10]

The editor should specify whether the text is being edited for the first time or whether had been printed earlier. In the latter circumstance, it is worthwhile to mention the need for the present edition.

***The constituted text***

The editor will do well if he speaks of the critical principles he adopted, particularly, if he had made any innovations. He must spell out the nature of difficulties and problems he faced and how he got over them. He must discuss the emendation that he might have proposed and the interpolation that he might have detected and rejected. If there has been any earlier attempt by any scholar in emending any part of his text, it is advisable for the editor to acknowledge it with proper reference. Not only will the editor be relieved of the onus but also there will be the due recognition of the effort of a fellow scholar.[11]

Certain methods are to be followed in presenting the constituted text. Because no definite rules are laid down for this, it will be necessary to set out the methods adopted. It is possible that a text might be edited for the second time.

Then providing a concordance to the earlier edition or cross reference to the earlier edition enhances the reference value.

Eg. Cr. edn. of *Mahābhārata* gives cross reference to Bombay, Kumbhakonam and Calcutta editions on every page. In the *Nāṭyaśāstra* edited by Manomohan Ghosh, references to Bombay (NSP), Baroda and Kashi editions are given on every page.

### *Critical Apparatus*

When a text is constituted, only one reading is accepted out of several readings that may be available. Those rejected readings are also to be presented along with the text. This collection of rejected readings is called critical apparatus. This is usually given as foot-notes on the same page on which the related text appears. Some editors choose to give the critical apparatus at the end of the volume. But this is not convenient. However, if an editor comes across new manuscript/s after the work is completed, the new readings may be given at the end so that scholars may be benefitted. Franklin Edgerton, for example, received certain collations 'much too late for inclusion in critical apparatus' of Sabhāparvan of the *Mahābhārata;* so they have been given at the end.[12]

The text part for which various readings are noted is marked with a superior figure. The numerals run in a sequence separately on each page. Some editors particularly of Kannada texts, prefer to put the superior figures on either side of the text part which has the readings. The relevant siglum must invariably accompany the readings.

Eg.(1) *sa* [5]*vyāpāro dhvaniruktaḥ, sa eva* [6]*yadāha.* (*Dhvanyāloka-Locana*, p.63)

(2) *cadura* [2]*śikhe*[2]*yanu hākida.* (Narasimhachar (1964), p. 183)

Editors of Sanskrit texts also sometimes follow this latter method.

Eg.: *...jayati śrīmat-ṣaḍakṣarī-*[1]*vidyā*[1]*;*
[2]*jayati*[2] *saḍa*[3]*ṅga*[3] *bhaktir ...*
*(Anubhavasūtra, 1.2 bc) /*

When the readings are too many, another method is employed. The *Mahābhārata*, for instance, has various readings for every pada. So it is not necessary to employ any superior figure in the text part. The critical apparatus has separate paragraphs for each stanza the number of which is given at the beginning. After a note for the stanza as whole, if any, the readings, for each pada indicated by the letters *a b c* and *d* are given with their sigla.

Example :

Eg.7. a) $B_{3.4}$ $D_6$ mahārāja for mahāteja.
b) $K_{3.4}$ B except ($B_{3.4}$) $Dn_2$ M magadhādhi-pateḥ- d) $D_5$ dhṛta (marg. added for omission (hutiḥ). - After 7,$K_3$ reads $8^{ab}$ (for the first time), followed by (accidental) repetition of most of $7^{cd}$

10. G $M_2$ om. 10 (cf. v.l. 5,9). $Ñ_1$ S om. the ref. - a) $S_1$ vyavasitam. - b) $K_2$ niḥkṛtim $G_2$ Samupasthitam.

(Sabhāparvan 17.7, p.95 and 58.10, p.283, respectively).

The editor of a text will have certainly, a greater facility in the selection of reading because he deals with the evidence directly. And the work is carried out with utmost objective outlook. But in spite of the attempt on the part of the editor to be objective to the core, the editor will be prone to bring in the subjective element. In other words, acceptance of a reading may not always be objective. Therefore, it is utmost important to place before the scholars, all the evidence relied on. The scholars can then judge the editorial endeavour. That is why the editor of a text is required to give a detailed note on each and every manuscript and other sources utilised as well as to give the critical apparatus.

### *Editorial Signs*

In the constituted text, a reading might have been accepted doubtfully or there might be a conjectural emendation, a lacuna might have been completed and so on. To indicate these, certain signs and symbols are employed. However there are no hard and fast rules laid down. Paul Mass has given a set of signs. V.S. Sukthankar has added/modified a few.[13] They are:

[ ] Square brackets enclose the editor's completion of an attested lacuna, say, caused by physical damage. - addition to manuscript reading. (Sukthankar).

< > arrow heads enclose the editor's completion of a surmised lacuna.

{[ ]} flower and square brackets enclose conjectural athetisation.

{ } flower brackets enclose the part deleted conjecturally.

( ) parenthesis enclose the text which may not have been in the original. (Sukthankar).

† dagger indicates irremediable or false localised corruption.

* asterisk indicates conjectural emendation.

~ wavy line placed below the text when it is less than certain (Sukthankar)

* * indicates loss due to injury to manuscript. (Sukthankar)

¤ ¤ indicates citation from commentary.

### *Higher Criticism*

An editor of a text will be in a position to discuss better the date, life and works of the author concerned. He can also dwell on the sources of the author and can appreciate the position of the work in its field. Hence, it is desirable that the editor shall devote some space in the introductory part to this aspect of study of the work.

A brief history of the field of the text should be written so as to highlight the place and value of the contribution of the work on hand. The nature and title of the work, the personality of the author, his place, life, date and works are to be discussed. The possible sources of the author could be indicated. Along with a critique of the work, the possible influence of the present work on the later works in the field may be pointed out. Commentaries, if any, on the work are to be taken note of. Providing a detailed table of contents goes a long way in helping the reader to appreciate the work edited.

*Indexes*

It is desirable that the editor comes to the help of research student and scholars in retrieving information from the work quickly. This is possible by compiling varieties of indexes. No doubt this is a tedious and mechanical job. But it leads easily to the many facets of the work, and the work can be used to the maximum by scholars engaged in research and lexicography. Possible types of indecies that can be compiled may be indicated here :

1. Index verborum (alphabetical register of all words in the text).
2. technical words (may be classified). This can be in the form of a glossary too.
3. Words peculiar to the text (may be glossarial or not).
4. Peculiar or ungrammatical forms of words.
5. Borrowed words.
6. Deśi words.
7. Words bearing on flora, fauna, geography etc.
8. Names cited.
9. Titles of works cited.
10. Citations or quotations (with sources indicated in the text or not).
11. Pithy sayings culled from the text.
12. Stanzas: pratīka-index or pāda-index (all pādas or odd pādas only).
13. Metres of stanzas.
14. Topics in general.

The fourth edition of *Arthaśāstra* (Mysore) has several of the above indices. The *Nyāyamañjarī-Granthi-bhaṅga* (Ahmedabad) has an index of philosophy terms. Index verborum, for example, was compiled for *Mahābhāṣya* and *Arthaśāstra*.

## Notes and References

1. Katre, p. 38.
2. Narasimhachar (1964), p. 142 ff.
3. *Abhijñāna-Śākuntalam*, 1.13.
4. Katre, p.73.
5. *Prabhulīlā*, for instance, is based on codex unicus. Many of its verses are not intelligible. The editor was certainly in a position to say if the difficulty was due to the scribe and could have suggested emendations. See *Prabhulīlā* ed. G. Marulasiddiah, Mysore: Prasaranga, University of Mysore, 1966.
6. Katre, p. 72.
7. Ibid., p. 47.
8. *Mahābhārata*, Araṇya-parva, Pune: BORI, 1942, p.813.
9. Katre, p. 66.
10. *Anubhūtisūtra* of Māyideva, Ed. H.P.Malledevaru, Mysore: Oriental Research Institute, 1983.
11. Narasimhachar (1964), p. 214. Paul Mass (*Textual Criticism*, p. 23) is quoted in the footnote: "It is the practice to indicate the authorship of conjectures. But justice and necessity demand that mention should also be made of the scholar who first explained the transmitted text or pointed out the corruption. In both cases a selection only should be given."
12. *Mahābhārata*, Sabhāparva, Ed. Edgerton, Pune: BORI, 1944.
13. Katre, p.8 4f and Sabhāparva, Intd.

# NOTES ON SOME MSS. COLLECTIONS

## CENTRAL ASIAN

### 1. Bakshali Manuscripts

A manuscript of birch bark leaves was found at Bakshali near Mardan in 1881 by an Inspector of Police. It was received by Hoernle through several local officials. Hoernle presented the manuscript to Bodleian Library in 1902. The manuscript consists of 70 leaves and some mere scraps. Style of writing is not uniform. According to Kaye, the manuscript dealing with mathematics dates from 12th century A.D.

Ed. Kaye, G.R., New Delhi : Archaeological Survey of India, New Imperial Series, 43, parts i & ii, 1927; part iii, 1933.

### 2. Bower Manuscripts

So called because Lietenant Bower was responsible for the preservation of this find. Some manuscripts were dug out of a stūpa-like structure near Kuchar in Central Asia. A.F. Rudolf Hoernle concludes that the main portion belongs to about 475 A.D., while the other portion can be dated 425 or even earlier. He distinguishs 5 distinct portions. (1) consists of 31 leaves and is a medical work. (2) Five leaves another medical treatise perhaps part of a longer work. (3) Five leaves, a sort of collection of proverbial sayings. (4) Six leaves, appears to be a collection of proverbial sayings but the condition is very bad. (5) Four leaves, relates how the charm against snake bite was given to Ānanda by the Buddha in Jetavana. Together with some detached and unconnected leaves there are 56 bhūrja leaves. The size varies: some are 23 X 5 cms. and others 29 X 6.5 cms.

### 3. Kharoṣṭhi Dhammapada or Prakrit Dhammapada

This is a birch bark manuscript. A French traveller Dutreuil de Rhins acquired a part of it in Khotan 1892. A month later another French traveller M.Grenard collected what he believed to be the rest of the manuscript. Before these two French men laid their hands on the manuscript, a larger portion of it had been sold to the agent of the Russian Consul General at Kashgar, M.Petrowsky. However, Petrowsky mediated to see that his collection were sent to Imperial Academy at St.Petersburg. The portion collected by Dutreuil de Rhins is in Paris. These are respectively called Petrowsky manuscripts and Dutreuil de Rhins manuscripts. The fragments go back to c. 200 A.D.

Rhys Davids (1899) refers to this codex as Gosinga Kharosthi Manuscript because the codex is considered to have been found in the Kohmari cave (Gosinga Vihara) on the Gośṛṅga hill. However, this find spot is doubtful since Stein who visited the cave could not find any evidence to the effect.

While the Russian scholars Serge d'Oldenberg edited the larger portion, Senart and later Barua (Calcutta University) edited the other portion, under the title *Prakrit Dhammapada*. (See also Shashi Bala (1980)).

### 4. Macartney Collection

Some scraps of manuscripts were presented to G.Macartney, Special Assistant for Chinese affairs at Kashgar to Lt.Col. A.C.Talbot, British Resident of Kashmir by the Manager of the Chinese Foreign Commerce, Kashgar. The fragments consists of 145 pieces in number, 13 of which are birch bark, 9 palm leaf and the rest paper. Two distinct types of Brahmi can be seen on the whole: Central Asian and North Indian (Gupta).

The manuscripts are grouped into six sets: Set (1) found in the same site as that Bower and Weber manuscripts; two scripts as noted above can be seen. Set (2) : found at Aksufil, north-east of Khotan. Set(3) found at Jabu Kum, about 50 miles north-east of Khotan. Set(4) found at Karakul Mazan

Khojan, about 50 miles east of Guma. Set(5) found in the desert at Kuk Gumbaz, east of Guma Set(6) picked up from the ground at Kuk Gumbaz.

Hoernle (1897) who has reproduced several of these folios, opines that the manuscript 1 b belongs to 2nd century AD. The material is a soft kind of paper. Another peculiarity is that the pagination is on the obverse, a feature found mostly in the manuscripts of South India.

### 5. Turfan Fragments

In 1902 a German expedition to tour Turfan was organised under Grunwedel and Huth. Two further expeditions were organised with state cooperation in 1904-07. It was led by Le Coq and Grunwedel. The library remains which the expedition unearthed were sent to Berlin. The most important of them consists of 144 pieces of palm leaf. The fragments were discovered by Le Coq in a cave temple at Mingai. The script is identical with the script of the inscription of Northern Ksatrapas and Kushans. Thus these fragments represent the earliest palm leaf documents. They contain parts of two plays attributed to Aśvaghoṣa. Lüders edited with pains-taking patient work of putting together the fragments. The dramas were published in the volume *Bruchsuecke Buddhistischer Dramen* first of the series Kleiners Sanskrit Texte in 1911 under the patronage of Koniglich Preussische Turfan-Expedition. Lüders was also the editor of other volumes published in this series devoted to Turfan expedition.

### 6. Weber Manuscript

An Afghan merchant who found some manuscripts near Kuigar about 100 kms. south of Yarkhand, within Chinese territory, gave them to F.Weber, Moravian Missionary in Leh in Ladhak. The collection has nine (possibly seven) manuscripts which can be grouped into two on the basis of the script. Nos. 1 to 4 are in North-Western Gupta characters (similar to Bower Ms.), while Nos. 5-9 are in Central Asian Nāgarī. The material is paper which is also of two kinds. Hoernle (1893) concludes none of these manuscripts is later than 700 A.D. They may be dated c. 500 A.D., contemporary with or anterior to Bower Ms.

**7. Gilgit Manuscripts :**

The manuscripts were deposited within the vault of a stupa near Gilgit. It was a chance discovery by somebody. But by the time the Wazir of Gilgit took charge of the treasure a good poriton of the manuscripts as well as its painted covers had been removed. The remaining bundle of leaves are now in Government custody in Kashmir. The manuscripts are not later than 7th century A.D. on the basis of palaeography. Thus this is the earliest manuscript discovered within our country. The style of writing is comparable to that of Tibetan xylograph. The language is Buddhist Hybrid Sanskrit. Aurel Stein first announced the discovery in *Statesman* of July 24, 1931. In the following year M.Hackin wrote an article on them in *Journal Asiatique* 14-15 (1932) after visiting the spot of discovery.

The first volume, *Gilgit Manuscripts* was edited for the Government of Kashmir (1939) by G.Nalinksha Datt assisted by D.M. Bhattacharya and Shive Nath Sharma Vidyavaridhi.

**8. Godfrey Manuscripts**

The fragments of paper manuscripts are said to have been dug up in the vicinity of Kuchar. Some Pathan merchants who were helped to cross the Leh trade route which was flooded at Kargil in July 1895 by Capt. S.H. Godfrey, British Joint Commissioner of Ladhak, presented the manuscripts to him. This collection consists of 71 pieces most of which are mutilated. Hoernle (1897) has reproduced them partially.

**9. Avesta Codex K5**

Best and complete as well as the oldest manuscript for the restoration of Avesta text. 327 folios numbered in Devanāgarī numbers 27.5 x 22.5 cms.; 17 lines per pages; contains Yasna with Pahlavi translation. Folio 326b has the colophon in Pahlavi and Sanskrit, mentioning the name of the copyist, the place (Cambay and date (AY 692, Sam. 1379 ; Nov. 17, 1323 A.D.).

Reproduced chromo-photographically by Copenhagen Royal Library in Rask collection in which the manuscript is found.

**10. Horiuzi Manuscript**

Palm leaf (28 x 5 cms., 7 lines per page) containing Buddhist texts; *Prajñāpāramita-hṛdaya-sūtra* and *Uśṇīṣa-vijaya-dhāriṇī*. It is written in script resembling Gupta script. Hence, Buhler opines, it is not later than 1st half of 6th cent. A.D. Accordingly to Dani (1963), however, it is not earlier than 700 A.D. The tradition says: the manuscript was with a Chinese priest living in the mountain Nan-yo in Hank(Ko) province of China; it was brought to Japan in the 37th year of Prince Umayado i.e., 609 A.D.; This Prince who died in 621 A.D. established the eleven famous monasteries including Horiuzi. The manuscript, copied by Ziogon in 17th century, was with Horiuzi as late as 1727 when the priest Zakumio, editor of 'Thousand Sanskrit and Chinese Words' (Chinese-Sanskrit-Japanese Vocabulary) wrote in the preface: In the monastery of Horiuzi in Yamato, there are preserved the 'Prajñāpāramita-hṛdayasūtrā' and 'Sonshio-dharaṇi', written on two palm leaves, handed down from Central India, and at the end of these, the fourteen sounds of the Siddham (alphabet) are written.

The texts have been edited by Max Muller and Nanjio Anecdot Oxon. I iii. To this is appended palaeographical remarks by Bühler.

**11. Mahābhārata Śāradā Codex**

The manuscript (No. 159 of 1875-76, purchased by G. Bühler in Kashmir for the Government of Bombay) of 114 folios in Śāradā script contains fragment of Ādiparva, whole of Sabhāparva and part of Vanaparva. The codex probably belongs to 16th or 17th century. It represents the shortest version known (textus simplicior) of the Mahābhārata. The siglum 'S' is given to it in the critical edition.

### 12. Mahābhārata Nepali Manuscript

A palm leaf manuscript about 700 years old has been acquired by Rajaguru Hemaraj Panditji of Nepal. The codex measures 21"X2" and 7 lines per page are written uniformly. It is complete and contains the Ādiparva of the Mahābhārata.

### 13. Paippalāda Manuscript

In 1875 Maharaja Ranbir Singh of Jammu and Kashmir sent birch bark manuscripts of the Atharvaveda of Paippalā-daśakhā to William Muir, the then Lieutenant Governor. He in turn despatched it to Rudolf Roth of Germany. The manuscript went to Tübingen University in 1895 when Roth died. The most priceless codex being codex unicum for Kashmiri recension of *Atharvaveda*. The codex is in 275 birch bark leaves 25X20 cms. (text space 20X15 cms.); written on both sides with indelible ink; Śāradā script; about 450 years old. It is reproduced by chromo-photography by Bloomfield and Garbe (Baltimore, 1901).

### 14. Dhavala Manuscripts

During the times of king Amoghavarṣa Nṛpatuṅga (814-871 A.D.) of Karnataka, an elaborate commentary on Ṣaṭkhaṇḍāgama of Puṣpadanta-Bhūtabali was written. This work is held in high esteem among the Jaina works as containing the words of Mahāvīra himself. On the first five Khaṇḍas of this work, Vīraṣeṇa wrote his commentary *Dhavala* extending to 72,000 granthas. He also wrote, *Jaya-dhavala,* a commentary on Kaṣāya-pāhuḍa of Guṇadhara. *Jayadhavala* has 20,000 granthas and is incomplete. Vīraṣeṇa passed away before he could complete it. His disciple Jinasena continued and completed it by writing 40,000 granthas.

The language of the original works is Śaurasenī, Jain Śaurasenī, to be more precise. The commentary is in the same language but there is more free mixture of Sanskrit. The only copy of this voluminous work (1,32,000 granthas in all) of Vīraṣeṇa-Jinasena is preserved in tact in Moodbidri

(Karnataka). The palm leaf codex is written with ink in the Kannada characters of the 9th century. Hence the codex can well be regarded as the autograph copy. It consists of 1478 leaves. A microfilm of the entire manuscript is available in the University of Mysore.

# LIST OF MANUSCRIPTS LIBRARIES

## INDIAN

| | | |
|---|---|---|
| 1. | Agartala | : Tripura Śikṣā Bibhāga |
| 2. | Agra | : Jaina Temple |
| 3. | Ahmedabad | : B.J.Institute of Learning and Research |
| 4. | | : Brahmacari Vadi |
| 5. | | : Gujarat Vidyapitha Granthalaya |
| 6. | | : Lalbhai Dalapatbhai Institute of Indology |
| 7. | | : Ahmednagar College Manuscripts Library |
| 8. | | : Sanatan Dharma Sabha |
| 9. | Ajaigarh | : State Library |
| 10. | Aliganja | : Sri Santinatha Jaina Temple |
| 11. | Aligarh | : Muslim University |
| 12. | | : Subhanallah Oriental Library |
| 13. | Aliyoor | : Adinatha Grantha Bhandar |
| 14. | Allahabad | : Ganganatha Jha Kendriya Sanskrit Vidyapitha |
| 15. | | : Ganganatha Jha Research Institute |
| 16. | | : Hindi Sahitya Sammelan |
| 17. | | : Municipal Museum |
| 18. | | : University Library |
| 19. | | : Uttar Pradesh State Archives |
| 20. | Alwar | : Government Museum |
| 21. | | : Library of H.H.the Maharaja of Alwar |
| 22. | Amritsar | : Guru Nanak Dev University Library |
| 23. | | : Khalsa College |
| 24. | | : Sikh Itihas Research Board |
| 25. | Annamalai Nagar | : Annamalai University |
| 26. | Arrah | : Jaina Siddhantha Bhavan |
| 27. | Aurangabad | : Balavant Vachanalaya |

| | |
|---|---|
| 28. Badami | : Sri Sivayogamandira |
| 29. Bandha | : Chanda Das Sahitya Sidhan Institute |
| 30. Bangalore | : Sri Chamarajendra Sanskrit College |
| 31. | : Sri Vidyadhisha Sanskrit Manuscripts Library |
| 32. | : University Library |
| 33. | : Sri Uttaradi Mutt Granthalaya |
| 34. | : B.M.Sri. Foundation |
| 35. Baroda | : Arya Jambusvami Jaina Muktabai Jnana Mandira |
| 36. | : Atmananda Jnana Mandira |
| 37. | : Jaina Jnana Mandira |
| 38. | : Oriental Institute (MS University) |
| 39. Berhampur (Orissa) | : University Library |
| 40. Bhagalpur | : Bhagavan Pustakalaya |
| 41. Bharatpur | : State Library |
| 42. Bhaskeri | : Subrahmanya Pracya Vidyapitha |
| 43. Bhor | : Palace Library |
| 44. Bhuvaneswar | : Orissa State Museum |
| 45. | : Utkal University Library |
| 46. Bikaner | : Abhaya Jaina Granthalaya |
| 47. | : Anup Sanskrit Library |
| 48. | : Library of H.H. the Maharaja of Bikaner |
| 49. Bodh Gaya | : The Buddha Gaya Library |
| 50. | : Magadha University |
| 51. Bombay | : Sri Ailka Pannalal Digambara Jaina Sarasvati Bhavan |
| 52. | : Anantacarya Indological Research Institute |
| 53. | : Bharat Samsodhan Mandala |
| 54. | : Bharatiya Vidya Bhavan |
| 55. | : Bombay Asiatic Society |
| 56. | : Forbes Gujarati Sabha |

57. Bombay : Jaina Svetambara Conference
58. : Jama Masjid Madrassah-e-Muhmmadiya
59. : K.R.Kama Oriental Institute
60. : Maharashtra Archives
61. : Marathi Samsodhana Mandala
62. : Mulla Firoze Library
63. : Parsi Pancayat
64. : University Library
65. Burdwan : Palace Library
66. : University Library
67. Calcutta : Asiatic Society
68. : Bangiya Sahitya Parishad
69. : Bengali Manuscripts Library
70. : Bishop's College Library
71. : National Library
72. : Private Library of the Maharaja Tagore Castle
73. : Sanskrit College
74. : Sanskrit Sahitya Parishad
75. : Sri Sri Gaurang Grantha Mandira
76. : University, Post Graduate Dept. of Sanskrit
77. : Victoria Memorial Museum
78. Calicut : University, Department of Malayalam
79. : University, Department of Sanskrit
80. Cambay : Santinatha Jaina Bhandara
81. Chamba : Bhuri Singh Museum
82. Chhani : Jaina Svetambara Jnana Mandira
83. Chhatarpur : Palace Library
84. Cochin : Sukritindra Oriental Research Institute
85. Coochbehar : Sahitya Sabha
86. : State Library
87. Darbhanga : Sri Kamesvara Singh Sanskrit University
88. : Mithila Institute of Post-graduate Studies & Research in Sanskrit Learning

89. Darbhanga : State Chandradhari Museum
90. Datia : Sri Pitambara Pitha
91. Delhi : Archaeological Survey of India Library
92. : Digambara Jaina Sarasvati Bhandara Nayamandir, Dharmpura
93. : Indian Institute of Islamic Studies
94. : International Academy of Indian Culture
95. : Jamia Milia Islamia
96. : Mahavira Jaina Pustakalaya
97. : National Archives
98. : National Museum
99. : University Library
100. Devaband : Kitubkhana Darul-ulm
101. Devaprayag : Pracya Vidya Academy
102. Devasram : Sri Devakumar Jain Oriental Library
103. Dharam puram : Abhinam Library
104. Dharamsala : Central Tibetan Secreṭariat
105. Dharmasthala: Sṅ Manjuunatha Temple
106. Dharwar : Kannada Research Institute
107. Dhilaoli : Jaina Temple
108. Dhulia : V.K.Rajawade Samsodhana Mandala
109. Dibrugarh : Sri Samartha Vagdevata Mandira
110. Dwaraka : Dwaraka University Library
111. Dwaraka : Dwarkadhish Sanskrit Academy and Indologcal Research Institute.
112. Guwahati : Assam, Department of History and Anti quarian Studies
113. : Kamapura Anusandhan Samiti
114. : Narayan Handiqui Research Institute
115. : Chamariya Satha
116. : University Library
117. Gaya : Sri Mannulal Pustakalaya
118. Gondal : Sri Bhuvanesvari Pitha
119. Gulbarga : Institute of Kannada Studies, University

| | |
|---|---|
| 120. Gwalior | : Jiwaji University Library |
| 121. | : Matrabhumi Karyalaya |
| 122. Haridwar | : Gurukul Kangri Visvavidyalaya |
| 123. Hombucca | : Jaina Matha |
| 124. Hoshiarpur | : Visvesvaranand Vedic Research Institute |
| 125. | : Visvesvaranand Visva Bandhu Institute of Sanskrit & Indological Studies |
| 126. Hospet | : Sri Uttaradimutt Granthalaya |
| 127. Hubli | : Moorusavira Matha |
| 128. Hyderabad | : Andhra Pradesh Government Oriental Manuscripts Library & Research Institute |
| 129. | : Gadval Samsthanam |
| 130. | : Idra-e-Ababiyate-Urdu |
| 131. | : Krsnadevaraya Andhra Bhasa Nilaya |
| 132. | : Newab Salar Jung Library |
| 133. | : Osmania University Library |
| 134. | : Salar Jung Museum |
| 135. | : State Central Library |
| 136. Imphal | : Manipur Government Secretariat |
| 137. | : Manipuri Sahitya Parishad |
| 138. | : Manipur State Kala Academy |
| 139. Indore | : Oriental Museum |
| 140. Jaipur | : Acarya Sri Vinayacandra Jnana Bhandara |
| 141. | : Amar Sastra Bhandar |
| 142. | : Jaina Grantha Bhandar |
| 143. | : Maharaja of Sawai Man Singh II Museum |
| 144. | : Maharaja Public Library |
| 145. | : Mahavir Bhavan |
| 146. Jaisalmer | : Jaina Bhandar |
| 147. Jambusar | : Jaina Temple |
| 148. Jammu | : Library of H.H.Maharaja Sri Hari-Singhji Bahadur |
| 149. | : Ragunatha Temple Library |
| 150. | : Sri Ranbir Sanskrit Research Institute |
| 151. Jamnagar | : Gujarat Ayurveda University |

152. Jamshoro : Sind University Institute of Sindhology
153. Jeypore : Palace Library
154. Jhalarapatan: Sri Ailak Pannalal Digambar Jain Sarasvati Bhavan
155. Jodhpur : Maharaja Man Singh Pustak Prakash
156. : Rajastani Research Institute, Chopasani
157. : Rajastan Oriental Research Institute
158. Karanja : Balatkara Gaṇa Temple
159. Karwal : Danasala Jaina Matha
160. Keladi : Keladi Museum Historical Research Bureau
161. Keonjhar : State Library
162. Keri : Gomantak Sanskrit Parishad
163. Kokinada : Telugu Academy
164. Kolhapur : Ayurvedic Chemical Works
165. Kolhapur : Jinasena Mutt
166. : The Mutt of Sri Laksmisena Bhattaraka Pattacarya Mahasvamin
167. Kota : State Library
168. Kumbhakonam : Sadhu Sesayya Oriental Library
169. Kumilla : Rammala Granthagar
170. Kurukshetra: Visvavidyalaya, Bharatiya Vidyasamsthan
171. Limbadi : Jaina Jnana Bhandara
172. Lucknow : Akhil Bharatiya Sanskrit Parishad
173. : Provincial Museum
174. : University Library
175. Ludhiana : Punjab Sahitya Akademy
176. Madhurantakam : Ahobila Mutt Sanskrit College
177. Madras : Adyar Library and Research Centre
178. : Board of Examiners Library
179. : College Library
180. : Connemara Public Library

181. Madras : Fort Saint George College
182. : Government Oriental Manuscripts Library
183. : Kuppuswami Sastri Research Institute
184. : University Library
185. : U.V.Swaminath Aiyar Library
186. : Sri Kallalagar Devasthanam Library
187. Madurai : Ramesvaram Devasthanam Pathasala
188. : Tamil Sangam
189. : Kamaraj University
190. Malladihalli : Anathasevasram Trust
191. Melkote : Sanskrit College
192. : Academy of Sanskrit Research
193. Moodbidri : Sri Veera Vani Vilasa Jaina Siddhanta Bhavana
194. Mysore : Institute of Kannada Studies, Mysore University
195. : Maharaja's Sanskrit College
196. : Oriental Library of the late Tippu Sultan
197. : Oriental Research Institute, Mysore University
198. : Parakala Mutt
199. : Sarasvati Bhandaram Library of H.H. The Maharaja of Mysore
200. Nabadwip : Sadharana Granthagar
201. Nabha : Sardar Kahnisingh Pustakalaya
202. Nadiad : Dahi Laksmi Library
203. Nagpur : Bhonsla Veda Sastra Mahavidyalaya
204. : University Library
205. Nalanda : Nava-Nalanda Mahavihara
206. Nanjangud : Sri Parimala Samsodhana Mandira
207. Nasik : Hansraj Pragji Thakersey College
208. Navsari : First Dastur Meharji Rana Library
209. Negapatam : Trichinopoly Krishna Iyar Collection
210. Nelbari (Assam) : Purva Bharati

| | |
|---|---|
| 211. Ollur | :Kumarapuram Palace |
| 212. Paingin | : Sri Kamalanatha Tirtha Sanskrit Grantha Sangrahalaya |
| 213. Panipat | : Jin Mandira |
| 214. Panna | : Private Library of the Maharaja |
| 215. Patan | : Hemacandracarya Jaina Jnana Mandira |
| 216. Patiala | : Central Public Library |
| 217. | : Moti Bagh Pustakalaya |
| 218. | : Punjabi Bhasa Vibhag |
| 219. | : Punjabi University |
| 220. | : Punjab State Archives |
| 221. Patna | : Bihar and Orissa Research Society |
| 222. | : Bihar Rastrabhaṣa Parishad |
| 223. | : Bihar Research Society |
| 224. | : Chaitanya Pustakalaya |
| 225. | : Khuda Baksh Oriental Public Library |
| 226. | : K.P.Jaiswal Research Institute |
| 227. | : University Library |
| 228. Pondichery | : Institute Francais d'indology |
| 229. Pudukottai | : Vani Vilas Veda Sastra Pathasala |
| 230. Pune | : Bhandarkar Oriental Research Institute |
| 231. | : Bharat Itihasa Samsodhana Mandala |
| 232. | : Deccan College |
| 233. | : Deccan College Post-graduate & Research Institute |
| 234. | : Fergusson College |
| 235. | : Mimamsa Vidyalaya |
| 236. | : Tilak Maharastra Vidyapitha |
| 237. | : Vaidika Samsodhana Mandala |
| 238. | : Veda Sastra Uttejaka Sabha |
| 239. | : University Library |
| 240. Raipur | : D.S.V.Sanskrit Mahavidyalaya |
| 241. Rajah-mundry | : Andhra Historical Research Society |
| 242. Rajapur | : Sanskrit Pathasala |

243. Rajashahi : Virendra Research Society
244. Rajkot : Saurashtra University
245. Rampur : Raza Library
246. Rangpur : Sahitya Parishad
247. Rewa : Private Library of the Maharaja
248. Sambalpur : University Department of History
249. Sangrur : Jind State Public Library
250. Santiniketan: Visvabharati
251. Sardarshahar:Gadia Pustakalaya
252. Sikar : Sri Mahavira Pustakalaya
253. Sravanabelaogola : Jaina Mutt.
254. Srinagar : Directorate of Library, Museum and Research
255. : Kashmir University Library
256. : Sanskrit Manuscripts Library, Kashmir University
257. Sringeri : Mutt of H.H.Sri Sankaracarya of Saradapitha
258. Sriperum-budur : Ubhayavedanta Sanskrit College
259. Srirangam : Ahobila Mutt
260. : Ranganathasvami Devasthanam Museum and Library
261. Surat : Chunilal Gandhi Vidya Bhavan
262. : Sri Mohanlal Jaina Jnana Bhandara
263. Svadi : Jaina Mutt
264. Sylhet : Ani Pandit Library
265. Thanjavur : Palace Library
266. : Tamil University
267. : Maharaja Serfoji's Sarasvati Mahal Library
268. Tirupati : Kendriya Sanskrit Vidyapitha
269. : Sri Venkatesvara Oriental Research Institute
270. : Sri Venketesvara University

271. Tiruvananta-puram : Curator's Office Library
272. : Maharaja's Palace Library
273. : Oriental Research Institute and Manuscripts Library, Kerala University
274. Tonk : Arabic and Persian Research Institute, Rajasthan
275. Trichur : Brahmasva Matham
276. : Brahmasva Vaddakke Matham
277. : Naduvil Matham
278. : Tekkamatham
279. Tripunithura : Government Sanskrit College
280. Tumkur : Sri Siddalingesvara Sanskrit College and Veda Pathasala
281. Udaipur : Sri Aurobindo Sangrahalaya
282. : Hindi Vidyapitha
283. : Nathadvara Library
284. : Sahitya Samsthan, Rajasthan Vidyapeetha
285. : Sarasvati Bhandar Library of H.H. the Maharaja of Udaipur, Mewar
286. Udavada : Dastura Kaioji Mirja Institute
287. Udipi : Krsnapur Mutt
288. : Mutt of Sri Madhvacarya Samsthan
289. : Pejavar Mutt
290. : Sanskrit College
291. : S.M.S.P. Sanskrit College
292. Ujjain : Scindia Oriental Institute
293. : Oriental Manuscripts Library
294. Vaishali : Pali Research Institute
295. Varanasi : Banaras Hindu University
296. : Bharat Kala Bhavan, Banaras Hindu University
297. : Goenka Sanskrit Mahavidyalaya Library
298. : Sri Jnansimhasana Mutt
299. : Nagari Pracarini Sabha University

300. Varanasi : Sampurnanand Sanskrit Uni. Library
301. : S.R.Gaekwad Library
302. : Sri Syadvada Digambara Jaina Mahavidyalaya
303. Varanga : Jaina Matha
304. Vengurla : College Library
305. Vijayawada : S.R.R.College
306. Vizianagaram : Maharaja's Sanskrit College
307. Vrindaban : Vrindaban Research Institute
308. Wai : Prajna Pathasala Mandala
309. Waltair : Andhra University Library
310. Warangal : Historical Research Society
311. : Kakatiya University
312. Yavatamala : Sardasram

## OUTSIDE INDIA

1. Aberystwyth : National Library
2. Berlin : Deutsche Staatsbibliothek
3. : Stastsbibliothek Preussischer Kulturbesitz
4. Berne : Musee Historique
5. Bonn : Universitatsbibliothek
6. Breslau : Staats Und Universitatsbibliothek
7. Calw : Hermann-Gundert Museum
8. Cambridge : Fitzwilliam Museum
9. : King's College Library
10. : University Library
11. : Trinity College
12. Canberra : Australian National University Library
13. Colombo : National Museum Library
14. : The Ceylon Government Oriental Library
15. Copenhagen : Bibliothecae Universitatis Havniensis
16. : Royal Library
17. Dacca : University Library
18. Darlington : Public Museum
19. Dublin : Trinity College

| | |
|---|---|
| 20. Edinburg | : New College |
| 21. | : University Library |
| 22. Erlangen-Nurnberg | : Universitatsbibliothek |
| 23. Evora | : Bibliotheca Publica |
| 24. Geneva | : University Library |
| 25. Glasgow | : Hunterian Museum |
| 26. Goettingen | : Universitats-bibliothek |
| 27. Gotha | : Landesbibliothek |
| 28. Halle | : Deutsche Morgenlandische Gesellschaft |
| 29. Heidelberg | : Sudasien Institute |
| 30. Kandy | : Oriental Library |
| 31. Karachi | : Anjuman Tarakoqi-e-Urdu |
| 32. | : Kutub Khanah-yi Hamdard |
| 33. | : Urdu Development Board |
| 34. Kathmandu | :Bir Pustakalaya |
| 35. | : Durbar Library |
| 36. Kazan | : Biblioteke Imperatorskago Kazanska Universiteta Charniascimsja |
| 37. Lahore | : Central Urdu Board |
| 38. | : D.A.V.College |
| 39. | : Museum Library |
| 40. | : Panjab Public Library |
| 41. | : Panjab University Library |
| 42. | : Research Society of Pakistan |
| 43. | : Shafi Mohammed Library |
| 44. Leiden | : University Library |
| 45. London | : British Museum |
| 46. | : India Office Library |
| 47. | : Royal Asiatic Society |
| 48. | : School of Oriental and African Studies, London University |
| 49. | : Wellcome Historical Medical Res. Library |
| 50. Lund | : Universitetsbibliotek |
| 51. Manchester | : John Rylands Library |

52. Mandalay : Palace Library
53. Mannanam : Vatican Library
54. Marburg : Staatsbibliothek
55. Melbourne : National Gallary of Victoria
56. Muenchen : Bayerische Staatsbibliothek
57. New York : Army Medical Library
58. Oxford : Bodlein Library
59. : Indian Institute
60. Paris : Bibliotheque Nationale
61. : Societe Asiatique
62. : Universite Sorbonne
63. Philadelphia : Free Library John Frederick Collection
64. Princeton : University Library
65. Providence : Brown University Library
66. Rangoon : Bernard Free Library
67. : Government High School
68. Rome : Bibliotheka Vaticana
69. Stockholm : State Ethnography Museum
70. Strasbourg : Bibliotheoue Nationale Universitaire
71. Stuttajurt : Linden Museum
72. Tokyo : University Library
73. Tuebingen : Universitatsbibliothek
74. Uppasala : University Library
75. Warzburg : University Library
76. Washington : Library of Congress
77. Wien : Universitatsbibliothek
78. Wolfenbuettel: Bibliothecae Regiae Dresdensis

# GLOSSARY

## SOME TECHNICAL TERMS

### (i) (English)

(Based on the Glossary in Katre (1944), pp.90ff)

*Accidental* : not deliberate; applied especially to errors which are not committed intentionally or consciously but occur due to chance.

*Abscript* : an insertion within the text, may be interlinear or marginal.

*Amorphous* : unorganised; applied to a text which is not fixed, such a text is also called a fluid text. In general it refers to popular texts like the epics and the purāṇas which exist already in different versions at different places before being reduced to writing.

*Amplification* : enlargement, addition of details; refers to the additional passages or interpolations found in a transmitted text.

*Anagrammatism* : transposition of letters; formation of words with the letters of adjoining words.

*Archetype* : original model; applied to the hypothetical common ancestor of a family or group of manuscripts. Ordinarily it is applied to any hypothetical common parent codex of any group of manuscripts or codices, irrespective of whether it is immediately derived from the autograph of the text before the breaking of its transmission into several strands or is only an intermediary hypothetical link in the transmission after the first division takes place in the transmission. But strictly speaking, continues Katre, it is better to reserve the name for that common source of all extant manuscripts in which the first divergence took place with reference to its transmission. For intermediate links the terms *Hyparchetypus* or *Sub-archetype* may be used.

*Athetisation* : conscious omission with a purpose; used when a portion of text which is conflated, is dropped if it is not intrinsically borne out.

*Authenticity* : validity of a reading as being original or not.

*Autograph* : the original copy of a text as written by the author himself, or the copy revised by the author in his own hand.

*Codex* (pl. codices) : a manuscript volume.

*Codex unicus* : single extant copy of a work.

*Conjecture* : the application of human ingenuity in proposing a reading in a text by process of common-sense guess sometimes beyond the evidence of manuscripts. Such a 'correction' of reading is called *'conjectural emendation.'*

*Collation* : the collection for comparison, of all the significant evidence; in codices and testimonia of a text, leading to the determination of the original reading.

*Colophon* : the tail piece of a codex or a section thereof, recording the ending of a section, part or the whole work itself as well as the name and other details of the author; it may also include the date.

*Conflation* : mixing; crossing the different lines of transmission of a text by a comparison of manuscripts belonging to independent lines of transmission.

*Constituted text* : 'transmitted text'; the text of the archetype arrived at on the evidence of extant manuscripts.

*Contamination:* crossing of two independant versions, sub-recensions or recensions or of two codices belonging to different versions or recensions.

*Corrector/Reviser* : the person, may be the scribe himself, who goes over a transcript and corrects the scribal errors by comparison with the exemplar.

*Corruption:* spoiling of a text by mistake, addition, omission etc., deliberately or accidentally.

*Critical Apparatus*: the critical material collated from the manuscripts of a 'transmitted text' on the evidence of which the critical recension is arrived at. Normally given as footnote below the constituted text.

*Critical Recension*: a text restored as far as possible to its original form, by following certain principles.

*Dittography*: accidental repetition of a letter, word or phrase while writing.

*Documental probability:* See Extrinsic probability.

*Ecletic* : selecting, choosing from various sources.

*Editio princeps*: The first or foremost edition; principal edition.

*Emendatio* : emendation, the third stage in classical philology of textual criticism; restoring the 'transmitted text' as far as possible to the original form.

*Examinatio* : Examination, the continuous study of the codices and noticing their peculiarities with a view to judging the trustworthiness of each codex.

*Exemplar* : a codex from which a transcript is directly made.

*Extant* : existing (codex).

*Extrinsic* (or External) probability: the probability that a reading can be derived from another due to the resemblance of script; Also Transcriptional/Documental probability.

*Gloss* : an explanation, by means of a marginal or interlinear note.

*Haphazard transmission:* see *Transmission*.

*Haplography*: omission of words or syllables with the same beginning or ending.

*Heuristics*: assembling of the manuscript, testimonia etc., and fixing their mutual relationship.

*Higher Criticism*: The fourth aspect of textual criticism.

*Homoeorarcta* : loss of lines between two lines which begin similarly.

*Homoeotraphon*: loss of letters, syllables, words, phrases or lines through similarity of writing.

*Homoeoteleuta*: loss of lines between two lines which end similarly.

*Hyparchetype* (sub-archetype) : the hypothetical source of extant manuscripts lower down in the transmission of the text than the archetype. It represents the second divergence in the line of tradition, the first starting with the archetype itself.

*Hypermetric* (verse): having redundant syllable/s.

*Hypothetical common ancestor:* a manuscript which is no longer extant but whose existence at some point of time is assumed to explain the relation found between the extant manuscripts.

*Illumination*: decoration of manuscripts with various designs, gold, colour etc.

*Immediate copy*: the copy made directly from the autograph.

*Interlinear*: between the lines.

*Interpolation*: literally, polishing or improvement by polishing; intentional insertion of words, passages etc. within a text.

*Interpretation* : exegesis, explanation, making out meaning of words/sentences.

*Intrinsic Probability* : the probability depending upon the meaning of the context.

*Lacuna* (pl. lacunae) : gap in a manuscript for some reason - some part missed accidentally or due to inability of the scribe to decipher the exemplar, or damage to the exemplar; or damage to the extant codex.

*Lemma* (pl. lemmata): a word at the beginning of a verse or sentence in a text cited by the commentator for reference.

*Lipography*: simple omission of any kind.

*Lower Criticism*: criticism applied to the verbal aspect of a text, to find what an author might have had written and does not address itself to how of it or the equipment of the author which is higher criticism.

*Manuscript*: hand-written copy of any text.

*Marginalia*: writing on the margins of a manuscript.

*Misch-codex*: a mixed or conflated manuscript; intermingling of different streams of independent versions.

*Original*: what is intended by the author.

*Pedigree of Codices:* chart in the form of family tree showing the interrelation of extant manuscripts. Stemma codicum.

*Presumptive variants*: the isolated reading in conflated manuscripts, which cannot be treated as corrupt due to lack of positive evidence and therefore to be taken as variants. Otherwise, such readings are not considered as variants.

*Probability*: two types: Extrinsic and Intrinsic. q.v.

*Protected Transmission*: See *Transmission.*

*Received text:* a text as it has come down in its normalised form, often called vulgate, a term applied to the Latin version of the Bible of Jerome - as opposed to the critical text or edition. *Textus receptus.*

*Recensio*: critical examination; restoration of the text to the original form as far as possible.

*Recension*: the first line of division of the transmission from the archetype. The secondary division of the recension would be sub-recension and further, version and sub-version.

*Redaction:* editing; putting into a literary form.

*Redactor:* editor.

*Reviser* : see *Corrector.*

*Scholium* (pl.scholia): commentary; originally, grammarian's marginal note on a word or phrase in a classical author.

*Scriptal fixation*: the reduction of a text existing in oral transmission only to written form for the first time.

*Siglum*(pl.sigla): a sign to identify a codex for easy reference in the discussion of the peculiarities etc. of the codices and in the critical apparatus; usually a letter of the alphabet (Roman, Devanāgarī etc.) accompanied by a numeral, regular or super-script or infra-script; assignment of an alphabet may be arbitrary or may be indicative of the script or the source.

*Solecism*: clear violation of grammar or accepted usage.

*Stemma codicum*: see *Pedigree.*

*Sub-recension* : the source of divergence when it is itself one of the different streams of transmission branching off from a recension.

*Sub-variant:* variant in the sub-recension or version, useful in the constitution of the text of the recension.

*Testimonium* (pl.testimonia): evidence other than direct or evidence of the manuscripts, for restoration of the transmitted text; found in quotations, commentaries, translation, adaptation, resume, parody and so on; hence this is indirect and is of partial nature.

*Textual Dynamics*: textual criticism of a *fluid* text represented by a *fluctuating* tradition, i.e. of a text not fixed at any period of its transmission but growing from time to time; expression coined by Sukthankar.

*Textual Statics*: textual criticism of a text fixed and rigid at the time of transmission.

*Textus ornator*: an ornate text; the recension or version or codex where the fuller text of a work is preserved.

*Textus simplicior*: a simple text, the recension or version or codex where the shorter text of a work is preserved.

*Textus receptus*: see *Received text.*

*Tradition* : the history of textual transmission.

*Traditional reading*: a reading supported both by the manuscripts and the testimonia. cf. transmitted reading.

*Transcript*: a copy of text made by hand.

*Transcriptional probability*: see *Extrinsic probability.*

*Transmission:* The survival of a text through a line of copies made from the original or intermediary copies; may be haphazard or protected; haphazard is that situation which is covert and where the copying is not supervised by some recognised authority, chances of corruptions are more; Protected is that situation which is overt, where bonafide persons are involved and copying done under some recognised authority.

*Transmitted reading*: a reading supported by manuscripts alone. cf. traditional reading.

*Transmitted text*: the text of the archetype.

*Varia lectione* (pl. Variae lectiones): Variant reading or variant.

*Variant*: one of the several readings which can be that of the text being constituted.

*Variant bearer*: a codex whose readings may be considered for the constitution of a text.

*Version*: branching off from the sub-recension or from the recension itself.

*Vulgate*: see Revised text

### (ii) Sanskrit

*akṣara* A letter: written or incised.

*akṣara-caṇa/-cuñcu/-jīvaka(-jīvika)/-jīvana*: professional scribe.

*akṣara-janan* : lekhanī.

*akṣara-jīvaka/jīvana* : see *akṣara-caṇa*.

*akṣara-tūlikā* : brush like pen for writing.

*akṣara-bhitti/akṣara-bhūmikā* : something with a plain surface to write on. cf. bhitti and lipyāsana.

*akṣara-mudrā* : abbreviation.

*akṣara-muṣṭikā* : art of communication through movement of fingers.

*akṣara-(vi)nyāsa* : writing.

*agaru-patra/-valkala* : bark of agaru tree.

*agrya-pāṭha* : see *pāṭha*.

*ajina* : parchment.

*atasī-valkala* : bark of atasī tree.

*anukramaṇī* : index; classified list.

*antaḥ-sambhāvyatā* : see *sambhāvyatā*.

*antara-patra* : book mark.

*anyathā-karaṇa* : changing, altering.

*apapāṭha* : see *pāṭha*.

*abuddhi-pūrvaka-dūṣana* : see *dūṣaṇa*.

*ayukta-pāṭha* : see *pāṭha*.

*avagraha* : mark of separation ('s') of component parts of a compound; 'hyphen'.

*asamagra* : incomplete.

*asāmpradāyika-pāṭha* : see *pāṭha*.

*āgantuka-pāṭha*. : see *pāṭha*.

*āgama-bhraṁśa* : break in tradition.

*ādarśa-pustaka* : see pustaka.

*ārṣa-pāṭha : see paṭha.*

*iṣika/iṣīka : a kind of read used as pen.*

*uddharaṇa* : quotations; citation.

*uddhṛta* : quoted, cited.

*upakrama* : beginning; a few lines in the beginning of a manuscript reproduced in a descriptive catalogue.

*upapradhāna-ādarśa* : sub-archetype.

*upalabdha* : extant, also labhya-.

*upasaṁhāra*: end. a few lines at the end of a manuscript reproduced in a descriptive catalogue.

*upādāna-sambhāra* : a set of writing and/or painting instruments including ink and paints.

*ūhātmaka-saṁskaraṇa*: see *saṁskaraṇa*.

*kakkhaṭī* : kaṭhinī.

*kacela* : cover/string keeping together leaves of a manuscript.

*kacchapī* : a form of codex ('tortoise-line').

*kajjala*: black soot.

*kajjala-rasa* : masi.

*kaṭhinī* : pot-stone steatite pencil. Also kakkhaṭī, khaṭī, etc.

*kaḍita* (Kannaḍa) : a form of codex, specially prepared with cotton cloth.

*kaṇṭaka/kaṇṭha*: stylus to incise on palm leaf. Also loha-kaṇṭaka.

*kambī*: a strip of metal/wood to keep track of the line while reading.

*karaṇika* : kāyastha.

*kaladhauta-lipi* : see *lipi*.

*kākapāda* : caret. Also haṁsapāda, svastika.

*kācana(ka)* : a string/tape which ties a bundle of leaves of a codex.

*kācanakin* : kośa.

*kāñcana-ketakī-dala* : leaf of golden ketakī flower.

*kāñcana-lekhanī* : golden pen.

*kāyastha* : official scribe. Also karaṇika.

*kārpāsika-paṭa* : cotton cloth for writing.

*kuñca/kuñci(kā)* : brush. See also *tūlikā*.

*kuṭila-lipi* : see *lipi*.

*kuṇḍalana* : encircling a blank space in a line indicating illegible or lost letter/s in the exemplar.

*kulakhaṇī* : bed, irresponsible, indescent scribe.

*kūcī* : =citralekhanī

*ketakī-patra* : petal of ketakī flower.

*kośa (1)/kācanakin* : codex. See also pustaka, pratilipi, mātṛkā.

*kośa* (2) : library.

*kośa-śuddhi* : trust-worthiness/correctness of a codex.

*kraya-cīrikā* : sale deed written on a cloth.

*krimi* : worm, book-worm.

*krimi-daṣṭa* : worm-eaten.

*kroḍa-patra* : marginal notes; post-script; supplement. cf. prāntalekhana.

*khaṭī/khaṭinī/khaṭikā/*

*khaṭīdala/khaṭinī-dala* : =kaṭhinī.

*khaṭikā-samudgaka* : box with chalk/crayons.

*kharatāla* : =tāḍa.

*gaṇḍī* : a form of Ms.: thickness corresponding to length; square.

*guṭka* : a Ms. of small size (15x20 cms.) paper sheets stitched in the middle or sides.

*guṇḍika-lipi* : see *lipi*.

*goḍavaca* : a herb used in preservation of Mss.

*gorocana* : yellow pigment to erase a letter or to paint.

*grantha-pāta* : lacuna; loss/omission of a word, a passage or a page.

*grantha/grantha-saṅkhyā/ śloka-saṅkhyā* : unit of 32 letters in speaking about the bulk of a work; also useful in fixing the rate for purchase of Mss. and for manual transcription of Mss. Obtained by multiplying the number of letters in a line, the number of lines in a page and the number of pages and dividing the product by 32.

*granthāgāra/granthālaya* : library. Also Sarasvatī-bhaṇḍāra etc., paṭṭaśālā, śāstra-śālā.

*ghuṇa* : termite-like insect infecting wood; lyctus brunneus.

*ghuṇa-sambhūta-lipi/ghuṇākṣara* : see lipi.

*citta-doṣa* : intentional error. cf. dṛṣṭi-doṣa. See also dūṣaṇa.

*citra-lekhanikā/kūcī* : paint brush.

*cīra* : bark, rough and thick. cf. valkala.

*cīrikā* : cotton cloth prepared for writing, 'document'. vol. cīṭhikā.

*chadana* : cotton cloth cover of Ms.

*chedapaṭi/chivaḍi/śṛpāṭikā* : a form of Ms. thin book of a few leaves; 'book-let'.

*tamāla-rasa* : juice of tamāla leaves, used for writing messages to be delivered immediately.

*tāḍa/tāla* : narrow, thick yellowish variety of palm leaf, *Borassus flabellifernis*. Also kharatāla.

*tāḍī/tāla* : broad, thin, brown variety of palm leaf, *Corypha umbraculifera* and *Corypha faliera*. Also śrītāla, tālipāt.

*tāmra-patra/-phalaka*: Copper plate for writing.

*teja(ḥ)-patra*: leaf of Larrus cassia.

*tūlī/tūlikā.* : a feather used for writing or to paint.

*tūlipāt/tālipāt* : = tāḍī.

*trīpāṭhī/trivalli* : a style of writing a text and its commentary; see also *pañcapāṭhī*.

*truṭika* : insect destroying books.

*truṭita* : broken, mutilated.

*daṇḍa* : a punctuation mark : full stop; vertical line, single or double (I II), virāma.

*durlipi* : see *dūṣaṇa*.

*duṣṭa-pāṭha*.

*dūṣaṇa* : error, mistake, mislection.
- *abuddhipūrvaka-* : Involuntary/mechanical error.
- *durlipi-* : writing wrongly.
- *pada-bheda-* : substitution, transposition.
- *bindu-*: omission/wrong use of nasal sign.
- *buddhi-pūrvaka-* : voluntary/intended error.
- *visarga-*: omission or wrong use of visarga.
- *vīthikā-*: Not maintaining the line of writing.
- *śṛṅgapatti-*: omission or wrong use of serifs or vowel signs.
- *hastavegaja* : error due to haste or running hand.

*dūṣikā* : brush.

*dṛṣṭi-doṣa* : visual/mechanical error. cf. cittadoṣa. See also dūṣaṇa.

*dhātu-rasa*: soft stone - usually red - used to write pictures in particular.

*navatikā* : paint brush (with 90 hairs).

*navīna-pustaka* : See pustaka.

*pañcapāṭhī*: a style of writing a text and its commentary; see also *tripāṭhī*.

*paṭa/paṭikā/ paṭṭa/paṭṭaka/paṭṭikā* : sheet like material for writing; copper plate, cotton cloth or palm leaf.

*paṭṭaśālā* : =granthāgāra.

*patitākṣara* : omission of letter.

*patra* : a leaf; a sheet of paper or of metal like copper.

*patra-saṅkhyā* : folio number.

*patrāñjana* : paste like black ink used to blacken the letters of an incised palm leaf.

*pada-bheda* : see dūṣaṇa.

*pariṣkaraṇa* : textual criticism (process).

*pariṣkartṛ.* : text- critical editor.

*pariṣkāra* : text- critical edition.

*pariṣkṛta* : critically edited.

*pāṭha* : a reading.

*agrya* - : best/preferable reading.
*apapāṭha* : wrong/erroneous reading.
*ayukta-* : inappropriate reading.
*asāmpradāyika-*: non-traditional reading.
*āgantuka-* : imported reading.
*ārṣa-* : vedic or epic usage (archaic).
*duṣṭa-* : bad/ corrupted reading.
*deśāntara-* : reading current in a different area.
*pustaka-* : reading in the book/Ms.; perhaps to distinguish from a reading transmitted orally.
*pramāda-* : erroneous reading in general.
*prācīna-* : older reading i.e., that found in older copies.
*bhrānta-*: confused reading.
*yukta-*: appropriate reading.
*sādhu-*: acceptable reading.

*sāmpra 'āyika-*: traditional reading.

*pāṭha-mīmāṁsā/-vimarśā* : critical editing.

*pāṭha-yojanā* : recension.

*pāṭha-lopa* : omission.

*pāṭha-vimarśā* : pāṭha-mīmāṁsā.

*pāṭha-saṁśodhana/-śodha* : selection of appropriate reading.

*pāṭha-saṁskaraṇa/-saṁskāra*: see saṁskāra.

*pāṭha-sākṣi-grantha*: testimonium.

*pāṭha-sāmya* : identity of reading.

*pāṭhādhikya* : additions.

*pāṭhāntara* : variant reading.

*pāṭhāntara-karaṇa* : substituting a different reading.

*pāṇḍu-lipi/-lekha(na)* : draft, drafting, manuscript.

*pānāvalī* : a form of Ms. oblong sheets stitched on the shorter side.

*punar-mudraṇa* : reprint.

*punar-lekhana* : dittography.

*purātana-pustaka* : see *pustaka*.

*pustaka* : book, manuscript. See also kośa, pratilipi.
*ādarśa-* : exemplar.
*navīna-*: a recent copy.
*purātana-/prācīna-*: older copy (older copy)
*prāmāṇika-*: trustworthy copy.

*pustaka-pāṭha*: see *pāṭha*.

*pustakopacaryā* : care of book/manuscript.

*puṣpikā* : colophon.

*pothī/potho* : book with paper sheets centre stitched; pothi is smaller in size and thickness than potho. Book with unstitched oblong sheets.

*prakṣepa* : interpolation (voluntary).

*prakṣipta* : interpolated (voluntary). cf. viśrasta.

*prati* : copy.

*pratikaraṇa/pratilipi-karaṇa* : making a copy. cf. *lipyantarakaraṇa*.

*prati-nidhāna* : substitution.

*prati-pustaka* : a copy, a manuscript. Also kośa, pustaka.

*prati-lipi* : copy, manuscript, transcription.

*prati-lipi-/pustaka-vijñāna* : Manuscriptology.

*pratīka* : lemma.

*pradhāna-ādarśa* : archetype.

*upapradhāna-*: sub-archetype.

*pramāda* : error, corruption. Also skhālitya.

*pramāda-pāṭha* : see *pāṭha.*

*prāmāṇika-pustaka* : see *pustaka.*

*praśasti* : eulogy; laudation usually at the end of a work.

*prācīna-pāṭha* : see *pāṭha.*

*prācīna-pustaka* : see *pustaka.*

*prānta-lekhana* : marginalia. cf. kroḍapatra.

*phalaka* : plank or plate.

*bāhya-sambhāvyatā* : see *sambhāvyatā.*

*bindu* : see *dūṣaṇa*

*buddhipūrvaka-*: see *dūṣaṇa*

*bṛhannāla-sūcī* : a kind of read used as pen.

*bhāratī-mandira* : *sarasvatī-prāsāda.*

*bhitti* : a plain surface suitable especially for painting; literally, wall. See also Akṣara-bhitti. cf. lipyāsana.

*bhūrja-patra/-tvak* : birch bark.

*bhrānta-*: see *pāṭha.*

*manaḥ-śilā* : natural soft material used as paint. cf. *dhātu.*

*maṇi-samudga* : jewelled casket.

*maṣi-kupikā/-ghaṭa/-dhānī/-pātra/-bhājana/-bhāṇḍa/-mallikā* : ink-pot. Also *melananda, melandhu(ka).*

*masi-guṭikā* : ink-pill.

*mātṛkā* : manuscript. Also kośa, pustaka.

*mudrā-lipi* : incised letter; impressed letter.

*muṣṭi* : a mini manuscript as can be held in a fist.

*mṛt.* : earthen brick/tablet to write on.

*melā* : masi

*melananda/melandhu(ka)* : *masi-kupikā.*

*yukta-pāṭha* : see *pāṭha.*

*rūpakṛt* : sculptor particularly of stone (*Kan.*: *rūvāri*)

*rekhāpaṭi* : ruler.

*raupya-patra* : a silver plate.

*labhya-pratilipi* : extant copy.

*lipi* : writing, script.

*kaladhauta* : writing in gold.

*kuṭila-* : running hand, cursive; not easily decipherable.

*guṇḍika-* : writing with any powder.

*ghuṇa-sambhūta-* : letter like path cut by insect ghuṇa.

*mudrā-*: produced by pressing a die; incised.

*lekhanī-sambhūta-*: produced by a pen, 'pen-style'.

*śilpa* : incised on a metal sheet/stone 'stylus-style'

*lipi-kara/-kāra* : scribe.

*lipi-phalaka* : writing board, slate.

*lipi-bhrānti* : confusion of scripts.

*lipi-śālā* : elementary school.

*lipi-sajjā/-sambhāra/*
*-sādhana/-sāmagrī* : stationery. Also lekhana-sāmagrī.

*lipyakṣara* : writing letter.

*lipyantara-karaṇa* : transcribing into a different script. cf. *prati-lipi-karaṇa.*

*lipyāsana* : paper and the like. cf. Akṣarabhitti; ink-pot(?); low stand to keep the book while reading (?).

*lekhaka* : author. scribe.

*lekhaka-pramādar* : scribal error

*lekhana-kāṇḍa* : = lekhanī.

*lekhana-sāmagrī* : = lipi-sajjā.

*lekhana-sambhāvyatā* : See sambhāvyatā.

*lekhanī* : pen, writing instrument in general. Also lekhana-kāṇḍa, akṣarajananī.

*lekhanī-sambhūta-lipi* : see *lipi.*

*lekhya-kūrcikā* : brush like pen.

*lekhya-vastu* : paper and such material. cf. bhitti.

*lopa* : omission.

*loha-kaṇṭaka* : = kaṇṭaka.

*vaṭapatra* : banyan leaf.

*vaṁśa* : bamboo (chips).

*varjana* : rejection (of a reading).

*varti(kā)/varṇa-vartikā* : brush for painting.

*vartikā-karaṇḍa* : casket for brushes.

*varṇaka/varṇikā*: colours particularly for painting.

*valkala* : bark, soft like birch. cf. cīra.

*vācaka* : reader of a book.

*vicchedaka-skhālitya* : see *skhālitya*.

*viparyasta* : transposed.

*virāma* : daṇḍa, full stop.

*viśiṣṭa-skhālitya* : see *skhālitya*.

*viśrasta* : introduced; interpolated. cf. prakṣipta.

*visarga* : see *dūṣaṇa*.

*vīthikā* : see *dūṣaṇa*.

*vṛkṣa-tvak* : rough bark. cf. valkala, cīra

*veṣṭana* : binding (thread) of a codex.

*vyatyāsa* : interchange of letters in particular

*vyatyasta* : interchanged.

*vyākīrṇa* : conflated.

*vyākhyāna* : commentary.

*vyāsapīṭha* : a low stand to keep the book while reading, usually foldable. cf. śara-śalākā-yantra, lipyāsana.

*śambūka* : a conch shell - used as ink pot.

*śaya* : paper.

*śaraśalākā-yantra* : = vyāsapīṭha.

*śalākā* (1) : stylus. Also sūcī

*śalākā* (2) : bamboo chip with writing, used as passport.

*śalākā-yantra* : śaraśalākāyantra.

*śalabha* : cockroach or beetle.

*śāstra-śālā* : = granthāgāra.

*śilātala/śilā-phalaka*: dressed stone for writing.

*śilpa-lipi* : see *lipi*.

*śilpī* : artisan, sculptor.

*śuṇḍa* : a style of writing; tapering.

*śṛṅkhalā* : chain; perhaps the pen had a chain the other end being tied to the ink-pot.

*śṛṅgapatti* : see *dūṣaṇa*.

*śṛpāṭikā* : see *chedapaṭi*.

*śodha-patra* : collation sheet.

*śrī-tāla* : = tālī.

*śloka-saṅkhyā* : = grantha-saṅkhyā.

*saṁyojaka-skhālitya* : see *skhālitya*.

*saṁskaraṇa/pāṭha-saṁskaraṇa* : emending. (usually, edition).

*saṁskāra/pāṭha-saṁskāra* : emendation.

*śūhātmaka* : conjectural emendation.

*sācipāt* : bark of sāci tree.

*sadyaḥ-pratilipi* : immediate copy.

*sādhu-pāṭha*: see *pāṭha*.

*sandigdha-* : doubtful (about a reading).

*samagra* : complete.

*samāsapaṭi* : a device for marking straight lines on a palm leaf or a sheet of paper.

*samudga(ka)* : casket.

*sampādaka* : editor.

*sampādana* : editing.

*savimarśa-* : critical editing.

*sampādita* : edited.

*sampuṭa/sampuṭikā* : box/casket with a set of writing materials.

*sampuṭa-phalaka* (1) : codex with wooden side boards

*sampuṭa-phalaka* (2) : foldable wooden plane/boards, (two/three boards joined so as to fold them).

*sambhāvyatā* : probability.

*antaḥ-*: intrinsic probability.

*bāhya-/lekhana-* : extrinsic/transcriptional probability.

*sarasvatī-bhaṇḍāra/-bhāṇḍgāra/prāsāda* : = *granthāgāra*. Also bhāratī-mandira, paṭṭāśālā.

*savimarśa-sampādana* : see *sampādana*.

*sāmagrī-saṅkalana* : heuristics.

*sūcī* (1) : *śalākā* (1); nail.

*sūcī* (2) : index. cf. Anukramaṇī.

*skhālitya* : error, corruption. Also pramāda.

*sūcaka* - indicative error.

*saṁyojaka*- : conjective error.

*vicchedaka*- : separating error.

*viśiṣṭa*-: peculiar error.

*svarna-patra* : gold plate.

*svastika* : caret. cf. kākapada.

*svahasta-pratilipi* : autograph copy.

*svīkaraṇa* : acceptance (of a reading).

*haṁsapāda* : = kākapāda

*hasta-vegaja*-: see dūṣaṇa.

*hasta-lekha* : draft, copy writing.

# BIBLIOGRAPHY

## Texts


*Amarakośa*. Mysore, Prasaranga, University of Mysore, 1970.

*Arthaśāstra*. Kauṭilya. Ed. R. Shamasastri, Rev. Ed. N.S. Venkatanathacharya, Mysore, Oriental Research Institute, Vth edn. 1986.

*Āryamañju-Śrīmūla-kalpa*. Ed. T. Ganapati Sastri, Trivandrum 1920 (TSS).

*Bṛhatkathākośa*. Hariṣena. Ed. A.N. Upadhye, Bombay, Bharatiya Vidya Bhavan, 1943.

*Dāsabodha*. Sant Ramadas. 1947, 6th edn.

*Dīgha-nikāya*. Gen ed. Bhikkhu J.Kashyap. Pali Publication Board, Bihar Govt., 1958, 3 vols.

*Harṣa-carita*. Bāṇa. Nirnaya Sagar Press, 1946, 7th edn.

*Jātakaṭṭha-kathā*. Kashi, Bharatiya Jnanapitha, 1951. Vol.1.

*Kapphinabhyudaya*. Śivasvāmin. Ed. Gauri Sankar. Lahore : University of Punjab, 1937.

*Kādambarī*. Bāṇa. Ed: M.R. Kale, Bombay, Gopal Narayan & Co., 1928, 3rd rev. edn.

*Kāvyamīmāṁsā*. Rājaśekhara Ed. Dalal and Sastry, Rev. edn.: K.R.Sastri. Baroda, Oriental Institute, 1934.

*Kāvya-mīmāṁsā* (Kan. tr). K.Krishnamoorthy. Mysore: Sharada Mandira, 1969.

*Lalita-vistara*: Ed. P.C.Vaidya. Darbhanga, Mithila Institute, 1988.

*Lekhapaddhati*: Ed. Chimanlal Dalal Baroda, Central Library, 1925. 2nd edn.

*Mahāvagga*. Gen.Ed. Bhikkhu J. Kashyap. Pali Publication Board, Bihar Govt., 1956.

*Mahāvastu*. Ed. S. Bagchi. Darbhanga, Mithila Institute, 1973.

*Mahāvastu*. (Eng. Tr) J.J. Jones, London, Luzac & Co., 1949, vol. 1, Sacred Books of the Buddhists, vol. 16.

*Naranārāyaṇānanda*. Vastupāla. Ed. Dalal & Sastri. Baroda, Central Library, 1916.

*Pācittiya*. Gen ed. Bhikkhu J. Kashyap. Pali Publication Board, Bihar Govt., 1958.

*Paṇṇavaṇā-sutta*. Ed. Punya Vijaya Muni *et al*. Bombay, Jain Vidyalaya, 1969.

*Pārājika*. Gen. Ed. Bhikkhu J.Kashyap. Pali Publication Board, Bihar Govt., 1958.

*Prabandha-kośa*. Rājaśekhara-sūri. Santiniketan, 1935.

*Prabhāvaka-carita*. Candraprabhasūri. Ed. Hirananda M. Sharma. Bombay, Nirnaya Sagar Press, 1900. Part 1.

*Rājataraṅgiṇī*. Jonarāja. Ed. Raghunath Singh. Varanasi, Chowkhamba, 1972.

*Rāyapaseṇiya-sutta*. Rajkot, ABBS Jaina Sastroddhara Samiti, 1965-66, 2 parts.

*Samavāyaṅga*. Ed. Muni Kanhaiyalal 'Kamal'. Delhi, Agama Anuyog Prakashan, 1966.

*Vaijayantī*. Ed. Oppert. Madras.

*Yoginī-tantra*. Ed. Jivananda Vidya Sagar, Calcutta, 1987. 2nd edn.

## Studies

Agarwal, O.P. (1977): *Care and Maintenance of Museum objects*. Delhi, National Research Laboratory.

Agrawala, V.S. (1946): 'Notes from the Bṛhatkathākośa'. *Journal of U.P.Historical Society*, 19, pp. 78-79.

Agrawala, V.S. (1953): *India as Known to Panini*. Lucknow, University of Lucknow.

Agrawala, V.S. (1961): *Indian Miniatures - an album*. New Delhi.

Agrawala, V.S. (1964): *Heritage of Indian Art*. New Delhi: Publications Division, Govt. of India.

Agrawala, V.S. (1966): 'Devanāgarī lipi.' *Triveni* 11, 6. pp. 162-64.

Altekar, A.S. (1934): *Education in Ancient India*. Banaras, Indian Book Depot.

Anantarangachar, N. (1950): "Kannaḍa Granthasaṁskaraṇaathavā Grantha Sampādane". *Prabuddha Karnataka*, (Mysore), 31,2, pp. 93-115.

Apte, V.S. (1890): *Students' Sanskrit -English Dictionary*, Pooṅa. Repr. Delhi: Motilal Banarsidas, 1976.

Aufrecht, Th. (1891) : *Catalogus Catalogorum*. 3 parts, Heidelberg, 1891; Bonn, 1896, 1903. Repr. Weisbaden, 1962 (2 vols.).

Back, S.A. (1946): 'Book Worms'. *Ind. Arch.*, 1, pp. 126-34.

Banerjee, Satya Ranjan (1988): 'Prakrit Textual Criticism'. *Jain Journal*, 26.3, pp. 87-88.

Banerjee, Satya Ranjan (1989): 'New Vistas in Prakrit Studies.' *New Horizons of Research in Indology*. Pune: CASS, University of Poona, pp. 221-33.

Banerji, Suresh Chandra (1958): 'Epistolary and Documentary Literature in Sanskrit'. *Indian Historical Quarterly*, 34, pp. 226-250.

Bapat, P.V. (1950): 'Another Valuable collection of Buddhist Sanskrit Manuscripts', *Annals of the Bhandarkar Oriental Research Institute*, 33.

Bapat, P.V. (1952): 'A Pali Manuscript in an Indian script.' *Annals of the Bhandarkar Oriental Research Institute*, 33.

Barrow, W.J. (1959): *Manuscripts and Documents, their Deterioration and Restoration*. Sharlontles Ville: University of Virginia Press, Ann Arbor University Microfilms Institute.

Basu, Purnendu (1951): 'Common Enemies of Records'. *Ind.Arch.*, 5.1.

Basu, Purnendu (1960): *Archives and Records, What are they* ? New Delhi: National Archives of India.

Belvalkar, S.K. (1915): (Ed.) *Uttararamacarita*. Cambridge (Mass.): Harvard University Press. Harvard Oriental Series 21-23 Intd., texts tr.

Bhandarkar, D.R. (1922): 'The Origin of Indian Alphabet.' *Sir Asutosh Mookerji Silver Jubilee Volumes*, III, part-1, Calcutta.

Bharati, H.L.N. (1971): *Prācīna Hastapratigaḷu*. Mysore: Prasaranga, University of Mysore.

Bharati, H.L.N. (1988): *An Introduction to Indian Textual Criticism and Modern Book Publishing*. Mysore: Central Institute of Indian Languages.

Bhargava, K.D. (1959): *Repair and Preservation of Books*. New Delhi: National Archives of India. II edn. 1967.

Bhatta, C. Panduranga (1990) : 'Textual Criticism of the *Abhijñāna-śākuntala* on the basis of Kāṭayavema's commentary'. *Adyar Library Bulletin*, pp. 99-110.

Bhattacharya, B. (1946)a : 'Palm leaf Manuscripts and their Preservation.' *Ind. Arch*. 1, pp. 233ff.

Bhattacharya, B. (1946)b : 'Further note on palm leaf Manuscripts'. *Ind.Arch*., 1, pp. 325f.

Bhowmik, S. (1966): 'Conservation of Palm leaf Manuscripts.' *Baroda Museum and Picture Gallery Bulletin*, 19.

Birdeau, Madeleine (1968): 'Some more considerations about Textual Criticism.' *Purāṇa*, 10, pp. 15-23.0

Bordin, Ruth B. & Warner, Robert M. (1966) : *The Modern Manuscripts Library*, New York & London: The Scarecrow Press, Inc.

Bowers, G. (1968) : 'Textual Criticism'. *Encyclopaedia Britannica*, vol. 22. pp. 918ff.

Brown, W.N. (1933)a : *Miniature Paintings in Western India*. Washington.

Brown, W.N. (1933)b: *Story of Kalaka*. Texts, history, legends and Miniature Paintings of Svetambara Jains. Washington.

Brown, W.N. (1941): Manuscript *Illustrations of the Uttarādhyayana Sūtra*. (Reproduced and described). 150 figs. 46 plates. New Haven (Conn.) : American Oriental Society, Amercian Oriental Series. No. 21.

Brown, W.N. (1965): (Ed.) *Mahimna-stava* of Puṣpadanta. Pune: American Institute of Indian Studies.

Bühler, Georg (1896) : *Indian Palaeography*. Strassburg. Eng. tr. 1904. Repr. Indian Series Past and Present, 1962, Calcutta.

Bühler, G. (1898): *On the Origin of the Indian Brahmi Alphabet*. Strassburg. II edn.

Bühler, G. : The Bhattprohu Buddhist Inscription: *Ep.Ind.*, 2.25, pp. 323-29.

Burnell, A.C. (1874): *Elements of South Indian Palaeography*. Mangalore: Basel Mission Press. II edn. 1878. Enlarged and improved edn. 1968, Varanasi: Indological Book House.

Chakravarti. C. (1941): 'The Study of Manuscripts.' *Festschrift P.V.Kane*. Pune: Kane Publication Committee.

Chakravarti, S. (1946)a : 'A study of palm leaf Manuscripts'. *Ind.Arch.*, 1, pp. 12-17.

Chakravariti, S. (1946)b : 'A Review of the Lamination process.' *Ind.Arch.*, 1, pp. 304-12.

Chatterji, S.K. (1940): 'Two Sanskrit-Chinese Lexicons.' *New Indian Antiquary*, 2, pp. 740-67.

Chidananda Murthy, M. See under Sitaramaiah, M.V.

Chopra, Veena (1981) : 'Processing of Sanskrit Books : A study.' *Herald of Library Science* (BHU) 20, pp.160-72.

*Corpus Inscriptionnum Indicarum* Vol.3. Revised. New Delhi, Archeological Survey of India, 1981; 13 (p. 260), 27 (p. 294), 42 (p. 329) etc. clay seals from Nalanda. No. 32. (p. 139).

Dani, Ahmad Hasan (1963): *Indian Palaeography*. Oxford University Press.

Das, J.P. and Williams, Joanna (1991) : *Palm leaf Miniatures : The Art of Raghunath Prusti of Orissa*. New Delhi.

Dasgupta, Charuchandra (1958): *The Development of the Kharosthi Script*. Calcutta: Firma K.L Mukhopadhyaya.

Datta, Bimal Kumar (1970): *Libraries and Librarianship in Ancient and Medieval India*. Delhi: Atmaram.

Desai, P.B. (1956): 'The University of Valabhi'. *Quarterly Journal of Mythic Society*, 47, pp. 107-112.

Deveerappa, H.(1977): *Kannaḍa Hastapratigala Itihāsa*. Bangalore: Kannada Sahitya Parishat.

Dileep, K. (1969): 'The Art of Text-editing and Textual Criticism in Sanskrit Literature.' *Our Heritage*, 17, pp. 41-49.

Diringer, David (1948): *The Alphabet : A key to the history of Mankind*. New York: Philosophical Library.

Diringer, David (1958): *The Illuminated Book, its history and production*. London: Faber & Faber. II edn. 1967.

Diskalkar, D.B. (1977): *Selections from Sanskrit Inscriptions*. New Delhi: Classical Publishers.

Divanji, P.S. (1952): 'Textual Criticism as a Branch of Indology.' *Journal of Oriental Institute*, Baroda, 1, pp. 60-64; 138-150.

De Silva, W.H. (1938): *A Catalogue of palm leaf Manuscripts in the Library of Colombo Museum*. Colombo. Vol. 1.

Dutta, Nalinaksha (1932): 'A Buddhist Manuscript at Gilgit.' *Indian Historical Quarterly*, 8. ii, pp. 93-110.

Edgerton, Franklin (1924): (Ed.) *Pañcatantra*, New Haven (Conn): American Oriental Society.

Edgerton, Franklin (1926): (Ed.) *Vikrama's Adventures*. Cambridge (Mass): Harvard University Press. Part I (Tr. of 4 parallel recensions) and II (text), Harvard Oriental Series 24 and 27.

Emeneau, M.B. (1934): (Ed.) *Jambhāladatta's Version of Vetala Pañcaviṁśati*. New Haven: American Oriental Series 4, American Oriental Society).

*Ep(igraphia) Car(natica)* : Revised.Edn. Mysore: University of Mysore. Vols. 2, 3, 5 and 10. Ed. Rice: Vol.8.

*Ep(igraphia) Ind(ica)*: 2. 25, pp. 323-29, Bühler, G. 'The Bhattiprolu Buddhist Inscription (1-10).
4.5, pp. 54-57. Bühler, G. 'Taxila Plate of Paṭīka.' (1896-97).

4.49. pp. 332-49, Lüders, H. 'Kaḍaba plates of Prabhūtavarṣa.' (1896-97).
5.11 pp. 101-2: Maung Tun Nyein. 'Maunggun Gold Plates'. (1898-99).
8.5, pp. 24-36, Kielhorn, F. 'Tālaguṇḍa Pillar Inscription of Kākusthavarman.' (1905-06).
8.9, pp. 96-122. Hultzsch, E. 'Dhar Praśasti of Arjuna-varman: Pārijātamañjarī Nāṭikā of Madana' (1905-06).
8.25, pp. 241-260. Pischel, R. 'Two Prakrit poems at Dhar.' (1905-06).
11.25, pp. 266-72. Francke, A.H. 'The Tibetan Alphabet'. (1911-12).
12.28, pp. 226-237. Bhandarkar, P.R. 'Kuḍimiyāmalai Inscription on Music'. (1913-14).
17.17, pp. 310-327. Hirananda Sastri. ''Nalanda Plates of Deva-paladeva. (1923-24).
18.19, pp. 152-157. Hirananda Sastri, 'Brahmi Inscription on a wooden pillar from Kirari.' (1925-26)
20.7, pp. 71-89. Jayaswal, K.P. 'Hathigumpha Inscription of Kharavela.' (1929-30)
21.12, pp. 72-77. Hirananda Sastri. ''The clay seals of Nalanda.' (1931-32).
21.32, pp. 193-199. Chakravarti, K.N. ''Two brick Inscriptions from Nalanda''. (1931-32).
21.39, pp. 251-259. Sten Konow. 'Kalawan plate Inscription of the year 134'. (1931-32).
22.1, pp. 1-3. Jayaswal, K.P. 'The text of Sohgauura plate. (1933-34).
24.5, pp. 20-22. Ghosh, A. 'An Inscribed brick from Nalanda of the year 197'. (1937-38).
26.32, pp. 241-246. Altekar, A.S. 'Mangraon Inscription of Viṣṇugupta's times, the year 17'. (1941-42).
28.25, pp. 133-137. Ramachandran, T.N. ''An Inscribed pot and other Buddhist Remains in Salihundum.' (1949-50)
29.34, App. pp. 1-90. Chakravarti, N.P. and Chhabra, B.Ch. 'Rājapraśasti Inscription of Udaipur'. (1952-53).
30. App. 91 ff. -do- (1953-54).

31.4, pp. 25-30, Sastri, K.N. 'Three Paramara Inscription from Malava.' (1955-56).
33.55, pp. 299-302. Gopal, B.R. and Satyanarayana, R. 'Inscription from Bantvala'. (1959-60).
34.7, pp. 33-41. Sircar, D.C. and Sankaranarayanan, S. 'Dharwar plates of the times of Simhana'. (1961-62).
36.27, pp. 209-18. Srinivasan, P.R. and Subrahmanyam, V.S. 'Hanumakoṇḍa Niroṣṭhya-kāvya.' (1965-66).

Filliozat, Jean (1946): 'Manuscripts in Birch bark and their Preservation'. *Ind. Arch.* 1, pp.102-108.

Fleet, J.F. (1906): 'Inscription on the Piprahwa vase' I & II. *Journal of the Royal Asiatic Society*, pp. 149ff and (1907) pp.105ff.

Fleet, J.F.(1907): 'Inscription on the Sohgaura plate'. *Journal of the Royal Asiatic Society*, pp. 510-532).

Francis, Frank (1975): (Ed.) *Treasures of British Museum*. London: James and Hudson.

Francke A.H. (1912): 'The Tibetan Alphabet'. *Ep.Ind.* 11, pp. 266-72.

Govinda, T.R. (1965): 'Preservation and conservation of Museum objects'. *Marg*, 19, pp. 53-56.

Gaur, Albertina (1979): *Writing materials of the East*. London.

Gauri Shankar (1937): (Ed.) *Kapphiṇābhyudaya* of Śivasvamin. Lahore: University of Panjab.

Ghosh, Man Mohan (1979): (Ed.) *Karpūramañjarī*. Calcutta: University of Calcutta, II edn. 1948.

Ghosh, Manmohan (1967): (Ed.) *Nāṭyaśāstra*. Calcutta: Manisha, 2 vols. I (chs 1-27); II (28-36); 1956.

Gode, P.K. (1940): 'Textual criticism in the 13th Century.' *Woolner Commemoration volume*, pp.106-108.

Gode, P.K. (1941): 'A Brief Note on the History and Progress of Catalogues of Sanskrit and other Manuscripts in India and Outside (from A.D. 1800 to 1941).' App.II. Katre (1941), pp. 99-129.

Gode, P.K. (1943): '*The Kavīndrācārya-sūcī* - Is it a dependable means for the restoration of Literary History?' *New Indian Antiquary*, 6, pp. 41-42.

Gode, P.K. (1943): 'Studies in the Regional History of Indian Paper Industry.' *Bharatiya Vidya*, 5, pp. 87-95; Gode (1969), pp. 18-23.

Gode, P.K. (1944)a: 'Saint Ramadasa's Discourse on the writing and preservation of Manuscripts and its importance for the history of Indian Palaeography. *New Indian Antiquary*, pp.126-128.

Gode, P.K. (1944)b: 'Regional History of Indian Paper industry'. *Bharatiya Vidya* 6. vi, pp. 126-30; Gode (1969), pp. 24-30.

Gode P.K. (1944)c: 'Migration of paper from China to India AE 105-1500. App. to Joshi (1944), pp. 205-222; Gode (1961), pp. 1-12.

Gode, P.K. (1944): 'Studies in The Regional History of Indian Paper Industry (The Paper Manufacture as Harihar on the Bank of the Tungabhadra in AD/790 as described by capra. Edward Moor).' *Bharatiya Vidya* 5, pp. 87-95.

Gode, P.K. (1945): 'Some evidence about the location of the Manuscript Library of Kavindrācārya Sarasvatī at Benares in AD 1665'. - Edition of *Jagadvijayachandas* by C.K. Raja, Bikaner, Ganga Oriental Series, No. 2, pp xivii-lvii.

Gode, P.K. (1946): 'Some notes on the History of Ink-manufacture in Ancient and Medieval India and other countries.' *Prācyavāṇī* 3.iv, pp. 1-15; Gode (1969), pp. 31-47.

Gode, P.K. (1948): 'Some Puranic extracts quoted by Aparāraka (c. A.D. 1125) and Their bearing on the history of Indian Palaeography and education.' *Poona Orientalist*, 13, pp. 10-14.

Gode, P.K. (1949): 'Recipe for hair dyes in the Navanītaka (c. 2nd cent. AD) and their close affinity with the recipe for ink manufacture.' *Bharatiya Vidya*, 11, pp.40-48.

Gode, P.K. (1952): 'Use of cloth for letter writing at the court of Harṣa (606-649).' *Hiriyanna Commemoration Volume*, pp. 15-21; Gode (1969), pp. 13-17.

Gode, P.K. (1961) : *Studies in Indian Cultural History*, Vol.4, pt l. Pune: Collected Works Publication Committee.

Gode, P.K (1969): *Studies in Indian Cultural History*, vol. 6, pt. 3. Pune: Collected Works Publication Committee.

Goel, O.P. (1953): 'Repair of documents'. ***Ind.Arch.***, 7, pp. 160-65.

Goldstucker, Th. (1965): *Pāṇini: his place in Sanskrit literature*, Varanasi: Chowkhamba.

Gopal, B.R. (1982): 'Śāsana Sampadane'. Sitaramiah and Seshasastri (1982): pp. 141-148.

Gough, A.E. (1878): *Paper relating to the Collection and Preservation of the Records of Ancient Sanskrit Literature in India*. Calcutta: Govt. of India.

Goyal, S.R. (1985): *Kautilya and Megasthanes*. Meerut: Kusumanjali Prakashan.

Gunda Jois, K. (1982): 'Kannaḍa Moḍi lipi'. Sitaramiah and Seshasastri (1982), pp. 385-91.

Gupta, B.A. (1905): 'Moḍi character' *Indian Antiquary*, 34, pp.27ff.

Gupta, C.B. : 'Conservation of paper materials'. Delhi : National Research Laboratory.

Gupta, R.C. (1954): 'How to fight white ants?' *Ind. Arch.* 8, pp 121-9.

Guy, John : *Palm leaf and paper illustrated Manuscripts of India and Southern Asia*. National Gallery of Victoria.

Harisagar, Muni (1946): 'Palm leaf Manuscripts in Jaisalmer'. *Ind.Arch.*,1, pp. 33 ff.

Hegde, M.L. (1982): 'Hastapratigala Mackenzie saṅgraha Sitaramaiah and Seshasastri (1982), pp. 243-52.

Hoerning (1883): 'List of Pali Manuscripts in the British Museum'. *Journal of Pali Text Society*, 1882-1905. Repr. Delhi: Caxton Publishers, 1985, pp. 133-144.

Hoernle, A.F.R. (1891): 'An instalment of the Bower manuscripts'. *Journal of Asiatic Society of Bengal*, 60, pp. 135-195.

Hoernle, A.F.R. (1893): 'Weber Manuscripts'. *Journal of Asiatic Society of Bengal*, 62, pp. 1ff.

Hoernle A.F.R. (1897), *'Three further collections of Ancient Manuscripts from Central Asia'* (Fragments, Godfrey and Macartney Mss). *Journal of Asiatic Society of Bengal*, 66, pp. 213-60.

Hoernle, A.F.R. (1901): 'A report on the British Collection of Antiquities from Central Asia' Part II. *Journal of Asiatic Society of Bengal*, 70 Extra No. (App. transliteration of Weber Ms. and Macartney Ms.)

Hoernle A.F.R. (1916): *Manuscript remains of Buddhist Literature found in Eastern Turkestan*. Oxford. 2 vols.

Hughes, A.W. Mekenny (1953): 'Protection of books and Records from insects.' *Ind.Arch.*, 7, pp. 41-43.

Hultzch, E. (1905): 'Dhar Praśasti of Arjunavarma: Parijātaharaṇanāṭikā of Madana.' *Ep.Ind.*, 8,9, pp.96-122.

*Ind(ian) Arch(ives)*:

1, 1946 pp.12ff. Chakravarti, S. 'A Study of palm leaf Manuscripts'.

pp. 33ff Harisagar Muni, 'Palm leaf Manuscripts in Jaisalmer'

pp. 102ff Filliozat, Jean, 'Manuscripts in Birch bark and their preservation'.

pp. 126ff Back, S.A. 'Book Worms'.

pp. 181ff Ranganathan, S.R. 'Laws of Archival Science'.

pp. 233ff Bhartacharya, B. 'Palm leaf Manuscripts and their preservation.

pp. 304ff Chakravarti, S. 'A Review of the Lamination process'.

5, 1951 pp. 1ff Basu, Purnendu, 'Common Enemies of Records'.

7, 1953 pp. 3ff Saletore, B.A. 'Medieval Hindu Archives'.

pp. 41ff Hughes, A.W.M. 'Protection of books and records from insects'.
pp 160ff Goel, O.P. 'Repair of documents'.

Jagirdar, Sitaram (1978) : *Kannaḍa Grantha-Sampādana-Paricaya*. Rangampet (Gulbarga) : Kannada Sahitya Sangha.

Jain, Premsuman (1979): 'Prākṛta Pāṇḍulipiyo kī katipaya Viśeṣatāye'. Sarma (1979), pp. 88-94.

Janaki, S.S. (1980): 'Textual Variants in Alankara Sarvasva of Ruyyaka'. *Journal of Oriental Institute*, 30, pp. 78-95.

Janert, K. Ludwig (1965): *An Annotated Bibliography of the Catalogues of Indian Manuscripts*, Part 1. Weisbaden.

Janert, K. Ludwig (1983): 'Writing on Arrows'. *Surabhi: Sreekrishna Sharma Felicitation Volume*. Tirupati: Felicitation Committee.

Javaliya, Vrajamohan (1979): 'Pāṇḍulipiyo kā prati-lipikārya'. Sarma (1979), pp. 72-82.

Jha, Trilokanath (1964): 'The Problem of valia lections of Kalidasa's works.' *Journal of Oriental Institute*, 13, pp. 399-402.

Joshi, K.B. (1944): *Paper making as a cottage Industry*. Bombay. All India Village Industries Association, Warona.

Kalburgi, M. (1972): *Kannada Grantha Sampadane*. Dharwad: Samaja Pustakalaya. II edn. 1986.

Kalburgi, M. (1979): *Sāhitya Sampādane*. Madras: University of Madras.

Kamat, Jyotsnā (1982): 'Śilpadalli Tālegari Grantha-galu'. Sitaramaiah and Seshasastri (1982), pp. 179-82.

Kanjilal, Dileep Kumar and Kanjilal, Kripamayee (1974): 'Uncatalogued Sanskrit and other Manuscripts in Europe'. *Annals of the Bhandarkar Oriental Research Institute*, 55, pp. 43-53.

Kapadia, H.R. (1938): 'A Detailed Exposition of the Nāgari, Gujarāti and Moḍi scripts'. *Annals of the Bhandarkar Oriental Research Institute*, 19. 3, pp. 386-418.

Karve, C.G. (1960): 'Manuscript-curatorship under the Marathas'. *P.K.Gode Commemoration Volume,* Pune: Oriental Book Agency, pp. 199-202.

Kathpalia, Y.P. (1959): 'Hand Lamination with Cellulose Acetate.' *American Archivis,* July.

Katre, Sumitra M. (1941): *Introduction to Indian Textual Criticism.* Bombay: Karnataka Publishing House, II edn. 1954: Pune: Deccan College.

Katre, S.M. (1941)b: (Kan.Tr.) N.S. Lakshminarayana Bhatta, Bangalore: Harsha Vardhana Prakasana, 1968.

Kaul, Srikant (1957): 'Saṁskṛt ke Bhojapatra Granth.' *Visvajyoti* (Hoshiarpur), 7.i.

Kaye, G.R. (1927): *Bakshali Manuscripts.* A study in Medieval Mathematics. Calcutta. 3 vols. Archaeological Survey of India New Series, 43. (1927-33).

Kielhorn, F, (1891): 'Sanskrit plays partly prescribed as inscription at Ajmere'. *Indian Antiquary,* 20, pp. 201-12.

Kielhorn, F. (1905): 'Tālaguṇḍa Pillar Inscription of Kākustha-Varma.' *Ep.Ind.,* 8.5, pp.24-36.

Kishore, Ranbir (1961): 'Preservation and Repair of palm leaf Manuscripts.' *Ind.Arch.,* 14, pp. 73-78.

Kishore, Ranbir and Mehra, C.P. (1954): 'Use of Naphthelene as a fumigant for books and manuscripts in Libraries and Record Depositories.' *Ind.Arch.,* 8, pp.164-5.

Konow, Sten (1901) : (Ed.) *Karpūra-mañjarī.* Cambridge (Mass) : Harvard Oriental Society. Harvard Oriental Series 4.

Krishnamoorthy, K. (1974): (Ed.Tr.) *Dhvanyāloka* of Ānandavardhana. Dharwad : Karnatak University, Repr. Delhi: Motilal Banarsidas, 1982.

Krishnamoorthy, K. (1977): (Ed.Tr.) : *Vakroktijīvita* of Kuntaka. Dharwad: Karnatak University.

Krishnamoorthy, K. (1983) : 'Samskṛtadalli Hastapratiśāstra mattu grantha-sampādane'. Sitaramiah and Chidanandamurthy (1983), pp. 35-49.

Krishnamoorthy, K. (1988) : (Ed.&Tr.). *Dhvanyāloka-locana,* Delhi: Meherchand Lacchmandas.

Krishnamurthi, P.V. (1982) : 'Grantha-Arava Lipigalu'. Sitaramaiah and Seshasastri (1982), pp. 392-399.

Krishnamurthy, V.G. (1977) : 'Mackenize and his collection'. *Śrīkaṇthikā* (S. Srikanta Sastri Commemoration volume), Mysore, pp. 179-186.

Krishna Rao, M.V.N. (1984) : *Indus Script Deciphered.* Delhi: Agam Kala Prakashan.

Krishna Sastri, H. (1920): 'The Cave and Brahmi Inscriptions of Southern India.' I All India Oriental Conference, *Proceedings.*

Kudalkar, J.S. (1920) : 'The Jain Manuscript Bhandars at Patan - A final word on their search.' I All India Oriental Conference, *Proceedings.*

Laksminarayana Bhatta, N.S. (1968): *Bhāratīya Grantha Sampādana Śāstra Paricaya.* Tr. of Katre (1941).

Lakshminarayana Bhatta, N.S. (1982) : 'Prācīna Padya-kṛtigala sampādaneyalli chandojñānada agatya.' Sitaramaiah and Seshasastri (1982), pp. 117-134.

Law, Bimal Charan (1933) : *History of Pali Literature.* London: Kegan Paul, Trench, Trubner & Co. 2 vols.

Levitt, Stephen Hillyer (1979): 'Orthographic confusion between bh and t in Devanagari manuscripts.' *Journal of Asiatic Society of Bengal,* 21, pp. 27-30.

Luders, H. (1911): *Bruchstucke Buddhisticher Dramen.* Berlin.

Macdonell, Arthur Anthony (1904): (Ed.). *Bṛhaddevatā.* Cambridge (Mass.) : Harvard Oriental Society. Harvard Oriental Series 5 & 6.

Mahalingam, T.V. (1974): *Early South Indian Palaeography.* Madras: University of Madras.

Mahantadevaru, K.S. (1965): 'Hastapratigala Saṁrakṣaṇe mattu melmn.' *Prabuddha Karnataka,* (Mysore), 47, pp. 13-22.

Maive, A. (1904): *Materials used to write before the invention of Printing*. Washington.

Majumdar, M.R. (1939) : 'Newly discovered Miniature of the Gujarati School of Painting.' *New Indian Antiquary*, 2, pp. 311-16.

Majumdar, P.C. (1956): 'Birch-bark and Clay-coated Manuscripts'. *Ind.Arch.*, 11, i-ii.

Malledevaru, H.P. (1983) : (Ed.) *Anubhūtisūtra* of Māyideva. Mysore: Oriental Research Institute.

Marathe, N.B. (1986) : 'Prācīna-bhāratīya-lipayaḥ.' 33rd All India Oriental Conference, Calcutta. (Section: Indian Linguistics).

Marshall, J.H. (1914) : 'The Date of Kaniska'. *Journal of Royal Asiatic Society*, pp. 973-86.

Mass, P. (1958) : *Textual Criticism*. Oxford. (Eng.tr.)

Mehra, C.P. See Kishore.

Menariya, Purushottamlal (1979): 'Pāṇḍulipi Vijñān'. Sarma (1979), pp. 83-87.

Mirashi, V.V. (1967): 'A Disputed reading in Kalidāsa's Meghaduta' *Indian Antiquary* (III series), 2, pp. 1-10.

Misra, B.N. (1968) : 'Certain Peculiarities in Book-making in Sanskrit Literature.' *Herald of Library Science* (BHU), 7, pp. 20-26.

Mitra, Rajendra Lal (1948): 'A Report on the search of Manuscripts in Indian Repositories.' *Ind. Arch.* 2, pp. 27-35.

Mohan, G.S. (1982) : 'Telugu Hastapratigalu'. Sita ramaiah and Sesha Sastri (1982), pp. 192-197.

Monier-Williams, Monier (1899): *Sanskrit-English Dictionary*.

Mookerjee, Radha Kumud (1947): *Education in Ancient India*. London: Macmilan & Co. II edn. 1951.

Muller, F. Max & Nanjio Bunyin (1884): *The Ancient Palm leaves containing the Prajña-Pāramita-hṛdaya and the Uṣnīṣa-Vijaya-Dhāriṇī*. Oxford. with an appendix on Palaeographical rules on the Horiuzi palm leaf

Manuscripts by Buhler pp. 63-85. Anecdota Oxoniensia, Aryan Series, vol. I, pp. iii.

Murray, G. (1980) : 'Paul Wills -Conserving our Artistic Heritage,' PHP Asian Edition, August.

Nanjio. See Muller & Nanjio.

Narasimhachar, D.L (1964) : *Kannaḍa Grantha Sampādane.* Mysore: Sharada Mandira. 3rd imp. 1976.

Narasimhachary, N.C.V. (1987): *'Mallinātha vyākhyā apapāṭhāś ca'. Journal of Sanskrit Academy* (Hyd.), pp. 17-30.

New Catalogus Catalogorum. Madras: University of Madras, 12 vols. Published. 1949 to 1992.

Norman, K.P. (1983) : *History of Pali Literature,* Wiesbaden : Otto Harrosowitz.

Ojha, Gaurishankar, H. (1918): *Bhāratīya Prācīna Lipi-mālā.* Ajmer (2nd edn), Repr. 1971, Delhi: Munshiram Manoharlal.

Oldenberg, H. *See* Rhys Davids, T.W. and Oldenberg, H.

Pandey, Raj Bali (1952) : *Indian Palaeography,* Part I. Varanasi : Motilal Banarsidass. II edn. 1957.

Pandurangi, K.T. (1978) : *Wealth of Sanskrit Manuscripts in India and Abroad.* Bangalore.

Parabrahma Sastri (1968): (Ed.) (*Siddhodvāha*). Hyderabad: Dept. of Archaeology and Museum, Govt. of Andhra Pradesh.

Parthasarathi, R.K. (1974) : 'The Pauṣkara-saṁhitā on Library Science'. *Charudevasastri Felicitation volume.* Delhi, pp. 629-32.

Perumal, P. (1988) : 'Study of Manuscript Libraries in Tamilnadu.' Tanjore : M.S.S.M. Library Society.

Pischel, R. (1905): 'Two Prakrit poems at Dhar.' *Ep.Ind.* 8, 25, pp 241-60.

Postgate, J.P. (1956): 'Textual Criticism.'*Encyclopaedia Britannica*, Vol. 22, pp. 6ff.

Pradhan, S.S. (1974) : 'Some Textual Problems in the Nirukta.' *Annals of the Bhandarkar Oriental Research Institute,* 55, pp. 83-91.

Prajapati, Manibhai, K. (1986) : *Bibliographic Survey of Catalogues of Indic Manuscripts.* Being a Union catalogue of Indian Languages manuscript catalogues available in Delhi. New Delhi : Indian National Trust for Art and Cultural Heritage Project.

Pungavanam, K. (1982) : 'Tamilu Hastapratigalu mattu avugala Mudraṇa'. Kan.Tr. M. Govindaraju. Sitartamaiah and Seshasastri (1982), pp. 183-191.

Raghavan, V. (1963) : *Manuscripts, Catalogues, Editions,* Bangalore.

Raghavan,V. (1977) : *Wealth of Sanskrit Manuscripts in India and Aborad.* Bangalore.

Raghavan, V. (1981) : 'The Illustrated Manuscript'. *Journal of Oriental Research,* 27, pp. 139-143.

Raja, K.Kunjunni (1976): 'Textual Criticism and Editorial problems in theory and practice.' *Annals of Oriental Research,* Madras, 26, pp. 1-10.

Ramachandra Rao, S.K. (1956): 'Reading and Editing of Manuscripts.' *Quarterly Journal of Mythic Society,* 65, p. 134.

Ramasastri, R. : See Rangaswami Iyengar.

Ramesh, K.V. (1984) : *Indian Epigraphy.* Delhi: Sundeep Prakashan.

Ranganathan, S.R. (1931): *Five Laws of Library Science.* Madras : Library Association. 2nd edn. Bombay: Asia, 1963.

Ranganathan, S.R. (1946): 'Laws of Archival Science. *Ind.Arch.,* 1, pp. 181ff.

Rangaswami Iyengar, H.G. and Ramasastri, R. (1950): (Ed.): Śaivaparibhāṣā of Śivāgrayogīndra. Mysore: Oriental Research Institute.

Rao, S.R. (1978) : 'Methodology of Decipherment of the Indus script.' *Journal of Sri Venkatesvara Oriental Research Institute,* p. 3ff.

Rao, V.T.S. (1982): 'Tālegari granthagalalli Citra-vinyāsa' Sitaramaiah and Seshasastri (1982), pp. 410-416.

Reddy, Devarakonda (1982): 'Kaḍata'. Sitaramaiah and Seshasastri (1982), pp. 213-216.

Rhys Davids, T.W. (1881) : (Tr.) *Buddhist Suttas.* Oxford University Press. Repr. Delhi: Motilal Banarsidass, 1965. Sacred Books of the East, Vol.11.

Rhys Davids, T.W. (1899) : 'The Gosinga Kharosthi Manuscript'. *Journal of Royal Asiatic Society,* pp. 426-28 (correspondence).

Rhys Davids, T.W. and Oldenberg, H. (1881) : (Tr.) *Vinaya Texts.* Part 1. Oxford University Press. Repr. Motilal Banarsidass, 1965. Sacred Books of the East Vol. 13.

Richards, F.J. (1916): 'Dravidian Affinities and their Sequel.' *Quarterly Journal of Mythic Society,* 7, pp. 243-84.

*Roopa Lekha*: Vol. 41. pp. 101-108 : 'A palm leaf illustrated manuscript of the Pañcarakṣa sūtra in The National Museum.'

Sachau, Edward, C. (1886) : *Alberuni's India.* London : Routledge & Kegan Paul. Ind. Repr. 1964. New Delhi, S. Chand & Co.

Saletore, B.A. (1953) : 'Medieval Hindu Archives.' *Ind.Arch,* 7, pp. 3-7.

Sampat, R.N. (1975) : 'Report on Palm leaf and cadjan manuscripts.' Madras : *Bulletin of Institute of Traditional Culture,* pp. 259-280.

Sampatkumara Ramanuja Iyar, Yadugiri Yatirāja (1982) : 'Purāṇagalalli Granthalekhana-vicāra'. Sitaramaiah and Seshasastri (1982). pp., 172-178.

Sandesara, Bhogilal J. (1953): *Literary Circle of Mahāmātya Vastupāla and its contribution to Sanskrit Literature.* Bombay: Bharatiya Vidya Bhavan.

Sankalia, H.D. (1972): *The University of Nalanda.* Delhi. 2nd edn. Rev. & enlarged.

Sannaiah, B.S. (1970) a: 'Olĕ granthagalu'. *Prabuddha Karnataka,* (Mysore), 42, pp. 93-102.

Sannaiah, B.S. (1982)b: 'Kendra Hastaprati- bhaṇḍārada Āvaśyakate'. Sitaramaiah and Seshasastri (1982), pp. 374-78.

Sannaiah, B.S. (1971) : *Grantha-Saṁrakṣaṇa*. Mysore: Prasaranga, University of Mysore.

Sannaih, B.S. (1992) : *Hastaprati-śāstra-vicāra*. Bangalore : BMSri Pratisthana.

Saran, Sarasvati (1961) : *India's National Writing*. Delhi : Munshiram Manoharlal.

Sharma, I. Karthikeya (1967): 'The Origin of Indian scripts'. *Indian Antiquary* (III series), pp. 34-39.

Sarma, K.V. (1966): 'Vedic textuo-linguistic studies.' *Visvesvaranand Indological Journal*, 3, pp. 92-204.

Sarma, K.V. (1980) : 'The manuscripts of the Jade family of Varanasi and the literature output of the Jade authors.' *Bharatiya Vidya*, 40, pp. 26-34.

Sarma K.V. (1982) : 'Manuscriptology and Textual criticism in Medieval India.' *Indologica Taurinensia*, Torino, 10, pp. 281-288.

Sarma, K.V. (1965): 'Some new Techniques in collating manuscripts and Editing Texts.' *Indologica Taurinensia*, Torino, 13, pp. 289-296.

Sarma, Ram Gopal (1979): (Ed.) *Pāṇdu lipi- Sampādana-kalā*. Delhi: Prabhat Prakashan.

Sarma, S.R. (1950) : *Writing Materials in Ancient India*. Aligarh: Vivek Publications.

Sastri, K.N. (1955) : 'Three Paramara Inscriptions from Malwa.' *Ep.Ind.*, 31.4, pp. 25-30.

Satyendra (1978): *Pāṇḍulipi Vijñān*. Jaipur: Rajasthan Hindi Granth Akademy.

Schuyler Jr, Montogomery (1908) : 'Notes on the making Palm leaf manuscripts in Siam.' *Journal of American Oriental Society*, 29, pp. 281 ff.

Segal, Judith (1979): *Conservation of Palm leaves*. Stencilled notes of a Demonstration lecture in Mysore.

Sengupta, Benoyendra (1964): *Cataloguing, its theory & Practice*, Calcutta.

Seshasastri, R. (1982): 'Saṁskṛta Hastapratigalu.' Sitaramaiah and Seshasastri (1982), pp. 225-229.

Seshasastri R. and Sitaramaiah, M.V.: See under Sitaramaiah.

Shamasastri, R. (1906): *The Origin of Devanāgarī Alphabet'*. Repr. Delhi: Bharat Prakashan, 1973.

Sharma, Y.D. (1953) : 'Exploration of Historical sites (A) - Rupar.' (Ivory Seal). *Ancient India*, 9, pp. 123, pl. 48a.

Shashi Bala (1980) : 'A Sanskrit Manuscript of the Gupta period at the Hori-uji monastery in Japan.' *Visvesvaranand Indological Journal*, 18, pp. 309-14.

Shastri, Ananthakrishna (1920) : 'Sanskrit Manuscripts, their search and preservation.' I All India Oriental Conference, *Proceedings*.

Shastri, Haraprasada (1899): 'Note on palm leaf Manuscripts in the Library of His Excellency the Maharaja of Nepal'. *Journal of Asiatic Society of Bengal*, 66, pp. 310-16.

Shelvankar, R.S. (1933): *A Report on the Moḍi Manuscripts in Sarasvati Mahal Library, Tanjore*. Madras : University of Madras.

Shivaganesha Murthy, R.S. (1984) : 'Contributions to the History of Indian Textual Criticism'. *Mysore University Arts Journal*, 46, pp. 26-30.

Shivaganesha Murthy, R.S. (1985)a: : 'Textual Criticism and Commentators - Mallinātha.' *Journal of Sanskrit Academy* (Hyderabad), pp. 57-68. (AIOC, Jaipur 1982).

Shivaganesa Murthy, R.S. (1985)b: 'Textual Criticism and Sanskrit Commentators - Jayaratha.' All India Oriental Conference, Ahmedabad, *Summaries*.

Shivaganesha Murthy, R.S. (1986) : 'Contribution to the History of Sanskrit Textual Criticism'. *Sugandhā* (Volume presented to M.P.L. Sastry), Bangalore, pp. 194-99.

Shivaganesha Murthy, R.S. (1987) : 'Hastaprati-vijñāna:Kelavu Pāribhāṣika padagalu.' *Locana*, 5 pp. 40-47.

Shivaganesha Murthy (1990): 'Textual Criticism and Sanskrit Commentators.' 8th World Sanskrit Conference, Vienna (Austria).

Shivaganesha Murthy, R.S. and Vathsala, G.B. (1991) : 'Saṁskṛta-sāhityadalli Lekhana sāmagri ullekhagalu.' *Dhanya-jīvi* (Raghavendragurey' Felicitation Volume), Malladi-halli (Chitradurga).

Shyamaji Krishnavarma (1883) : 'Use of writing at Vedic period., *Transactions of Congress of Orientalists* VI, Leiden pp. 305 ff.

Sikdar, J.C. (1964) : *Studies in Bhagavatisūtra*. Muzaffarpur: Bihar Research Institute of Prakrit, Jainism and Ahimsa.

Sircar, Dinesh Candra (1965) : *Indian Epigraphy*. Delhi: Motilal Banarsidass.

Sitaramaiah, M.V. (1982) : 'Hastapratigala Saṅgraha.' Sitaramaiah and Seshasastri. (1982), pp. 217-222.

Sitaramaiah, M.V. (1983) : 'Hastaprati śāstrada samasyegalu.' Sitaramaiah and Chidanandamurthy (1983), pp. 4-9.

Sitaramaiah, M.V. and Seshasastri, R. (1982): (Ed.) *Maṇiha* (P.G. Halakaṭṭi Commemoration Volume). Bangalore: BMSri Memorial Foundation.

Sitaramaiah, M.V. and Chidananda Murthy, M. (1983) : (Ed.). *Hastapratiśāstra* (Manuscriptology) Seminar papers. Bangalore: BMSri Memorial Foundation.

Sivaramamurti, C. (1952) : *Indian Epigraphy and South Indian Scripts*. Bulletin of the Madras Government Museum. NS. Gen.Secn. vol.3, No. 4.

Sivaramamurti, C. (1970) : *Indian Painting*. New Delhi: National Book Trust.

Smith, Vincent (1902) : 'Indian Documents on Parchment.' *Journal of Royal Asiatic Society*, pp. 232-33 (correspondence).

Srikanta Sastri, S. (1934) : 'Studies in Indus scripts'. *Quarterly Journal of Mythic Society*, 24, pp. 224-30; 335-42.

Srikanta Sastri, S. (1954): *Bhāratīya Saṁskṛti*, Mysore: Prasaranga, University of Mysore.

Srinivasan, P.K. and Subrahmanyam, V.S. (1965): 'Hanuma-Koṇḍa Niroṣṭhya-Kāvya Inscription.' *Ep.Ind.*, 36. 27, pp. 209-248.

Subramanian, T.N. (1957): (Ed.) *South Indian Temple Inscriptions*. Vol. 3, pt. 2, with notes. Madras: Govt. Oriental Manuscripts Library.

Subrahmanyam, V.S.: See Srinivasan, P.K.

Sukthankar, Vishnu, S. (1933) : *Prolegomena* to the Critical Edition of Ādiparva. vol. 1. Pune: Bhandrkar Oriental Research Institute.

Todarmal (Late). (1928) : (Ed.) *Mahavīracarita*. London : OUP for Panjab University, Lahore. Prepared for Pub. A Macdonell.

Unithiri, N.V.P. (1983) : 'Commentorial Literature in Sanskrit.' *Journal of Kerala Studies*, 10.

Upadhyaya, Vasudeva (1961) : *Prācīna Bhāratīya Abhilekho kā Adhyayan*, Delhi: Motilal Banarsidass.

Upadhye, A.N. (1943) : (Ed.) *Bṛhatkathākośa*. Bombay: Bharatiya Vidya Bhavan.

Upadhye, A.N. (1975) : 'A point for the Text-critic'. *Sanskrit and Indological Studies* (V. Raghavan Felicitation Volume), pp. 449-51.

Upadhye, A.N. (1983) : *Upadhye papers*. Prasaranga, University of Mysore.

Varadaraja Rao, G. (1969) : 'Grantha Sampādane.' *Prabuddha Karnataka*. (Mysore), pp. 723-743.

Vathsala, G.B. See under Shivaganesha Murthy, R.S.

Velankar, Hari Dev (1944) : *Jinaratnakośa*. Vol.I: Works. Pune : Bhandarkar Oriental Research Institute.

Velankar, Hari Dev (1966) : 'Sanskrit Manuscripts: their acquisition, preservation and utilisation.' *Bharatiya Vidya*, 26, pp.1-14.

Venkatasubbaiah, A. (1911) : *The Kalās*. Madras: Vasanta Press, Adyar.

Venkatasubbaiah, A. (1917) : '12th Century University in Mysore.' *Quarterly Journal of Mythic Society*, 7, pp. 157-76.

Venkatasubbaih, G. (1982) : 'Grantharacanākālada nirṇaya.' Sitaramaiah and Seshasastri (1982), pp. 149-162.

Vishvabandhu (1964) : 'Vedic textus linguistic studies'. *Visvesvaranand Indological Journal*, 2, pp. 1-8; 5 (1967), pp. 13-14.

Visvabandhu and Sarma, K.V. (1976): (Ed.) *Vedic textus-linguistic Studies*. Hoshiarpur: Visvesvaranand Vedic Research Institute.

Wakankar, L.S. (1985) : 'The Origin of Brahmi Script - An informative Review.' *Quarterly Journal of Mythic Society*, 76, pp. 183-192.

Warner, R.M. See Bordin.

Walters, Thomas (1961) : *On Yuan Chwang's Travels in India*. Ed. T.W. Rhys Davids and W. Bushell. London : RAS, 2 vols. Ind. Edn. Delhi : Munshiram Manoharlal vol. 1.

Winternitz, M. (1926): 'The Art of writing and the transmission of Indian Literature.' *History of Indian Literature*, Vol. I, Part 1. Tr. S. Ketkar. University of Calcutta, pp. 26-35.

Witzel, Michael (1976) : 'On the reconstruction of the authentic Paippalada Samhita.' *Journal of the Ganganatha Jha Samskrta Kendriya Vidyapitha*, 32, pp. 137-68.

# Index


Abhinavagupta, 57
*Abhījnāna-Śākuntalam*, 55, 63-64, 153, 169
*Abhīlaṣitārthacintāmaṇi*, 143
Āgama, 133
Aggarwal, V.S., 23
Ajanta, 53
Akbar, 41
Alberuni, 31-32
Allahabad pillar inscription, 42, 59
*Amarakośa*, 32, 45-46
Amarāvati, 133
Amṛtananda, 147
Andhra Pradesh, 60
Aṅga-līpi, 9
*Anubhavasūtra*, 164-65
*Āpastamba-Dharma-sūtra*, 107
*Arthaśāstra*, 6, 12, 19, 25, 29, 32, 45, 55, 102, 119, 125, 127, 144, 168
Aśoka, 2, 12, 42
Aśokan edicts, 2
Aśokan scripts, 3
Aśokan inscription, 17
Aśvaghoṣa, 31
*Atharva Veda*, 33, 57
Australia, 83
Badli inscription, 2
Bagchi, P.C., 35
Bālabodha, 14
Bakshali manuscripts, 33
Baṇa, 46, 53, 62, 66, 117, 119, 128
Banerjee, S.R., 162
Bantavala inscription, 60
Baroda, 71
Basavapurāṇa, 23, 108, 119
Benfey, 4, 52
Benaras, 71
*Bhāgavata-Purāṇa*, 36, 118
*Bhāgavata-Purāṇa Mahimna-stotra*, 108
*Bhagvad-gīta*, 33, 36, 58
*Bhagvati-sūtra*, 10
Bhandarkar, D.R., 18, 20
Bhandarkar, R.G., 70, 72
Bhandarkar Oriental Research Institute, 30
*Bhāratamañjari*, 145
Bhāravi, 39
Bhasa, 6, 45
Bhattacharya, B., 83, 101
Bhaṭṭanārāyaṇa, 53
Bhaṭṭiprolu relic casket inscription, 2
Bhaṭṭoji Dīkṣita, 144
Bhavabhūti, 53
Bhūrja-barks, 32
Bhūṣaṇa Bhaṭṭa, 128
Bhṛgukaccha, 76
Bīrch-Bark (*Bhūrja-Patra*), 31
Bloomfield, M., 57
B.M. Shri Memorial Foundation, 75
Bombay, 70
Bonn, 147
Bower manuscripts, 33, 56
Brahmajāla-sūtra, 8
Brāhmī script, 2, 3, 9, 10, 33, 61, 63
*Bṛhatkāthā*, 26, 145, 155

*Bṛhatkāthākośa*, 21, 61
British Library, 72
British Museum, 59, 63, 88
Buddha, 9, 12
*Buddhacarita*, 142, 147
Buddhist literature, 8
Buddhist manuscripts, 42, 108
Bühler, G., 4, 5, 69
Burma, 63
Burnell, A.C., 70
Calcutta, 59
Candragupta Maurya, 39
*Candraprabha-Vijaya-Kāvya*, 64
*Caurapañcaśīkā*, 54, 108
Chālukyan script, 61
*Chāndogya-Upaniṣad*, 19
Chatterji, S.K., 35, 45
Chedpati, 103
China, 10
Cīna-lipi, 9
Cola script, 60
Cullavagga, 9
Cunningham, A., 4, 39
Dakṣiṇa-līpī, 9
Darada-līpī, 9
Dasgupta, Charuchandra, 23, 61
*Daśakumāracārita*, 62
*Daśavaikālika-sūtra*, 103
Davids, Rays, 4, 18, 20, 22
*Deccan Herald*, 17, 58, 59, 62
Desilva, W.H., 28, 49, 56, 63, 117, 118
Devadhar, C.R., 19
*Devakota*, 142
*Devanāgarī*, 13, 14, 108, 118, 131, 133, 135
Devapaladeva, 75
Devarājayajvan, 141, 147
Devasthali, G.V., 62
*Devī-Purāṇa*, 44, 61
Dhammapada, 52
*Dharmābhyudaya*, 36
Dharmadāsa, 65
*Dharmavidhi*, 46
Dharwar, 148
Dhavala manuscripts, 57, 123
*Dhavanyāloka-locana*, 35, 123, 126, 128, 144, 156
Diringer, David, 5, 18, 76, 119
Drāvida-līpī, 9
*Dṛṣṭāntaśataka*, 129, 143
Durbar library, 30
Dwarkā, 13, 18
Edgerton, Franklin, 169
Firoz Shah Tughlak, 17
Fleet, J.F., 17
France, 72
Francis, F., 58, 119
Garbe, R., 57
Germany, 72
Gidwani, 100
Ghosh, Manmohan, 162
*Gīta Govinda*, 54, 66, 108, 144
Godfrey, 30, 33
Gosavi, P.G., 58
Goyal, S.R., 23
Greek, 3, 11
Griffith, R.T.H., 69
Gujarat, 14, 69, 108
Gupta, R.C., 86, 161
Gupta Script, 17, 33
Hanumanakonda, 60
Harappan Seals, 3
Harihara, 123
Harisagar Muni, 86, 102
Hariseṇa, 46, 121
*Harṣacarita*, 46, 61-62, 117, 119, 133
Hathigumpha cave inscription, 42, 59

Heidelberg 99
Hemachandra, 102, 144
*Hitopadeśa*, 154
Hiuen Tsang, 29
Hoernle, A.F.R., 27, 57
Hori-uzi monastery, 30
Hūna-lipī, 9
Hyderabad, 60
Indus script, 6
Jain Bhandara, 72, 108, 123
Jain, Hiralal, 133
Jain, Premsuman, 23, 62
Jaipur, 108
Jaisalmer Jain Bhandar, 30
Jammu, 15
Japan, 88
*Jātakaṭṭha-Kathā*, 62
Jaya, 131
*Jayamaṅgalā*, 164
Jīvananda Vidyasagar, 148
Jonarāja, 53, 119
Jones, Sir Williams, 68
Kācchapeśvara temple, 60
Kadamba plates, 37
Kadamba script, 40, 59
*Kādambarī*, 46, 66
Kalidāsa, 6, 32, 153
Kaliyuga, 11
*Kalpalatāviveka*, 144
Kamasūtra, 7, 19, 63
Kanārī lipī, 9
Kaniska, 38, 59
Kannaḍa, 14, 15, 71, 108, 109, 133
Karnataka, 14, 15, 17
*Karpūramañjarī*, 162
Kashmir, 11, 15, 37, 67, 70, 108, 119
*Kāṭahakajātaka*, 9, 22, 26
Katre, S.M., 115, 120, 131, 133, 169
*Kātyāyana-smṛti*, 47, 62
Kaul, Madhusudan, 120
Kauṭilya, 6, 12, 27, 119
*Kāvyālaṁkāra-sūtra*, 128, 130
*Kāvyamīmāṁsa*, 55, 119
*Kāvyaprakāśa*, 55, 141, 144
Kaye, G.R., 27, 55, 117
Kerala, 14, 72
Kharosṭhi script, 2, 9, 39
Kielhorn, F., 70
*Kirātārjunīyam*, 59
Krishnamoorthy, K., 144, 148
Kṣemendra, 120, 145, 155
Kumārapāla, 67
*Kumārasaṁbhava*, 32, 57, 160
Kunjunni Raja, C., 100
Kunte, K., 70
Kuppuswami Sastri Research Institute, Madras, 72
*Kūrma-Śatakas*, 43
Lahore, 73
*Lalitavistara*, 9, 14, 21, 47
*Laṅkāvatāra-Sūtra*, 30
Lassen, 4
Law, Bimala Charan, 56, 59
London, 63, 68, 72
Lüders, H., 30, 57
Macartney, G., 70
Madras, 68, 70, 71, 137, 147
*Mahābhārata*, 7, 33, 34, 36, 38, 49, 108, 114-16, 127, 130, 137, 141, 145, 154-55, 160, 165-66
*Mahābhāṣya*, 26, 119, 168
Maharaja Chamaraja Odeyar, Mysore, 71
Maharaja Serfoji, Tanjore, 71
Maharaja 'Svati' Tirunal Rama Varma, 72

Mahārāṣtrī, 161
Mahasthana stone plaque inscription, 2
*Mahāvastu*, 20, 22
*Mahāvīracarita*, 67, 132
*Mahindra-Vijaya-dima*, 126
Maheśvarī-lipi, 21
*Majjhīma-nikāya*, 9
Malayalam script, 39
Malledevaru, H.P., 169
Malleson, G.B., 70
*Mānasollāsa*, 143
Mandasor stone pillar inscription, 42
Maribasavaradhya, P., 148
*Mārkaṇḍeya Purāṇa*, 161
Marulasiddiah, G., 169
Mauryan Age, 12
Max Muller, 3,4
Megasthenes, 11
*Meghadūta*, 141
*Meghasandeśa*, 136
Meharauli Iron pillar, 41
Menariya, P.L., 23
Mirji Aṇṇāraya, 133
Mitramiśra, 18
Mitra, Rajendralal, 34, 48, 56, 63, 69, 70
Mookerji, Radhakumud, 22, 75
Monier Williams, M., 64
Murray, G., 102
Mysore., 55, 58, 59, 70, 71, 110, 133
Mysore Archaeological Reports, 59
Nagari script, 13, 36
*Naiṣadhīya-Carita*, 39, 59, 123
Nalanda, 11, 60, 67
Nandināgarī, 131
*Nandi-Sūtra*, 144
*Nārada-Smṛti*, 6
Narasimachar, D.L. 59-60, 165, 168
Nasik inscription, 46
*Nāṭyaśāstra*, 7, 19, 57, 73, 166
Nepal, 73, 108
Newari scripts, 42
Niṣītha-cūrṇī, 108
*Nyāyamañjarī-Granthi-bhaṅga*, 168
Ojha, G.H., 35, 60, 62
Oldenberg, H., 20
Oriental Research Institute, Mysore, 31, 84, 91-92, 102, 119
Orissa, 15
*Padmapurāṇa*, 145
*Pali Tripīṭaka*, 43, 48
Pañchapāṭhi manuscripts, 106
*Panchatantra*, 114, 116, 141, 154
Pandey, R.B., 23, 57, 59, 119
Pandurangi, K.T., 73, 75, 118
Pāṇini, 3, 7, 45
*Paṇinīya-sikṣa*, 18
Panjab, 15
*Paṇṇavaṇā-sutta*, 10-11, 22
*Parameśvaratantra*, 30
Parāśara, 11
*Pārijatāmañjarī*, 43, 60
*Parīkṣit*, 115
*Pārśvābhyudeya*, 145
Patañjali, 45
*Patañjali-carita*, 26, 119, 127
Pataliputra, 11
Paul Mass, 166
Persian inscriptions 41
Peterson, P., 36, 46, 70, 143
Piprahwa vase inscription, 2
Post-Harappan scripts, 6
*Prabhavāka-carita*, 55, 58, 77

*Pratityasamutpāda-sūtra*, 60
*Purāṇa-Prabanda Saṅgraha*, 120
*Pustakapāṇi*, 11
Raghavan, V., 91, 100, 102
*Raghuvaṁśa*, 18
Rājaśekhara, 82, 101, 119, 162
*Rājaśekhara-carita*, 118, 122
Rājaśekharasūrī, 123
Rajasthan, 63, 70, 108
*Rājataraṅgiṇi*, 66
Rāma, 7
Ramabhadra-Dīkṣita, 119, 127, 133
Ramasastri, R., 143, 147-48
*Rāmāyāṇa*, 7, 34, 48, 106, 108, 117, 125, 126, 130
Ramayya, N.V., 57
Ranganathan, S.R., 93
Ranvir Sanskrit Residential Institute, Jammu, 71
Rao, S.R., 6, 18
Ratnāsagara, 67
*Rāyapaseṇiya sūtta*, 10, 22, 24, 29, 51
*Ṛgveda*, 19, 108, 119
Rice, B.L., 70
*Sahṛdayāloka*, 136
*Saivaparibhāṣā*, 142
*Samavāyanga-sutta*, 10
Sampath, R.N., 28, 56
Sampurnanand Sanskrit University Library, 71
Saṁyuktāgama-sutta, 33
Sāñcipāṭor Samucipat, 33
Sanchi Stūpa, 44
Sankalia, H.D., 75
Śāradā script, 33, 131
Sarasvatī, 11
Saraswati Mahal Library, Tanjore, 70, 83
*Sāri-Puttappakaraṇa*, 31
Sarma, K.V., 76, 133
Sastri, (Pt) A. Mahadeva, 71
Sastri, Haraprasada, 70
Sastri, S. Kuppuswami, 100
Sastri, P.V. Parabrahma, 60
*Śatapatha-Brāhmaṇa*, 36
Satyendra, 51, 58-60, 67, 101, 117-18
Sayaji Rao Gaekwad Oriental Institute, 71
Schuyler, M., 56, 117
Segal, Judith, 56, 88-89, 101-02
Sengupta, Benoyendra, 102
Sharma, Y.D., 61
Shashi Bala, 57
*Sīddhāntākaumudī*, 130
*Siddhodvāha*, 60
Sikdar, J.C., 58
Singrauli stone inscription, 4
Sircar, D.C., 27, 46, 51, 58-59, 61, 63-64
Sitaramaiah, M.V., 73, 77, 101
*Śivamahīmnastotra*, 54
Sivaramamurti, C., 23, 55, 60, 119
*Śivatattva-ratnākara*, 143
*Skanda Purāṇa*, 30
Sohgaura copper plate, 2, 38
Someśvara, 144
Śriharṣa, 123
*Śrīkaṇṭha-carita*, 66, 119
Sri Lanka, 73
Srinivasan, C.S., 133
*Sritattvanidhi*, 108
Srivihara plate, 38
*Śṛṅgāra-pravāha*, 102
Stein, M.A., 63
Sten Konow, 162
Subandhu. 44, 50

*Subhāṣitavalī*, 143, 148
Śukra, 6
*Śukranitisāra*, 18
Sukthankar, V.S., 130-31, 137, 145, 166-67
*Suryaśataka*, 60
*Sutta-pīṭaka*, 8
*Taittirīya Upaniṣad*, 19
Talagunda piliar inscription, 42
Tāllapākam Aṇṇamācārya, 38
Tamil Nadu, 14
Taxila, 2, 29, 33, 39-40, 67
Thomas, Edward, 4
Tiruvantapuram, 72
*Uṇādisūtra*, 64
*Unnata-śikhara purāṇa*, 43
Upadhyaya, Vasudev, 23, 59, 75, 118-19
*Utpala-Parimala*, 126, 130
Varadacharya, K.S., 133
Vallabhadeva, 143
*Vārāhī-tantra*, 8, 17
Vāsavadatta, 64, 66
*Vāśiṣtha-Dharmasūtra*, 7, 19
*Vāsudevahiṇḍī*, 36, 38
Vedavyas, 114
Veezhināthan, N., 100
*Veṇīsaṁhāra*, 46, 62
Veṅkappayya Bhūpatı, 113
Venkatasubbaiah, 19
*Vijayaśri-Nāṭikā*, 60
Vijñāneśvara, 45
*Vikramorvaśiyam*, 32, 57
*Vinayapīṭaka*, 9, 47
*Vīramitrodaya*, 19
Viśakhadatta, 66
*Viṣṇu Dharmasūtra*, 7, 19
*Vyaṣasmṛti*, 119
*Vyavahāranirṇaya*, 18
*Vyavahāraprakāśa*, 18-19
Warangal, 60
Weber, 4, 52
Western Gaṅga Kings, 29
Western Gaṅga plates, 37
Whitney, 4
Winternitz, M., 34
*Yājñavalkya-sīkṣā*, 6, 18
*Yājñavalkya-Smṛti*, 45, 61
Yazdani, 5
Yogini-tantra, 55, 57, 59, 62-63

# SCRIPTS

*Alphabets and numerals*
(Arranged on the basis of shape similarity and in the traditional way)

1. Bengali
2. Grantha
3. Gujarati
4. Kaithi
5. Kannada
6. Maithili
7. Malayalam
8. Modi
9. Nandi Nagari
10. Sarada
11. Tamil
12. Telugu
13. Tigalari
14. Udiya

Charts prepared by:
Vidwan Haramba R. Bhat
(M.A., Dip.-in-Manuscriptology)

## बंगाली

| न | ह | ड | व | लृ | ए | थ | प | ग | ढ | न | द |
|---|---|---|---|---|---|---|---|---|---|---|---|
| ত | হ | ড | ব | ঌ | এ | থ | প | গ | ঢ | ন | দ |
| ओ | इ | ड. | ब | भ | ऐ | ध | घ | | ट | ण | स |
| ও | ই | ঙ | ব | ভ | ঐ | ধ | ঘ | | ট | ণ | স |
| औ | ई | उ | र | ल | ञ | फ | य | | च | | |
| ঔ | ঈ | উ | র | ল | ঞ | ফ | য | | চ | | |
| अ | | ऊ | क | श | | ख | म | | ठ | | |
| অ | | ঊ | ক | শ | | খ | ম | | ঠ | | |
| आ | | ज | झ | | | | ष | | | | |
| আ | | জ | ঝ | | | | ষ | | | | |
| अं | | छ | ऋ | | | | | | | | |
| অং | | ছ | ঋ | | | | | | | | |
| अः | | | | | | | | | | | |
| অঃ | | | | | | | | | | | |

| अ | आ | इ | ई | उ | ऊ | ऋ | लृ | ए | ऐ | ओ | औ |
|---|---|---|---|---|---|---|---|---|---|---|---|
| অ | আ | ই | ঈ | উ | ঊ | ঋ | ঌ | এ | ঐ | ও | ঔ |
| अं | अः | क | ख | ग | घ | ड. | च | छ | ज | झ | ञ |
| অং | অঃ | ক | খ | গ | ঘ | ঙ | চ | ছ | জ | ঝ | ঞ |
| ट | ठ | ड | ढ | ण | त | थ | द | ध | न | प | फ |
| ট | ঠ | ড | ঢ | ণ | ত | থ | দ | ধ | ন | প | ফ |
| ब | भ | म | य | र | ल | व | श | ष | स | ह | का |
| ব | ভ | ম | য | র | ল | ব | শ | ষ | স | হ | কা |
| कि | की | कु | कू | के | कै | को | कौ | | | | |
| কি | কী | কু | কূ | কে | কৈ | কো | কৌ | | | | |
| 1 | 2 | 3 | 4 | 5 | 6 | 7 | 8 | 9 | 0 | | |
| ১ | ২ | ৩ | ৪ | ৫ | ৬ | ৭ | ৮ | ৯ | ০ | | |

## ग्रन्थ

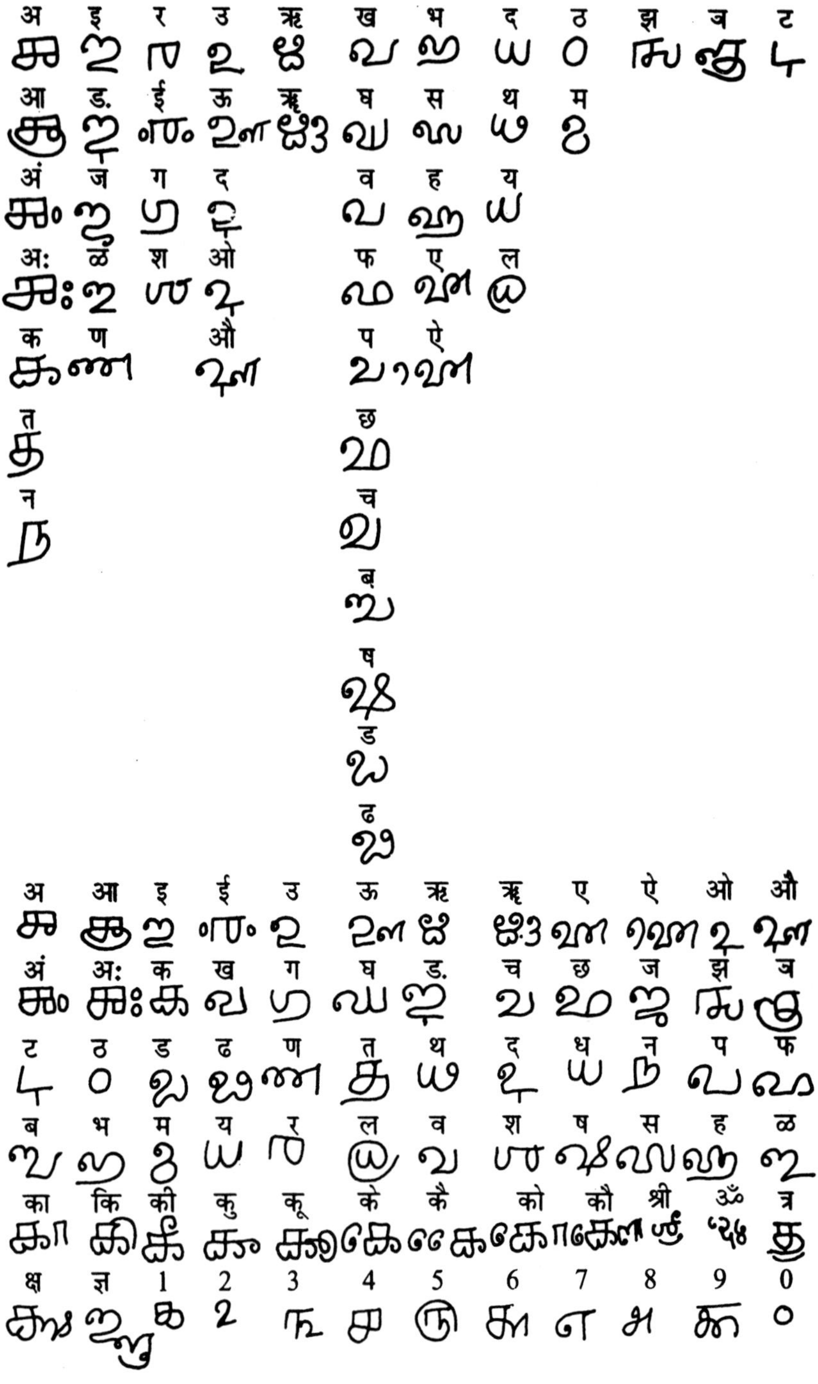
अ इ र उ ऋ ख भ द ठ झ ञ ट
आ ङ ई ऊ ॠ घ स थ म
अं ज ग द व ह य
अः ळ श ओ फ ए ल
क ण औ प ऐ
त छ
न च
ब
ष
ड
ढ
अ आ इ ई उ ऊ ऋ ॠ ए ऐ ओ औ
अं अः क ख ग घ ङ च छ ज झ ञ
ट ठ ड ढ ण त थ द ध न प फ
ब भ म य र ल व श ष स ह ळ
का कि की कु कू के कै को कौ श्री ॐ त्र
क्ष ज्ञ 1 2 3 4 5 6 7 8 9 0

# गुजराती

| च | द | ऋ | ऌ | ठ | ळ | ग | ज | ट | त | प | र |
|---|---|---|---|---|---|---|---|---|---|---|---|
| ચ | દ | ઋ | ઌ | ઠ | ળ | ગ | જ | ટ | ત | પ | ર |
| अ | इ | ॠ | भ | ङ | ख | ञ | व | ढ | न | ष | श |
| અ | ઇ | ૠ | ભ | ઙ | ખ | ઞ | વ | ઢ | ન | ષ | શ |
| आ | ई | | म | ड | | झ | | | ल | य | स |
| આ | ઈ | | મ | ડ | | ઝ | | | લ | ય | સ |
| ए | घ | | | क | | | ण | | | थ | |
| એ | ઘ | | | ક | | | ણ | | | થ | |
| ऐ | ध | | | फ | | | | | | | |
| ઐ | ધ | | | ફ | | | | | | | |
| ओ | छ | | | ह | | | | | | | |
| ઓ | છ | | | હ | | | | | | | |
| औ | उ | | | | | | | | | | |
| ઔ | ઉ | | | | | | | | | | |
| अं | ऊ | | | | | | | | | | |
| અં | ઊ | | | | | | | | | | |
| अः | ब | | | | | | | | | | |
| અઃ | બ | | | | | | | | | | |

| अ | आ | इ | ई | उ | ऊ | ऋ | ॠ | ऌ | ए | ऐ | ओ |
|---|---|---|---|---|---|---|---|---|---|---|---|
| અ | આ | ઇ | ઈ | ઉ | ઊ | ઋ | ૠ | ઌ | એ | ઐ | ઓ |
| औ | अं | अः | क | ख | ग | घ | ङ | च | छ | ज | झ |
| ઔ | અં | અઃ | ક | ખ | ગ | ઘ | ઙ | ચ | છ | જ | ઝ |
| ञ | ट | ठ | ड | ढ | ण | त | थ | द | ध | न | प |
| ઞ | ટ | ઠ | ડ | ઢ | ણ | ત | થ | દ | ધ | ન | પ |
| फ | ब | भ | म | य | र | ल | व | श | ष | स | ह |
| ફ | બ | ભ | મ | ય | ર | લ | વ | શ | ષ | સ | હ |
| ळ | का | कि | की | कु | कू | के | कै | को | कौ | | |
| ળ | કા | કિ | કી | કુ | કૂ | કે | કૈ | કો | કૌ | | |
| 1 | 2 | 3 | 4 | 5 | 6 | 7 | 8 | 9 | 0 | | |
| ૧ | ૨ | ૩ | ૪ | ૫ | ૬ | ૭ | ૮ | ૯ | ૦ | | |

# कैथी

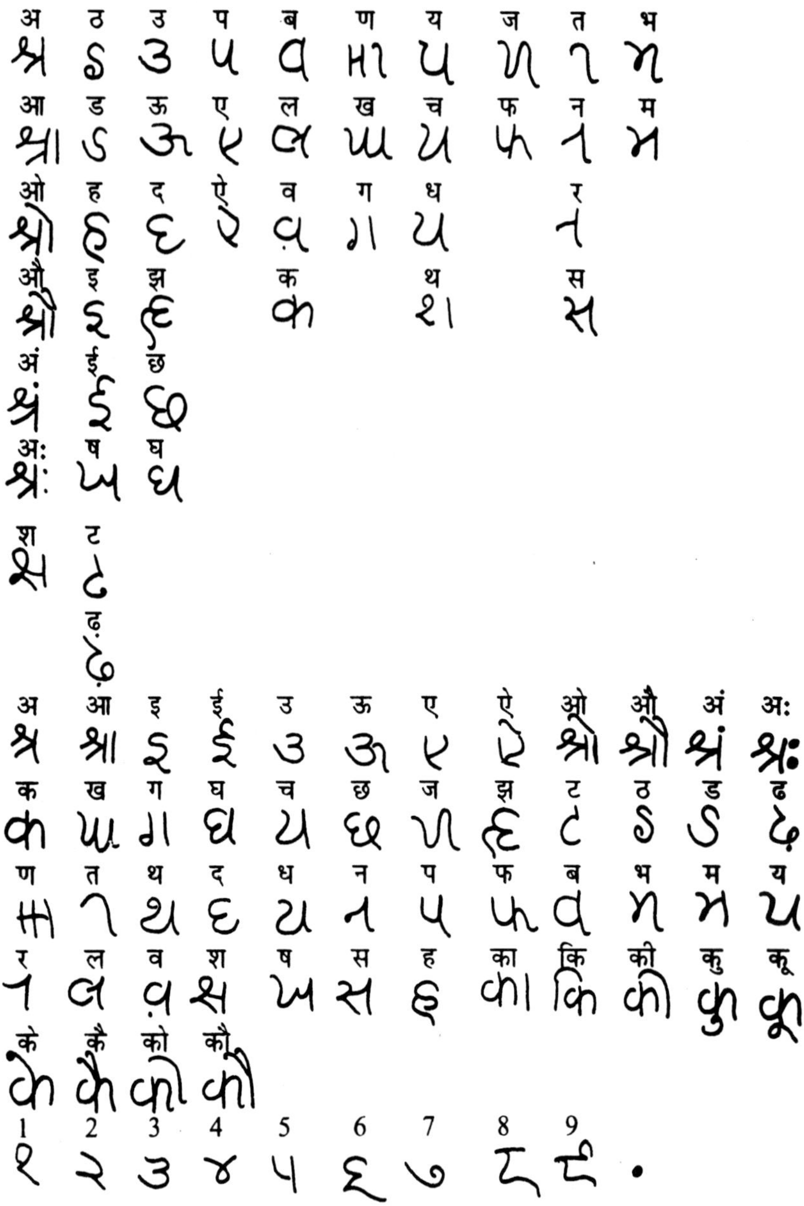
अ ठ उ प ब ण य ज त भ
आ ड ऊ ए ल ख च फ न म
ओ ह द ऐ व ग ध र
औ इ झ क थ स
अं ई छ
अः ष घ
श ट
ढ़
अ आ इ ई उ ऊ ए ऐ ओ औ अं अः
क ख ग घ च छ ज झ ट ठ ड ढ
ण त थ द ध न प फ ब भ म य
र ल व श ष स ह का कि की कु कू
के कै को कौ
1 2 3 4 5 6 7 8 9

# कन्नड़

| | | | | | | | | | | |
|---|---|---|---|---|---|---|---|---|---|---|
| ल ಲ | इ ಇ | र ರ | उ ಉ | ए ಎ | ओ ಒ | ट ಟ | ग ಗ | त ತ | श ಶ | ळ ಳ |
| अ ಅ | ञ ಞ | ठ ಠ | ऊ ಊ | ए̄ ಏ | ओं ಓ | ण ಣ | न ನ | | | |
| आ ಆ | | ई ಈ | | ऐ ಐ | औ ಔ | ड ಡ | स ಸ | | | |
| अं ಅಂ | | य ಯ | | व ವ | ङ ಙ | ढ ಢ | | | | |
| अः ಅಃ | | झ ಝ | | छ ಛ | ज ಜ | द ದ | | | | |
| | | ळ ೞ | | म ಮ | ज्ञ ಜ್ಞ | ध ಧ | | | | |
| | | क ಕ | | प ಪ | च ಚ | थ ಥ | | | | |
| | | क्ष ಕ್ಷ | | फ ಫ | ब ಬ | | | | | |
| | | ऋ ಋ | | ष ಷ | भ ಭ | | | | | |
| | | ॠ ೠ | | घ ಘ | ख ಖ | | | | | |

| | | | | | | | | | | | |
|---|---|---|---|---|---|---|---|---|---|---|---|
| अ ಅ | आ ಆ | इ ಇ | ई ಈ | उ ಉ | ऊ ಊ | ऋ ಋ | ॠ ೠ | ए ಎ | ए̄ ಏ | ऐ ಐ | ओ ಒ |
| ओ ಓ | औ ಔ | अं ಅಂ | अः ಅಃ | क ಕ | ख ಖ | ग ಗ | घ ಘ | ङ ಙ | च ಚ | छ ಛ | ज ಜ |
| झ ಝ | ञ ಞ | ट ಟ | ठ ಠ | ड ಡ | ढ ಢ | ण ಣ | त ತ | थ ಥ | द ದ | ध ಧ | न ನ |
| प ಪ | फ ಫ | ब ಬ | भ ಭ | म ಮ | य ಯ | र ರ | ल ಲ | व ವ | श ಶ | ष ಷ | स ಸ |
| ह ಹ | ळ ಳ | का ಕಾ | कि ಕಿ | की ಕೀ | कु ಕು | कू ಕೂ | कृ ಕೃ | के ಕೆ | कें ಕೇ | कै ಕೈ | को ಕೊ |
| कों ಕೋ | कौ ಕೌ | श्री ಶ್ರೀ | ॐ ಓಂ | क् ಕ್ | र्क ರ್ಕ | त्र ತ್ರ | क्ष ಕ್ಷ | ज्ञ ಜ್ಞ | | | |
| 1 ೧ | 2 ೨ | 3 ೩ | 4 ೪ | 5 ೫ | 6 ೬ | 7 ೭ | 8 ೮ | 9 ೯ | 0 ೦ | | |

## मैथिल

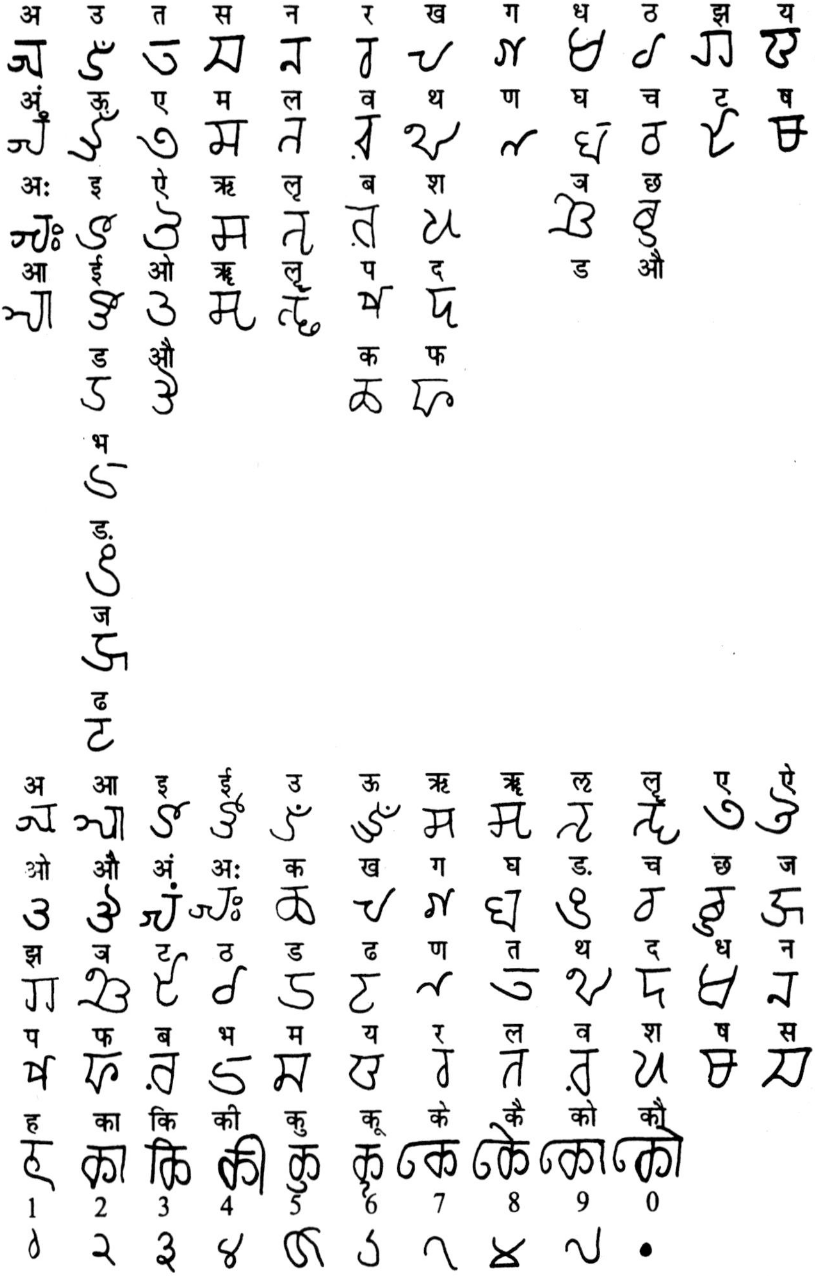

अ उ त स न र ख ग ध ठ झ य
अं ऊं ए म ल व थ ण घ च ट ष
अः इ ऐ ऋ लृ ब श ञ छ
आ ई ओ ॠ ॡ प द ड औ
ङ औ क फ
भ
ङ
ज
ढ
अ आ इ ई उ ऊ ऋ ॠ ऌ ॡ ए ऐ
ओ औ अं अः क ख ग घ ङ च छ ज
झ ञ ट ठ ड ढ ण त थ द ध न
प फ ब भ म य र ल व श ष स
ह का कि की कु कू के कै को कौ
1 2 3 4 5 6 7 8 9 0

**मलयालम**

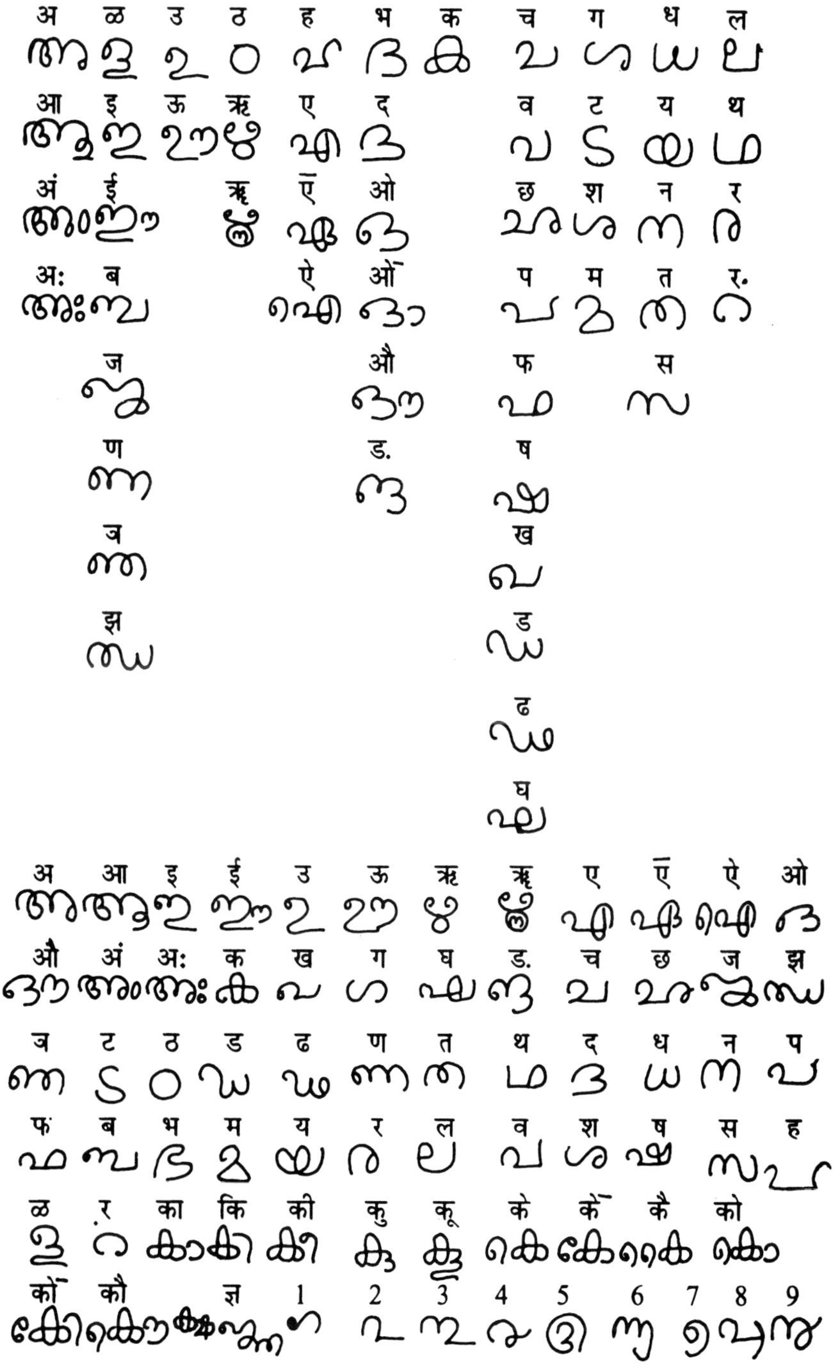
अ ळ उ ठ ह भ क च ग ध ल
आ इ ऊ ऋ ए द व ट य थ
अं ई ॠ ए ओ छ श न र
अः ब ऐ ओं प म त ऱ
ज औ फ स
ण ङ ष
ञ ख
झ ड
ढ
घ
अ आ इ ई उ ऊ ऋ ॠ ए ए ऐ ओ
औ अं अः क ख ग घ ङ च छ ज झ
ञ ट ठ ड ढ ण त थ द ध न प
फ ब भ म य र ल व श ष स ह
ळ ऱ का कि की कु कू के कें कै को
कों कौ ज्ञ 1 2 3 4 5 6 7 8 9

## मोडी ( मराठी )

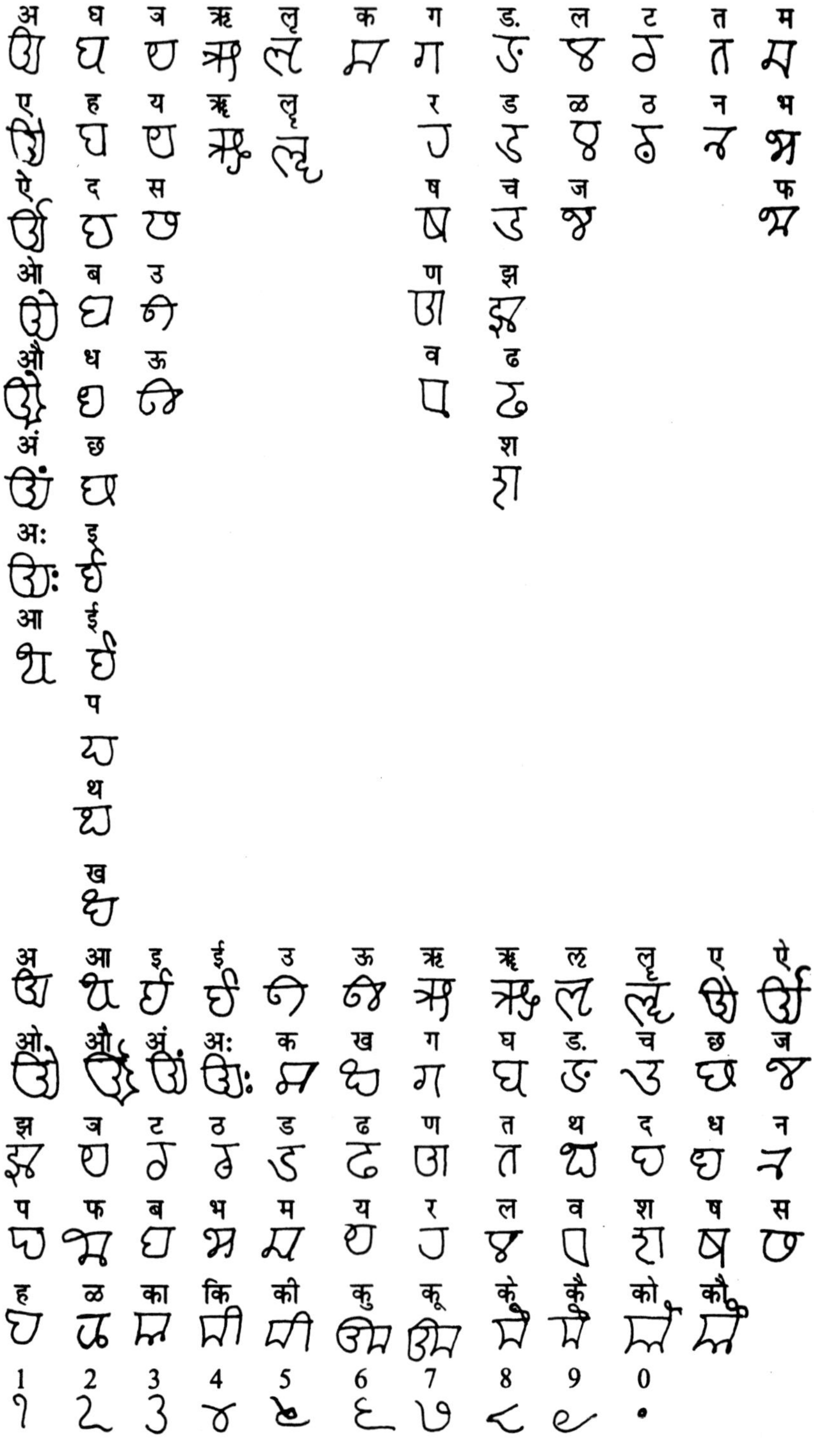
अ घ ञ ऋ लृ क ग ङ. ल ट त म
ए ह य ॠ लॄ र ड ळ ठ न भ
ऐ द स ष च ज फ
ओ ब उ ण झ
औ ध ऊ व ढ
अं छ श
अः इ
आ ई
प
थ
ख
अ आ इ ई उ ऊ ऋ ॠ ल लृ ए ऐ
ओ औ अं अः क ख ग घ ङ. च छ ज
झ ञ ट ठ ड ढ ण त थ द ध न
प फ ब भ म य र ल व श ष स
ह ळ का कि की कु कू के कै को कौ
1 2 3 4 5 6 7 8 9 0

# नन्दिनागरी

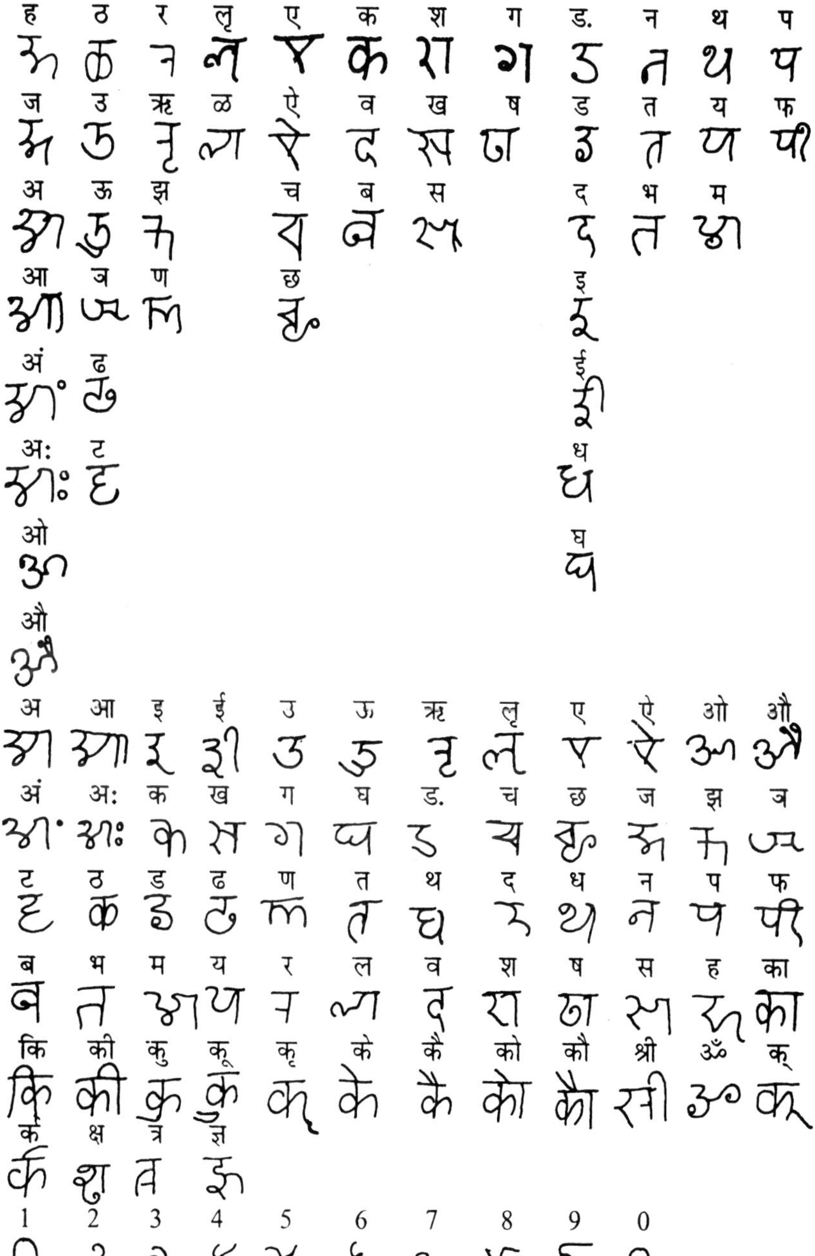
ह ठ र लृ ए क श ग ड. न थ प
ज उ ऋ ळ ऐ व ख ष ड त य फ
अ ऊ झ च ब स द भ म
आ ञ ण छ इ
अं ढ ई
अः ट ध
ओ घ
औ
अ आ इ ई उ ऊ ऋ लृ ए ऐ ओ औ
अं अः क ख ग घ ड. च छ ज झ ञ
ट ठ ड ढ ण त थ द ध न प फ
ब भ म य र ल व श ष स ह का
कि की कु कू कृ के कै को कौ श्री ॐ क्
र्क क्ष त्र ज्ञ
1 2 3 4 5 6 7 8 9 0

# शारदा

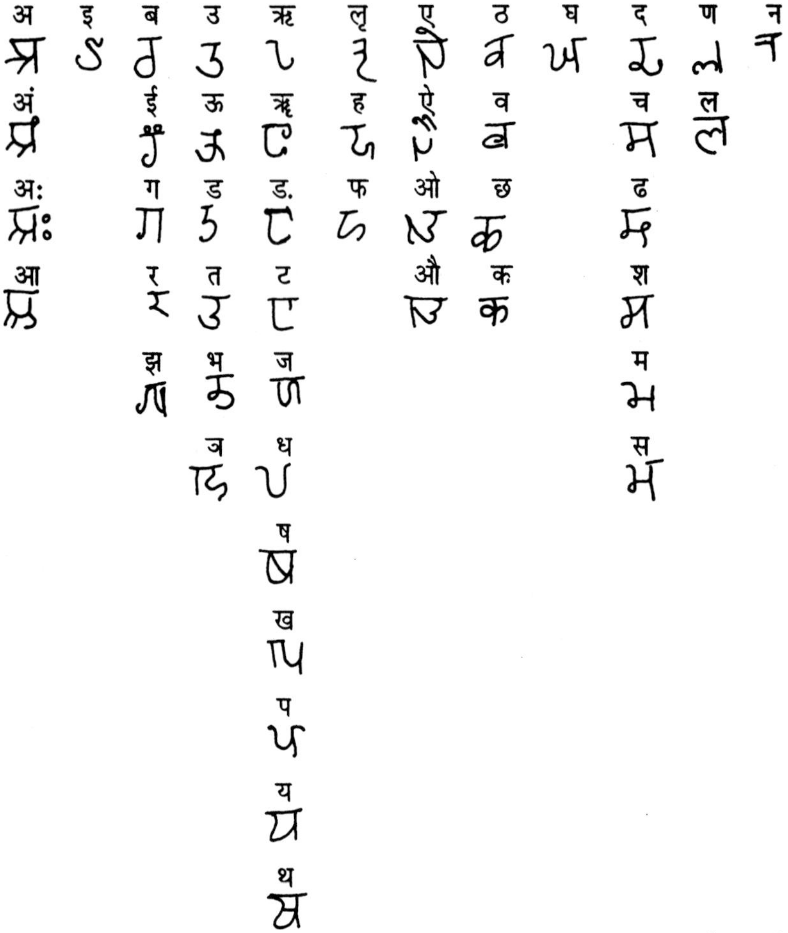
अ अं अः आ
इ
ब ई ग र झ
उ ऊ ड त भ ञ
ऋ ॠ ङ ट ज ध ष ख प य थ
लृ ह फ
ए ऐ ओ औ
ठ व छ क
घ
द च ढ श म स
ण ल
न

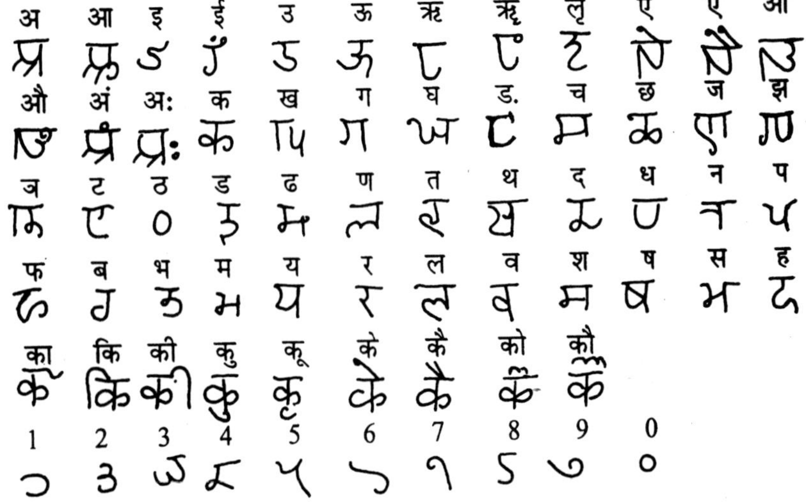
अ आ इ ई उ ऊ ऋ ॠ लृ ए ऐ ओ
औ अं अः क ख ग घ ङ च छ ज झ
ञ ट ठ ड ढ ण त थ द ध न प
फ ब भ म य र ल व श ष स ह
का कि की कु कू के कै को कौ
1 2 3 4 5 6 7 8 9 0

## तमिल

| | | | | | |
|---|---|---|---|---|---|
| अ | उ | ए | ओ | च | ट |
| அ | உ | எ | ஒ | ச | ட |
| आ | ऊ | ए̄ | ओ | क | प |
| ஆ | ஊ | ஏ | ஓ | க | ப |
| इ | ल | ञ | औ | त | भ |
| இ | ல | ஞ | ஔ | த | ம |
| ई | व | ण़ | | न | य |
| ஈ | வ | ன | | ந | ய |
| | | ण | | ङ | र |
| | | ண | | ங | ர |
| | | ळ | | | ऴ |
| | | ள | | | ழ |
| | | ऱ | | | |
| | | ற | | | |
| | | ऐ | | | |
| | | ஐ | | | |

| | | | | | | | | | | | |
|---|---|---|---|---|---|---|---|---|---|---|---|
| अ | आ | इ | ई | उ | ऊ | ए | ए̄ | ऐ | ओ | ओ | औ |
| அ | ஆ | இ | ஈ | உ | ஊ | எ | ஏ | ஐ | ஒ | ஓ | ஔ |
| क | ङ | च | ज | ट | ण | त | न | प | म | य | र |
| க | ங | ச | ஞ | ட | ண | த | ந | ப | ம | ய | ர |
| ल | व | ऴ | ळ | ऱ | ण़ | का | कि | की | कु | कू | के |
| ல | வ | ழ | ள | ற | ன | கா | கி | கீ | கு | கூ | கெ |
| के̄ | कै | को | कौ | ॐ | | | | | | | |
| கே | கை | கொ | கௌ | ௐ | | | | | | | |
| 1 | 2 | 3 | 4 | 5 | 6 | 7 | 8 | 9 | 10 | 11 | 20 |
| ௧ | ௨ | ௩ | ௪ | ௫ | ௬ | ௭ | ௮ | ௯ | ௰ | ௰௧ | ௨௰ |
| 100 | 1000 | | | | | | | | | | |
| ௱ | ௲ | | | | | | | | | | |

## तेलगू

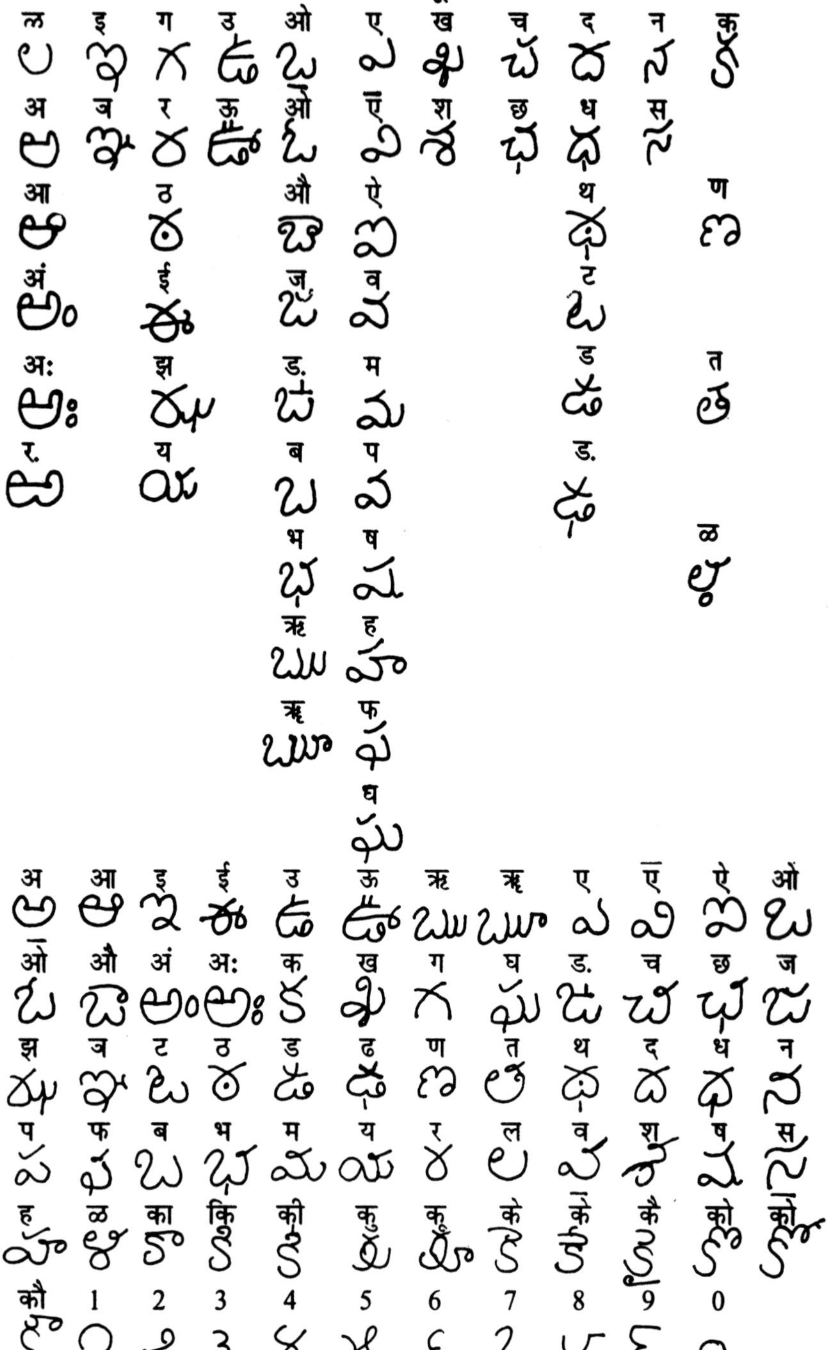

ल इ ग उ ओ ए ख च द न क
अ ज र ऊ ओ ए श छ ध स
आ ठ औ ऐ थ ण
अं ई ज़ व ट
अः झ ड़ म ड त
ऱ य ब प ड़
भ ष ळ
ऋ ह
ॠ फ
घ
अ आ इ ई उ ऊ ऋ ॠ ए ए ऐ ओ
ओ औ अं अः क ख ग घ ड. च छ ज
झ ञ ट ठ ड ढ ण त थ द ध न
प फ ब भ म य र ल व श ष स
ह ळ का कि की कु कू के के कै को को
कौ 1 2 3 4 5 6 7 8 9 0

# तिगलारी

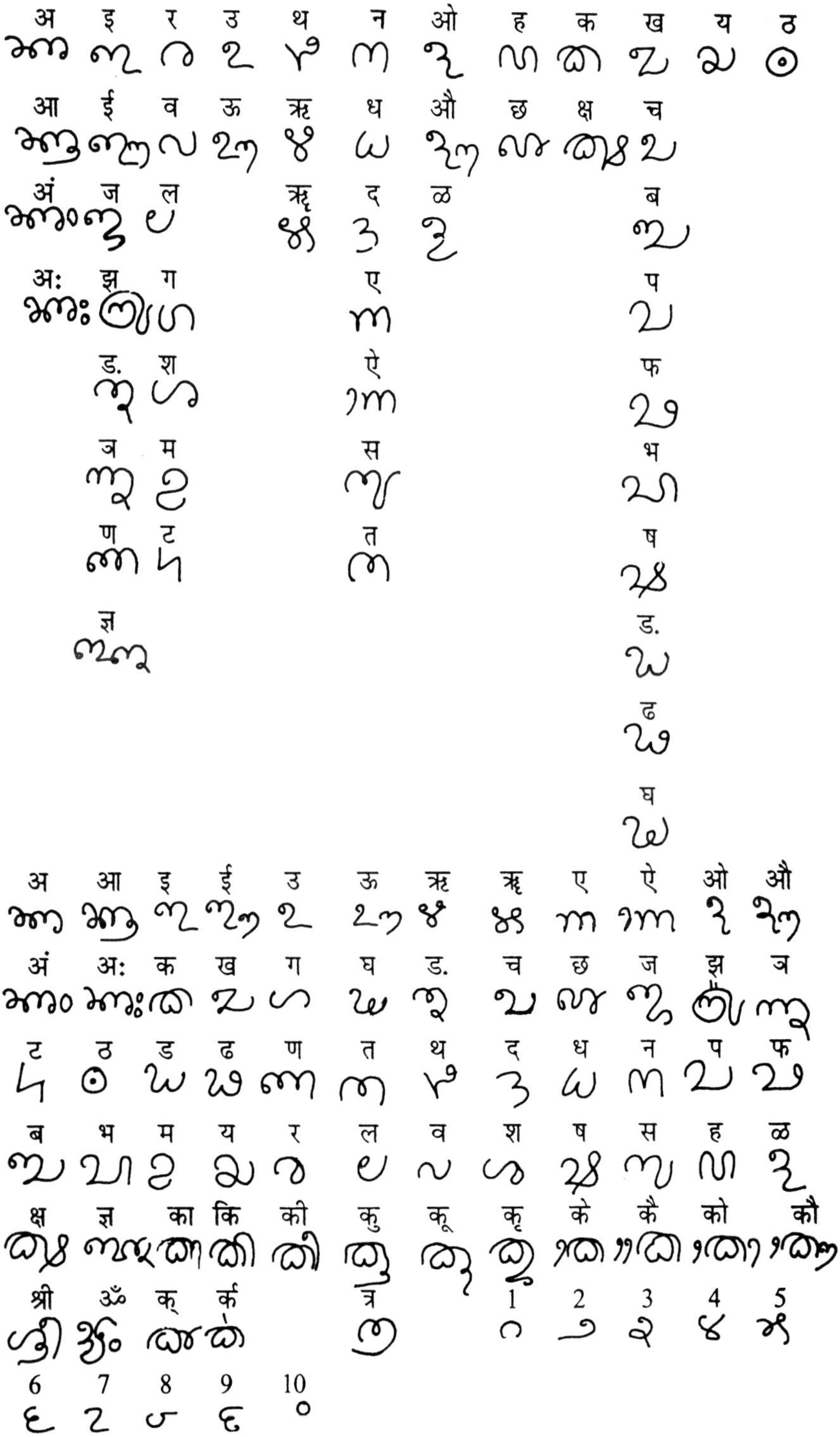

अ इ र उ थ न ओ ह क ख य ठ
आ ई व ऊ ऋ ध औ छ क्ष च
अं ज ल ॠ द ळ ब
अः झ ग ए प
ङ. श ऐ फ
ञ म स भ
ण ट त ष
ज्ञ ङ.
ढ
घ
अ आ इ ई उ ऊ ऋ ॠ ए ऐ ओ औ
अं अः क ख ग घ ङ. च छ ज झ ञ
ट ठ ड ढ ण त थ द ध न प फ
ब भ म य र ल व श ष स ह ळ
क्ष ज्ञ का कि की कु कू कृ के कै को कौ
श्री ॐ क् र्क त्र 1 2 3 4 5
6 7 8 9 10

# उडिया

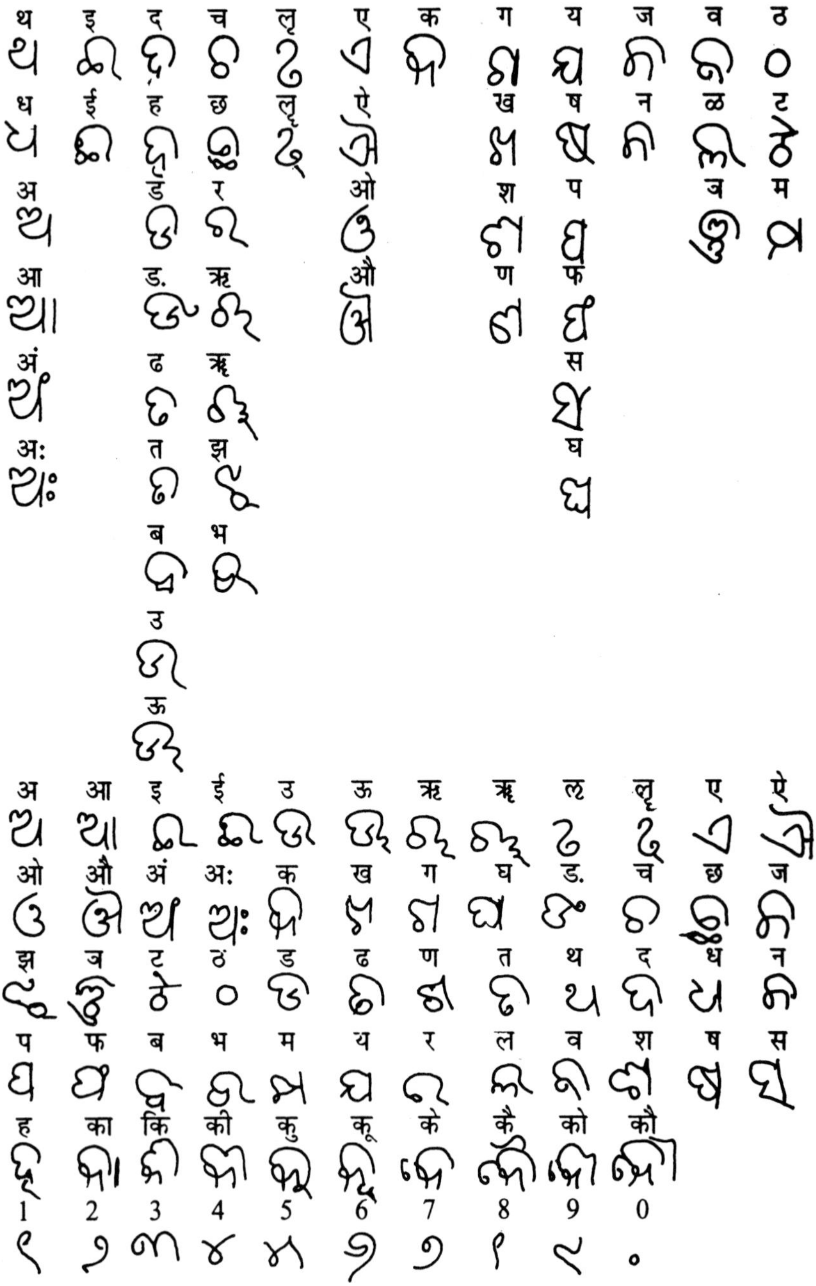
थ ध अ आ अं अः
इ ई
द ह ड ड. ढ त ब उ ऊ
च छ र ऋ ॠ झ भ
लृ लॄ
ए ऐ ओ औ
क
ग ख श ण
य ष प फ स घ
ज न
व ळ ञ
ठ ट म
अ आ इ ई उ ऊ ऋ ॠ ऌ ॡ ए ऐ
ओ औ अं अः क ख ग घ ङ. च छ ज
झ ञ ट ठ ड ढ ण त थ द ध न
प फ ब भ म य र ल व श ष स
ह का कि की कु कू के कै को कौ
1 2 3 4 5 6 7 8 9 0

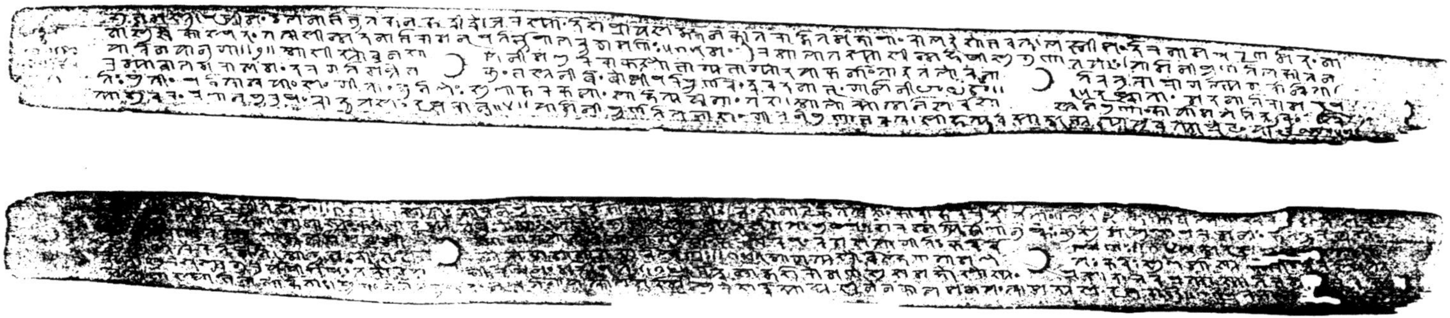

Pl. 1. Nāgarī Script, Bīlhaṇacaritam

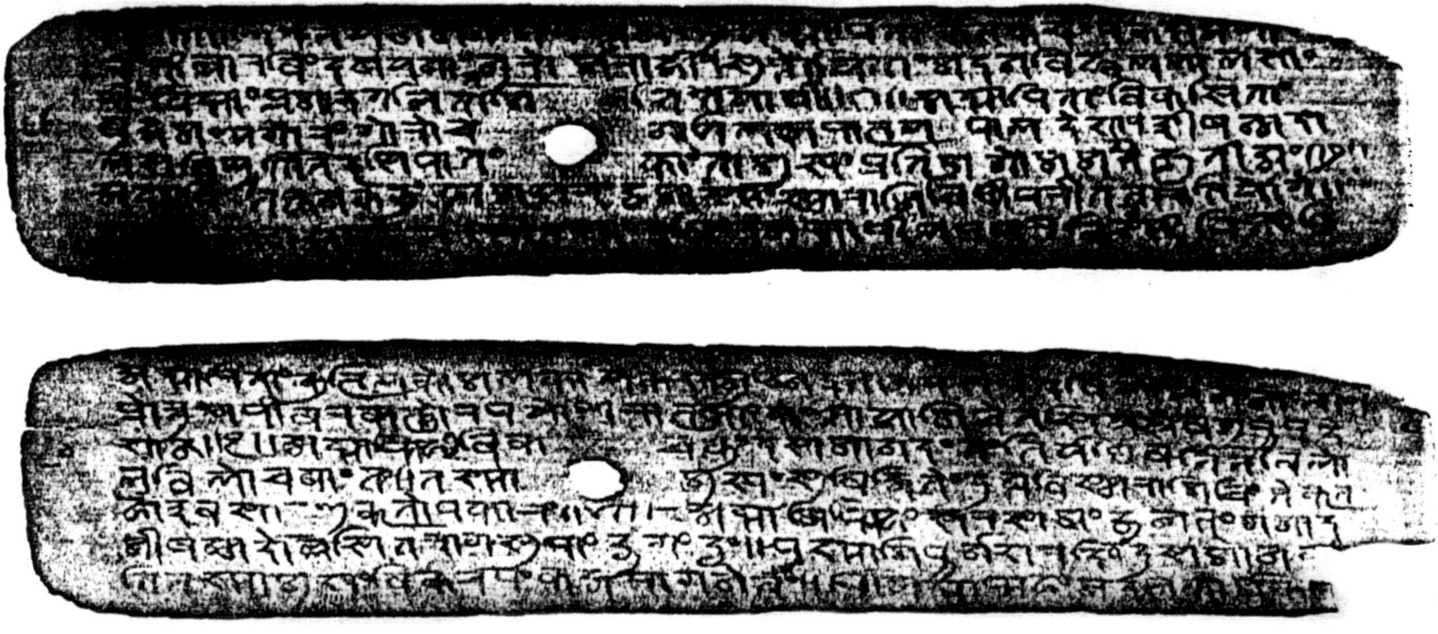

Pl. 2. Nāgarī Script, Bīlhaṇacaritam

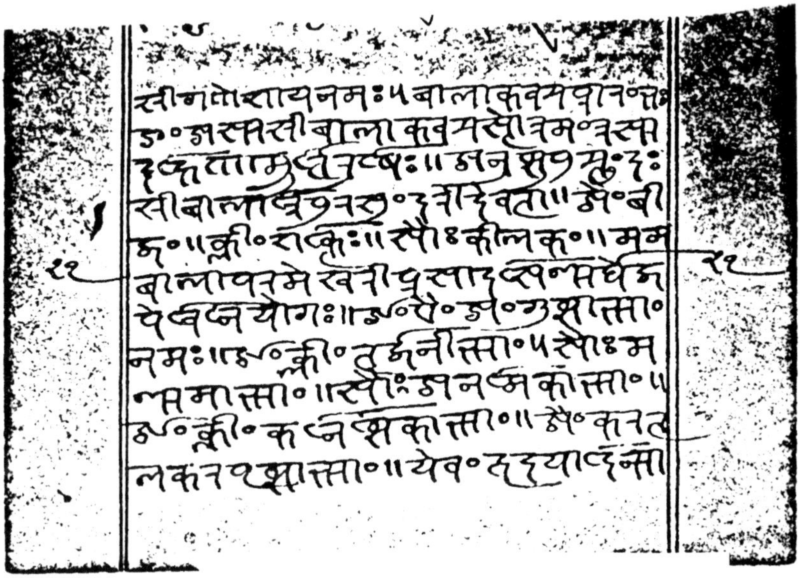

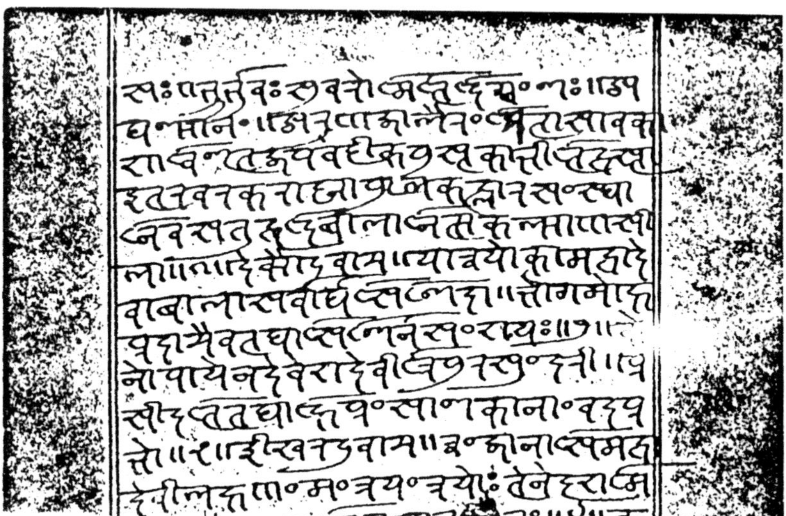

Pl. 3. Nāgarī Script, Bālakavacam (Paper Mss.) Mysore)

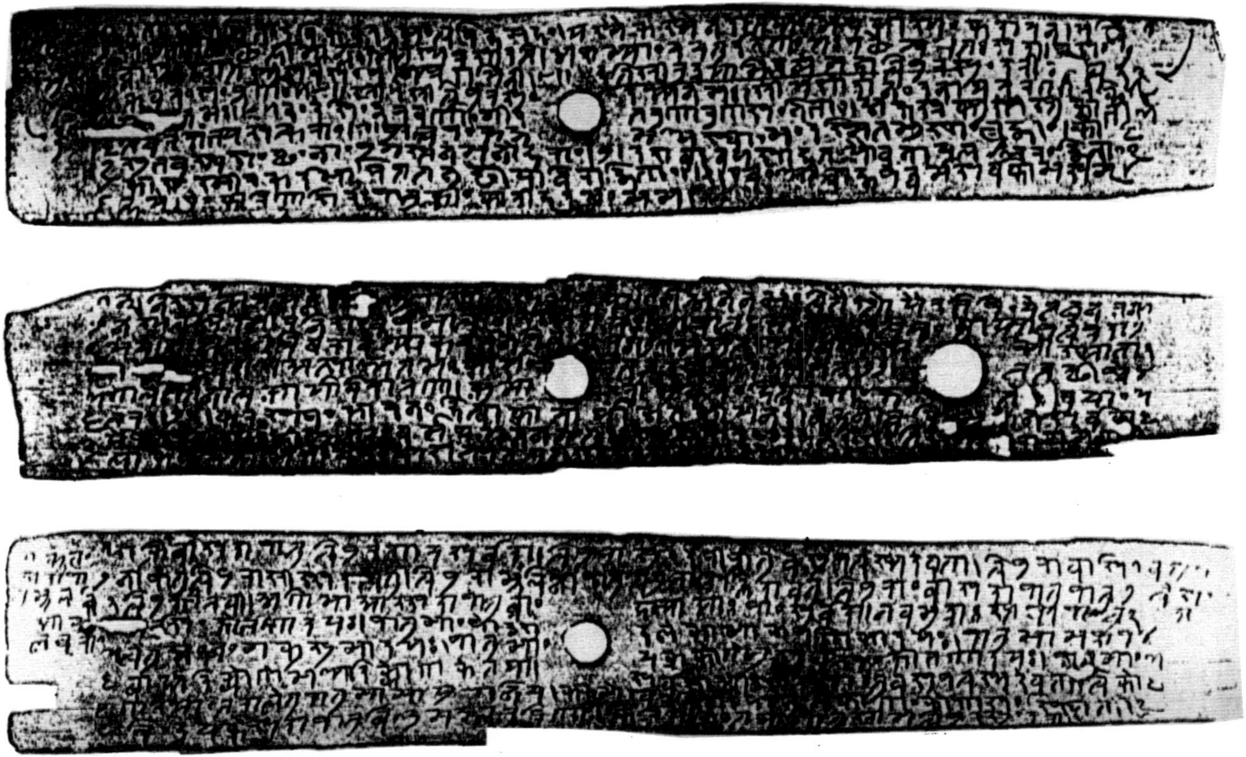

Pl. 4. Nāgarī Script

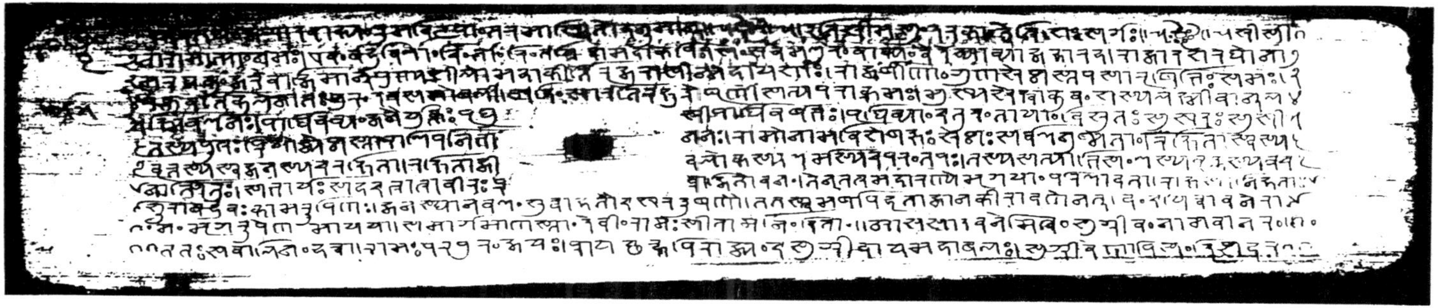

Pl. 5. Nandi-Nāgarī Script, Vālmīki Rāmāyaṇa, 31st Canto in Sundara Kāṇḍa

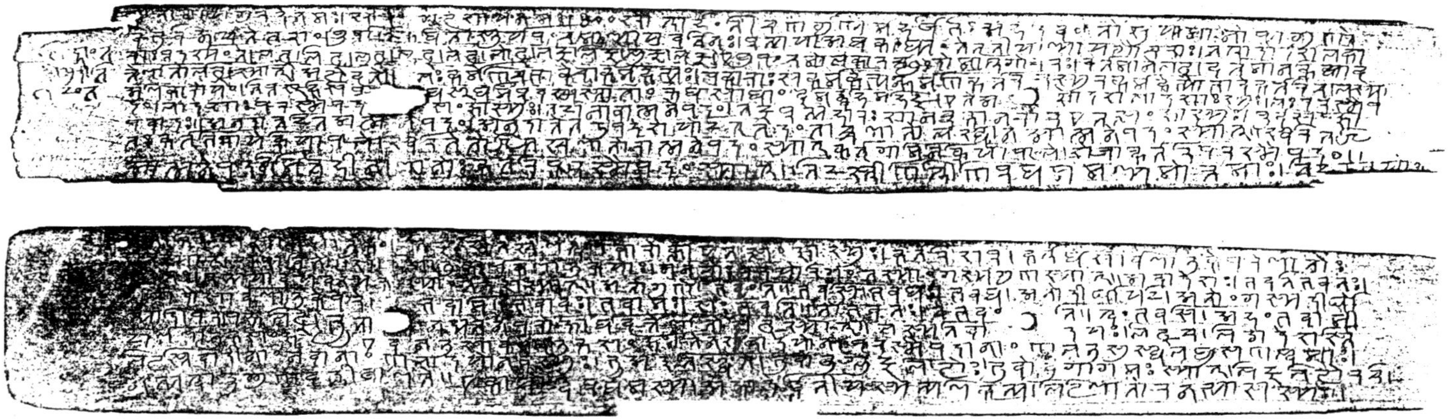

Pl. 6. Nāgari Script, Sīddhānta Kaumudi

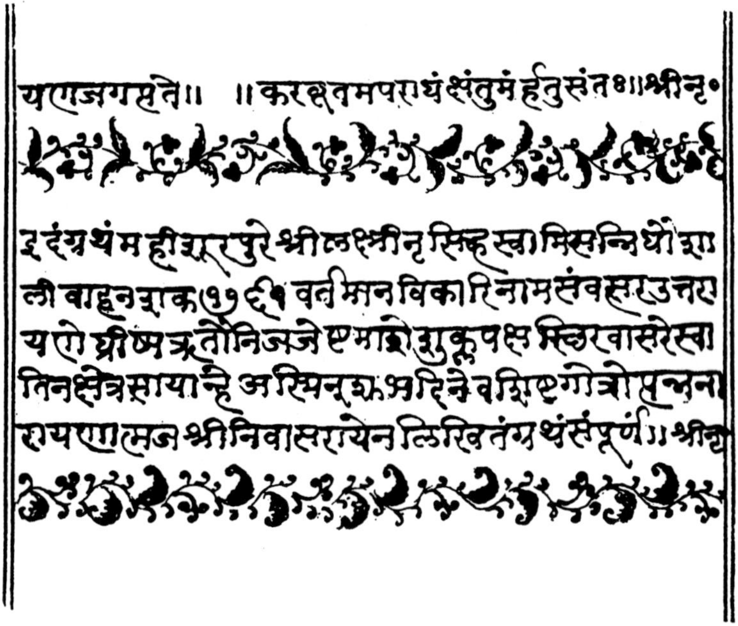

यणेजगस्ते॥ ॥करक्षतमपराधं क्षंतुमर्हंतुसंत॥ श्रीनृ०
इदंग्रथं महीशूरपुरे श्रीलक्ष्मीनृसिंहस्वामिसन्निधौ शा
लीवाहनशाक १७८१ वर्तमान विकारिनाम संवत्सर उत्तरा
यणे ग्रीष्मऋतौ निजज्येष्ठमासे शुक्लपक्षे स्थिरवासरे स्वा
तिनक्षत्रे सायान्हे अस्मिन् शुभदिने वसिष्ठगोत्रो पन्नन
रायणात्मज श्रीनिवासरायेन लिखितं ग्रंथं संपूर्णं॥ श्रीनृ

Pl. 7. Nāgari Script

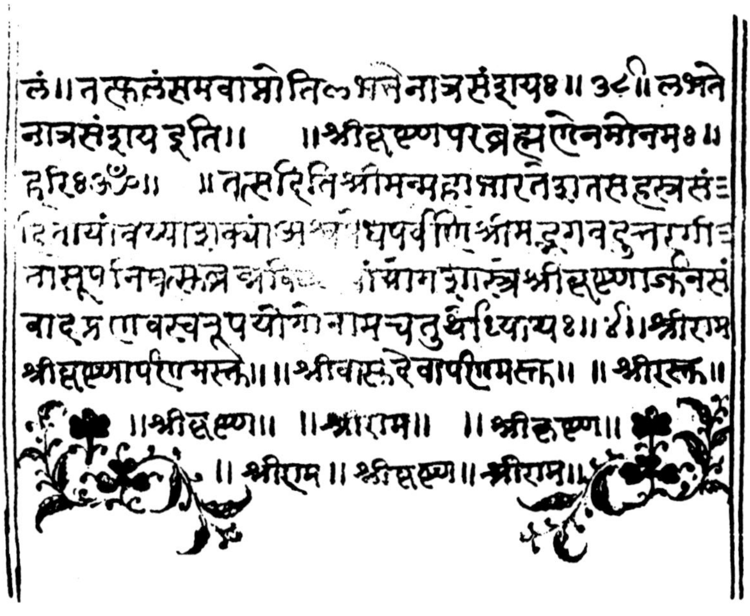

लं॥ न फलं समवाप्नोति लभते नात्र संशयः॥ ३८॥ लभते
नात्र संशय इति॥ ॥श्रीकृष्णपरब्रह्मणे नमो नमः॥
हरिः ॐ॥ ॥तत्सदिति श्रीमन्महाभारते शतसहस्रसं
हितायां वैयासिक्यां भीष्मपर्वणि श्रीमद्भगवद्गीता
सूपनिषत्सु ब्रह्मविद्यायां योगशास्त्रे श्रीकृष्णार्जुनसं
वादे ज्ञानवस्तुरूपयोगो नाम चतुर्थोध्यायः॥ ४॥ श्रीराम
श्रीकृष्णार्पणमस्तु॥ ॥श्रीवासुदेवार्पणमस्तु॥ ॥श्रीरस्तु॥
॥श्रीकृष्ण॥ ॥श्रीराम॥ ॥श्रीकृष्ण॥
॥श्रीराम॥ श्रीकृष्ण॥ श्रीराम॥

Pl. 8. Nāgarī Script

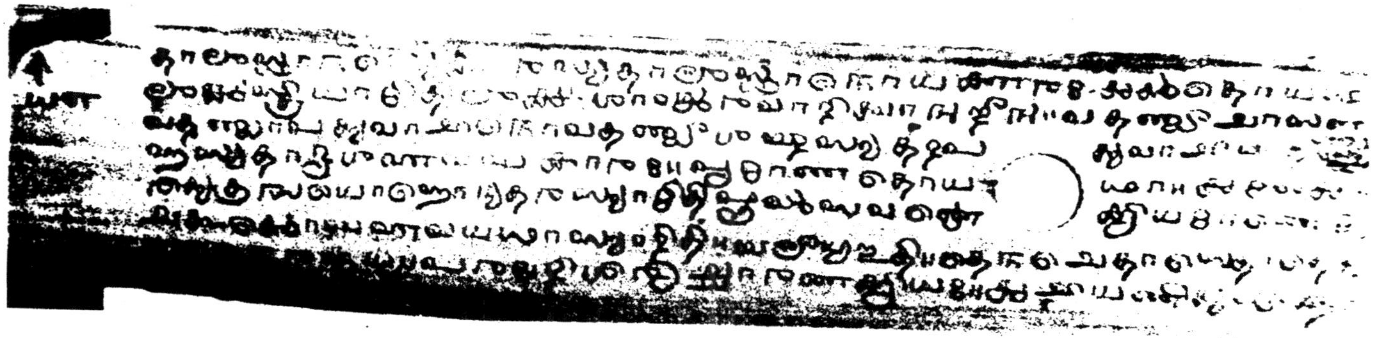

Pl. 9. Grantha Script, Sīddhānta Kaumudi

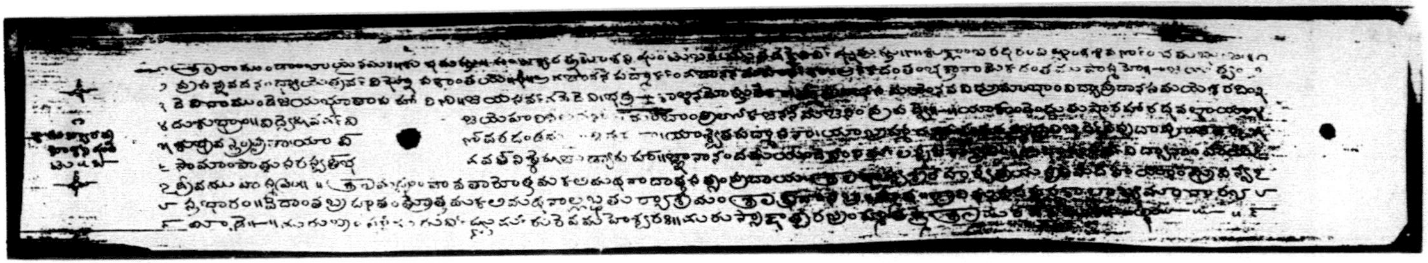

Pl. 10. Kannada Script. Sankhya Ratnakośa

Pl. 11. Kannada Script, Gīta Govinda

Pl. 12. Copper Plate with dotted lines

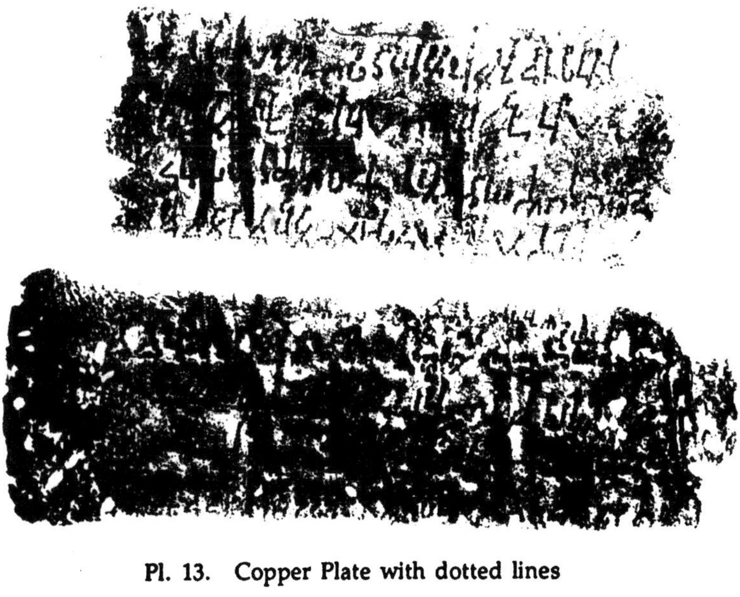

Pl. 13. Copper Plate with dotted lines

Pl. 14. Sohgaura Copper Plate, 4th cent. B.C.

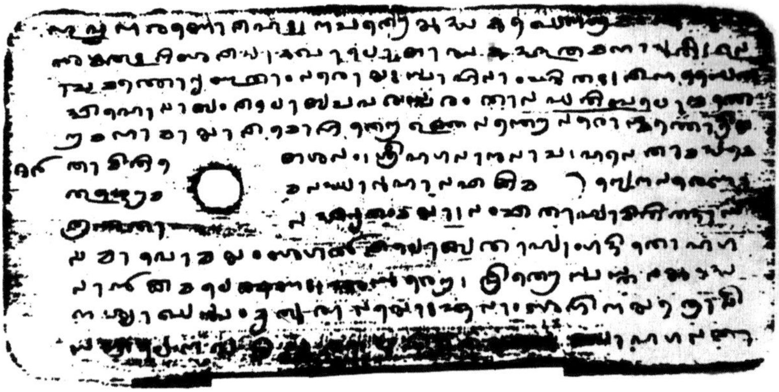

Pl. 15. Tulu Script, Devīmāhātyam

Pl. 16. Malayalam Script

Pl. 17. Kannada Script, Deśavarṇanam

Pl. 18. Drawings in Palmleaf Manuscripts

Pl. 19. Drawings in Palmleaf Manuscripts

Pl. 20. Drawings in Palmleaf Manuscripts

Pl. 21. Geometrical Patterns in writing

Pl. 22. Patterns in writing

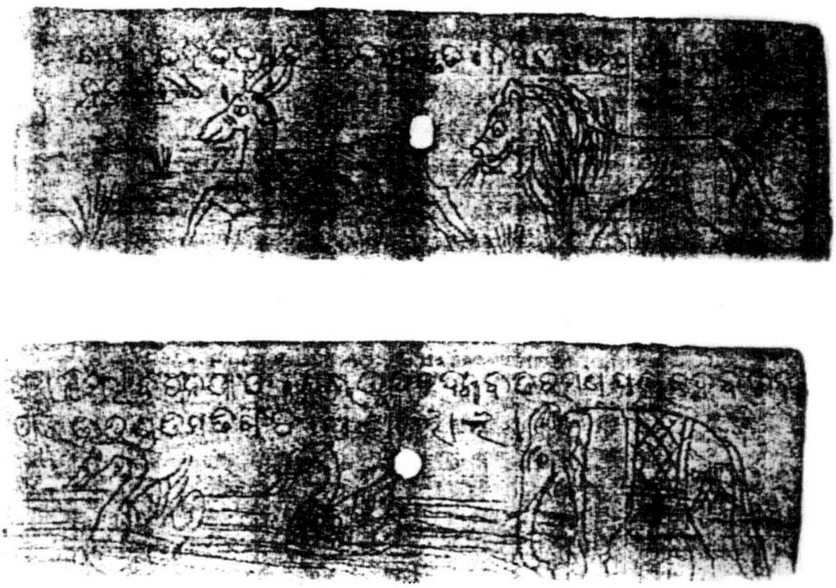

Pl. 23. Oriya manuscript containing Viṣṇusahasranamastotra, etc.

Pl. 24. Jaina Prakrit manuscript, Mahavira Preaching

Pl. 25. Jaina Prakrit manuscript, King Sanjaya stoots the deer

Pl. 26. A sage reading a palm-leaf manuscript

Pl. 27. Muttara [Image in stone of Piṅgala, attendant of Sūrya, holding pen in his right hand and an inkpot in left (Gupta Period)]

Pl. 28. Gautama at school, Ajanta Painting, Cave No. XVI, c. 6th cent. A.D.

Pl. 29. Sculpture showing Vaiṣṇava Guru and his royal disciple holding in his right hand a manuscript with his attending guards shown below.

Pl. 30. Scroll

Pl. 31. Knife with ivory handle

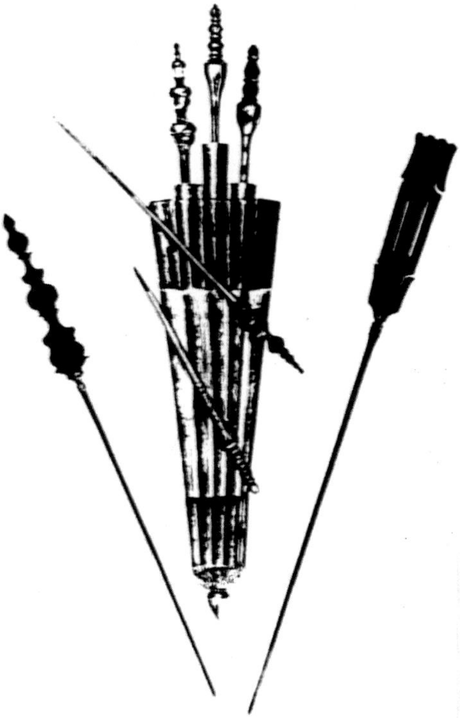

Pl. 32. Stylus used in writing on palmleaf and a stylus case

Pl. 33. Stylus

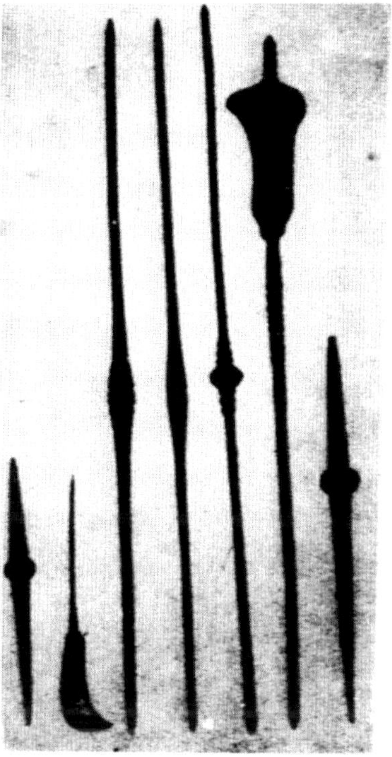

Pl. 34. Stylus

Pl. 35. Stylus

Pl. 36. Inkpot Top view

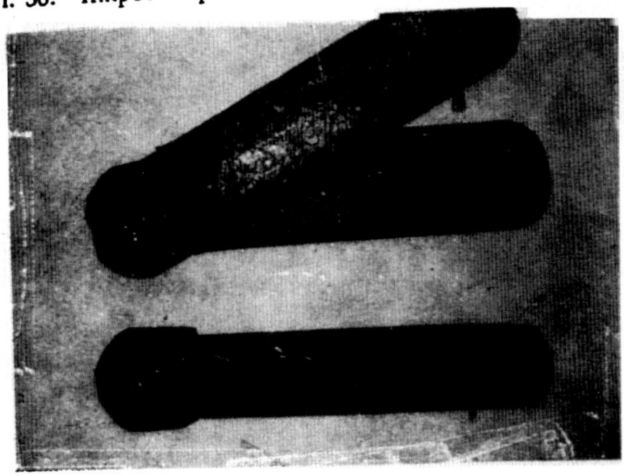

Pl. 37. Inkpot Front view

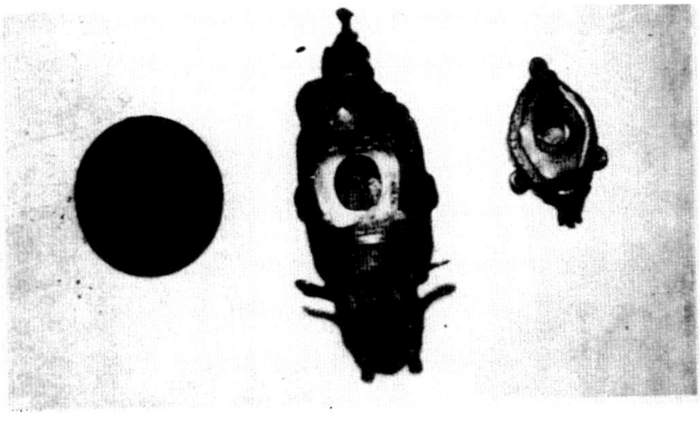

Pl. 38. Inkpot

Pl. 39. Headless Ṣaraswatı

Pl. 40. Khajuraho - Woman writing letter on palmleaf

Pl. 41. Lady writing inscription, Siva Temple, Bidar Dist.

Pl. 42. Pandit holding a palmleaf in the left hand explaining to a citizen, 16th cent.

Pl. 43. A saint holding a manuscript, decorated manuscript box is also seen

Pl. 44. A Jaina saint holding a palmleaf in left hand is seen with a disciple

Pl. 45. Jaina saint holding palmleaf under his left arm